FREEDOM FROM
THE MARKET

FREEDOM FROM THE MARKET

America's Fight to Liberate Itself from
the Grip of the Invisible Hand

MIKE KONCZAL

NEW YORK
LONDON

Requests for permission to reproduce selections from this book should be made through our
website: https://thenewpress.com/contact.

Published in the United States by The New Press, New York, 2021
Distributed by Two Rivers Distribution

ISBN 978-1-62097-537-4 (hc)
ISBN 978-1-62097-538-1 (ebook)
CIP data is available

The New Press publishes books that promote and enrich public discussion and
understanding of the issues vital to our democracy and to a more equitable world. These
books are made possible by the enthusiasm of our readers; the support of a committed group
of donors, large and small; the collaboration of our many partners in the independent media
and the not-for-profit sector; booksellers, who often hand-sell New Press books; librarians;
and above all by our authors.

www.thenewpress.com

Book design and composition by dix!
This book was set in Garamond Premier Pro

Printed in the United States of America

10 9 8 7 6 5 4 3 2 1

For Kendra, Vivian, and dreams about spring

No man or body of men who require such excessive labor can be friends to the country or the Rights of Man. [...] The God of the Universe has given us time, health, and strength. We utterly deny the right of any man to dictate to us how much of it we shall sell.

—"Ten-Hour Circular," calling for a maximum ten-hour work day, 1835

It is not till it is discovered that high individual incomes will not purchase the mass of mankind immunity from cholera, typhus, and ignorance, still less secure them the positive advantages of educational opportunity and economic security, that slowly and reluctantly, amid prophecies of moral degeneration and economic disaster, society begins to make collective provision for needs which no ordinary individual, even if he works overtime all his life, can provide himself.

—R.H. Tawney, *Equality* (1931)

[W]e need to understand the nature of the corporation—to make money—and come to love it, and yet, to keep it in its proper place, just as you can love a tiger, but know that it's not the sort of thing that should play with your kid.

—Lawrence Lessig, 2007

CONTENTS

INTRODUCTION

Over the past several decades, we've been fed an idea that free markets—the unregulated flow of goods, services, and labor—are the fundamental form of freedom, and that freedom itself functions like a market. The freedom of a business owner, the freedom to sell your labor, the freedom to buy the necessities of life like health and education—these are the market opportunities that keep us free and allow us to express ourselves as members of a society. This narrow, limited view has extended into all parts of our lives, becoming like the air that surrounds us.

America's market-oriented worldview is now breaking down. At a time of political upheaval, insecurity, and pandemics, people are hungry to reclaim a world outside the market. Their desires are animating politics, especially among younger voters, who are demanding that the government directly provide essential goods while also suppressing aspects of the market that threaten to swallow our lives whole.

These political demands are actually old ideas, though they've long since been forgotten. For two centuries, Americans have been fighting for freedom from the market. Their stories provide a powerful legacy to draw from and build upon.

All around us, this old fight against the free market rages anew. There was a short-lived social media account that emerged alongside the 2011 Occupy movement, a Tumblr page titled "We Are the 99 Percent" filled with stories of economic hardship. The number one problem people expressed, the fear that permeated the whole website, stemmed from student debt and debt from medical bills. What was drawing people into that political moment was the idea of a space beyond the marketplace, one that wasn't ruled by debt and precarity.[1] Later on, the desire for goods accessible outside the marketplace went crashing into the 2016 and 2020 Democratic primary battles. Suddenly there were debates everywhere about free college and free, universal, single-payer health care. Old questions about the workplace were being resurrected, including through the grassroots effort to pass a $15 minimum wage in states and cities. Previous gatekeepers, who wanted people's political imagination to keep to a more market-friendly, incremental approach, saw the debate simply move past them. That energy expanded even after Donald Trump's 2016 victory, motivating a whole new generation to run for office and change the political debate.

We see this energy reflected in recent polling about the appeal of socialism. "Exclusive Poll: Young Americans Are Embracing Socialism" reads one such headline. "Gen Z Prefers 'Socialism' to 'Capitalism' " reads another. An early 2019 poll found that nearly 50 percent of millennials and members of Generation Z would "prefer living in a socialist country." Sixty-one percent of those between the ages of eighteen and twenty-four have a positive reaction to the word "socialism," compared with less than 29 percent for those over fifty-five years of age. Younger people are more likely to believe that the government should provide universal health care and tuition-free college, though these opinions are broadly popular outside this age bracket as well.[2]

Conservatives respond to this development with a predictable mix of hyperventilation and condescension. Yet it is easy to miss the motivating force behind this new political energy and the skepticism over capitalism it has unleashed. Central to this stance is the rejection of what the historian Ellen Meiksins Wood calls "market dependence," where the market determines our access to all aspects of life. As Wood describes, under capitalism markets have a "historically unprecedented role in organizing human life and social reproduction, where people must go through the market to gain access to the most basic means of self-reproduction." What has changed about our era is how successful capitalism has become in colonizing our everyday lives, and how market dependency has bulldozed through efforts to check it.[3]

People have used markets for trading and exchange for centuries. What is unique today is how the economy has been restructured to extend and accelerate our reliance on markets into all aspects of society. For all the language about how markets open up opportunities, they also create dependencies as well. As Wood notes, what defines our current way of dealing with markets "is not opportunity or choice but, on the contrary, compulsion." The things we need to lead our lives are forced into markets where we are compelled to obtain them, at the mercy of private, profit-seeking actors and our own ability to pay. Many of our needs are left unmet or poorly provided for by the market—from health care to retirement security to providing for children—and more suffering is the result.[4]

When we understand that people are resisting dependency on markets it helps us see how they are also articulating a different idea of freedom. When citizens declare that health care is a human right, they are making a stand against market dependency. In this view there are still markets. Doctors and nurses get salaries, MRI machines and bandages are purchased, and so on. But it also holds that individuals should not be dependent on the market as the sole determinant of what care they get. Health care should go to those who are sick, not those who are sick and who also happen to have money. That market must be suppressed in favor of publicly provided health care.[5] When workers demand a living wage and control over the hours they work, they are making a statement that they aren't mere commodities, whose fortunes are determined by their dependency on the marketplace, but individuals who deserve a level of freedom that goes beyond this. When Franklin

Delano Roosevelt called for new freedoms, it was about putting limits on this kind of dependency. It's a way of harnessing the innovative features of markets, without being servants to them.

This book argues that true freedom requires keeping us free from the market. In some places this will require the government to provide key services directly and universally, rather than requiring citizens to rely on the marketplace. These services include social insurance, education, and health care, among others. Elsewhere it will mean suppressing the extent of the market, such as the number of hours we work or the ability of businesses to discriminate against their customers. The form this takes will depend on the contingency of everything from technology to the aspect of our life in question. But in all cases market dependency is a profound state of unfreedom, and freedom requires checks and hard boundaries on the ways markets exist in our society and in our lives.

Americans have always been aware of the stakes between markets and freedom. It is only recently that this historical awareness been obscured from our public memory. In our political battles through the centuries over land policy, free college, maximum working hours, public day cares, and more, Americans have understood that market dependency can be a source of unfreedom and is something that needs to be contained. But in recent years, our historical consciousness has been clouded by glib libertarian fantasies where the government played no role in checking the market before the Progressive Era and the New Deal. In this fairy tale, there was no need for the state, especially the federal state, in creating capitalism itself, and no role it played in determining who would benefit from this nominally private marketplace. This is wrong, and we need to recover our genuine history of American freedom. We have forgotten that free programs and keeping things free from the market are as American as apple pie.

It is important for us to recover this, because what is dysfunctional about our current economy and politics comes from extreme market dependency. Over the past fifty years, both our personal lives and our economy have been forced ever more deeply into market dependency. Those who have carried out this project aren't adhering to some vision of limited government. They have been unapologetic about using the state to make us more dependent on markets. Where markets did not exist, they have been forced and created. Where checks existed, they've been attacked. It's been a strip-mining of society, leaving us and our politics exhausted, depleted, and desperate for fundamental change. Moreover, as writers like Corey Robin and Eric Foner have argued convincingly, liberals and the left have lost a language of freedom that would help us describe this predicament, conceding the terrain to conservatives and those who see freedom only in the marketplace. But people are now becoming hungry for a new idea of freedom, one that is rooted in public programs that genuinely serve people and checking market dependency. Recovering this history is essential to moving our politics and our lives toward a better direction.[6]

The idea that freedom requires being free from the market cuts directly against the notion of freedom that is prevalent today. Now economic freedom, the freedom of buying, selling, and existing within markets, is seen as the only kind of freedom. As the philosopher Wendy Brown told the filmmaker and writer Astra Taylor, "Today, there is no meaning of equality and freedom other than the meaning that you see in the market. . . . But the market itself is a domain of inequality. It's a domain of winners and losers. And winners and losers are therefore the natural outcome of a fully marketized democracy."[7]

Today's idea of market freedom has two origin stories. The first comes from libertarians taking a distinction introduced by the British philosopher Isaiah Berlin to its extreme. In 1958 Berlin popularized the idea of negative and positive freedom, often referred to "freedom from" interference and "freedom to" do things. Negative freedom is defined as a kind of absence, where there are no obstacles preventing your actions. Positive freedom, on the other hand, is the freedom to achieve certain kinds of objectives, usually determined collectively as a group.[8]

One might think these are two sides of the same coin, or different aspects of the debate over how to balance our competing social goals of freedom and security. However, Berlin unhelpfully describes the two ideas as fundamentally at odds with each other. A new generation of libertarian and neoliberal thinkers would drive this wall between the two further. For them, negative freedom was not just an important goal of the government, it was the only legitimate one. Any kind of economic interference, be it regulations, taxes, public programs, or social insurance, would necessarily also undermine the idea of freedom.[9]

The other origin story deal coincides with the ascendancy of economists to the forefront of policymaking. Economists, even liberal ones, tend to have a particular view of the proper way to regulate and structure the marketplace, and that is solely by giving people money. In a 1970 essay, the liberal economist James Tobin contrasted two views of egalitarian thought. The first he called "specific egalitarianism," in which access to specific goods like health and education shouldn't be based on the ability to pay. The other, "general egalitarianism," was the view of most economists. General egalitarians believed that the government shouldn't change how the market creates goods through regulations, produce goods directly like education, or otherwise interfere with prices like with minimum-wage laws. Instead, if the government cared about equality, it should just give poor people cash and remain indifferent to how people spend it.

As Tobin described this newly influential view, "While concerned laymen who observe people with shabby housing or too little to eat instinctively want to provide them with decent housing and adequate food, economists instinctively want to provide them with more cash income." Liberal theories of justice under capitalism began to mirror this ideal, concentrating on thought experiments of the economy as one giant auction. In these debates the question of justice focused just on how much money each type of individual should get for bidding on these market goods, not the terms under which goods are created or accessed.[10]

The logical endpoint of this worldview is replacing all government programs with the provision of a basic income, such as a negative income tax, as the conservative economist Milton Friedman proposed. In a series of 1978 lectures, the philosopher Michel Foucault saw that this created a certain relationship in the economy. A basic income would be, according to its advocates, "socially effective without being economically disruptive" and would mean "giving up the idea that society as a whole owes services like health and education to each of its members." Concerns about inequality would only focus on the absolute poverty of the worst-off, a group that could be mentally segregated from the rest of society.[11]

For most people, however, this world meant that apart from the very poor, "the mechanisms of competition and enterprise" would "be allowed to function in the rest of society." Market dependency would be the rule for most people, as "above the threshold everyone will have to be an enterprise for himself or for his family." (It is precisely this detachment from a broader egalitarian agenda that makes many people skeptical when basic income proposals are brought up as a fix to all of society's problems.) In the increasingly dominant view of many economists, the whole point of egalitarianism is to ensure that market dependency can be sustained.[12]

This book is a history of people fighting against market dependency, and a story of how they formed arguments about freedom in order to do so. Over the centuries, Americans have articulated five broad, overlapping arguments for why freedom requires keeping us free from the market.

The first is the most straightforward: the distribution of goods in a market economy doesn't match what we need to live free lives. Health, education, and time are part of the necessary baseline for exercising our freedom, and as such it is necessary that all of us have access to them in roughly equal measure. These goods should not be distributed on the basis of who can afford to pay for them.[13]

The second argument is that the market is an unreliable provider of these essential goods. Sometimes companies just don't produce enough compared with what society needs. People demand free public colleges because it is clear that private higher education institutions would rather increase their prestige instead of provide mass education. Insurance companies want to preemptively discriminate against those who would most benefit from insurance. Simply subsidizing private businesses to do this work can easily end up in them capturing those resources rather than providing what is needed. Public programs instead do the opposite here, reducing costs and ensuring people get what they need. In addition, while any individual market for a good can fail to deliver what society needs, the problem is compounded when you look at how all those markets, put together, can fail during recessions and depressions. The problem of insufficient demand creates long periods of high unemployment and depressed output for no reason other than the failure of the market to coordinate all its activities. An important reason people have demanded protections from the marketplace is to offset the devastation caused by the business cycle, pain no individual causes themselves or can prevent on their own. Markets that can collapse in such ways are not suitable for the core elements of our freedom.[14]

A third argument is that freedom requires being free from arbitrary power and domination by the will of others. Americans have concluded that if others can interfere with your life in a wanton and capricious manner, you are not free. The marketplace is a site of profound domination and arbitrary power. This is obvious in the labor contract. In the abstract worldview of economics, workers simply sell their labor and bosses buy it, the same way one might sell and buy a pack of gum. But the workplace has always been one of the most important political battlefields for the definition of freedom. Workers put themselves under what the philosopher Elizabeth Anderson describes as the "private government" of bosses in the workplace, and these relationships, like any kind of government power, can be predatory and exploitative. While workers may have the choice to leave, many don't, either because of the lack of viable options in the larger economic environment or the terms of their contracts themselves. Bosses will always have an advantage because, under market dependency, workers need to work in order to survive, in order to have the resources to continue living.[15]

Abusive, arbitrary power extends from the labor contract to markets in general. Consider how Enron manipulated energy prices, or pharmaceutical investors have taken over rare, life-saving drugs and raised their prices beyond what ordinary people can afford. Consider families that have their equity in their home stripped through a deceptive financial product, an injustice that especially hits families of color. The philosopher Debra Satz describes these kinds of exchanges as "noxious markets." Markets like these can create harmful outcomes for individuals themselves or for society as a whole. They are characterized by instances where one side can take advantage of asymmetric knowledge, agency, power, or the vulnerabilities of a participant. People have always fought to suppress these kinds of markets in order to preserve their freedom.[16]

The fourth argument is that the expansion of markets to all of society turns all things into commodities, and leaves no rewards for things that don't function as commodities. As the political economist Karl Polanyi described in his book *The Great Transformation*, things like land, labor, and money aren't actual commodities. Instead each functions as a "fictitious commodity." Land isn't produced by anyone; it was already there. Money isn't made from one's efforts but comes from banks and states as a mechanism for accounting. As Polanyi writes, "Labor is only another name for a human activity which goes with life itself, which in its turn is not produced for sale but for entirely different reasons, nor can that activity be detached from the rest of life, be stored or mobilized." Society resists the commodification of all of these elements. Throughout the 1800s, a century before Polanyi, Americans made arguments when it came to land and working hours and money, understanding something was being stripped from their freedom when they were all determined solely by the marketplace.[17]

Sustaining human life requires resources that the market can't guarantee. Those who can't work, either because they are old, young, or disabled, still need to survive. A society based entirely around the market will not be able to reproduce itself in a healthy manner, because all societies rely on an infrastructure of care to replenish themselves. People aren't batteries that can be recharged in a factory. They are human beings who need care, love, and protection in order to function. Society needs resources to raise and care for children, work that doesn't claim any income from society. This care work of social reproduction is precisely a thing the market doesn't pay for; it can only borrow against, until the deficit it runs starts to strain all of us.[18]

The last reason people have given for why freedom requires the suppression of the market is that, contrary to the idea of negative freedom, the marketplace is a political project, a form of government that projects state power. Once you think about how a modern, capitalist economy operates, the idea of negative freedom doesn't carry any weight. Just as we debate whether or not the actions of the government will help or hinder freedom, the execution of the marketplace by the government needs to be democratically debated as well. There is no neutral way to have a market, and all choices matter, especially when it comes to how free we are. This was understood before the late 1800s, where the line between the economy and government wasn't drawn as sharply through law. The idea of economic freedom as an absolute right to contract had to be invented.

Money and property are the terms under which we manage

relationships among people. Those relationships are backed by the state, which ultimately enforces all contracts. Consider, for example, owning a house. You own your home because you can prevent other people from living in it or using it without your permission. It's not a vertical relationship between you and the physical structure—your house remains blissfully unaware of any legal contracts you have over it. Instead, it's a horizontal relationship between people. If you were to sleep on the front porch of someone's house, they could call the police to remove you. This is even more true in a modern economy, where the state structures capital and wealth claims so that they can easily be moved across time and space. From shares in a corporation to intellectual property, much of what constitutes wealth in our era doesn't reflect relationships to actual objects, but instead represents claims over profits and incomes, claims the government will ultimately administer. Once we see property in this sense, we understand that there's no way we can define it as anything other than a form of regulating interference among people.[19]

A free society will provide key goods in some realms and suppress markets in others. Sometimes this can be done with regulations and mandates, while other times it must be through the public directly providing the good itself. A free society also works to suppress domination in the marketplace: by giving workers a say in their workplaces that goes beyond simply being able to leave, by aggressively checking abuses from sellers, and by ensuring that work done outside the marketplace is compensated and provided for as well. All of these political goals can be done in a way that takes advantage of the innovation and dynamism of markets, while checking our dependency on them. The choice for this freer society is ours to make.

There are many ways to tell the story of freedom and markets. This is a work of history because history gives a flesh-and-blood urgency to what are often presented as abstract, academic fights.

When we only understand these problems using the tools of economics and public policy, we end up ascribing a naturalness to the market in a way that gives too much away. When we focus just on market failures and how the government can respond to them, we tend to assume that the market is both natural and should have primacy over the way we arrange our lives. When we use the current tools of philosophy to examine the expansion of markets into our lives, we tend to get lost in well-rehearsed debates about what should be for sale, rather than the life-or-death threat of the market that everyday people face. There are debates over whether sex work is degrading, without any underlying criticism of how waged work itself can be degrading. There are arguments over whether people should be able to purchase human organs or illegal drugs, but little about the injustice of a society where people die because they can't buy insulin.

History also has a wide range of stories to draw from. Chapters 1 through 3 discuss land, labor, and life, respectively, and the fictitious understanding of them as commodities. Advocates for free homesteads, limitations on working hours, and social insurance each faced significant opposition in trying to remove each of these spheres of life from the sole logic of the market. Chapter 4 looks at the New Deal, and how Social Security and the Wagner Act were able to redefine a new baseline of freedom against extraordinary odds.

Chapter 5 examines the remarkable case study of World War II day care centers. Because the military wanted bombers, not case files, they provided day cares to female workers without the humiliating stigma that normally went with charity and poverty-targeted programs. Women responded with political campaigns after the war ended to keep the day cares open. Chapter 6 is the story of how federal bureaucrats teamed up with civil rights activists and black medical professionals to use the brand new program of Medicare as a means to tear down Jim Crow and desegregate Southern hospitals. It was a clear example of how a public program can break down injustice in a way that markets will not on their own.

Chapters 7 and 8 tell the story in reverse, about how our age of neoliberalism expanded and embraced markets as a political weapon. Chapter 7 looks at how the notion of the public was stripped out of public corporations, the public domain, and public utilities. This was a revolutionary program carried out rapidly, replacing public obligation with an idea of freedom as private property instead. Chapter 8 looks at how free college, the norm for over a century, was replaced with student loans. This ideological transformation was built on forcing young students to become enterprises of themselves in a financial market, market dependency conjured out of thin air through the law.

Past generations of thinkers and activists built an intellectual arsenal of ideas and concepts about the role of the marketplace and human freedom that make current notions look thin. Indeed, making us forget we ever knew something different has been one of the major accomplishments of our age of market dependency. But that older tradition is waiting to be recovered. The overwhelming odds of the current moment can beat us down and leave us exhausted, unsure if anything can change. This nihilism leads to inaction. But history shows us that people have always faced overwhelming odds; they have also fought for what they believe is right. Sometimes they won.

1

FREE LAND

In 1846 the newspaper publisher Horace Greeley took on the cause of land reform. He threw his energy and enterprise into the idea that the federal government should freely give 160 acres of land in the West to anyone willing to work it. He announced his support with an editorial in his own newspaper, the rapidly rising *New-York Tribune.* In it, he outlined how making this land accessible outside the market would create a free citizenry. Dividing public land in the West "would rapidly cover the yet unappropriated Public Domain with an independent, substantial yeomanry, enjoying a degree of Equality in Opportunities and advantages such as the world has not seen." This would be not be a form of charity but rather an antidote to poverty. "Shame on the laws which send an able, willing man to the Alms-House or to any form of beggary," Greeley wrote, "when the Soil on which he would gladly work and produce is barred against Poverty and accorded by this Government of Freemen to those alone who have money to pay for it." He would become the most prominent voice for that movement until the Homestead Act passed sixteen years later.[1]

Greeley had clear villains in mind: a land monopoly and slaveholders seeking to dominate the free lands. He stated that the "right of owning property, or of owning land, is one thing; the right to own thousands and even millions of acres of land is another." He condemned "a system of Land Monopoly which robs the producer" of their work and "often dooms him to absolute

starvation on the soil he has faithfully and effectively tilled!"
More, even in 1846, Greeley saw that free homesteads would "erect
an almost impregnable barrier against the farther encroachments
of Slavery." In the 1850s he would continue to argue, alongside the
newly formed Republican Party he helped create, that homesteads
were the best way to stop the expansion of the Slave Power west
and its domination of the nation's politics.[2]

The broad-based accessibility of public wealth that Greeley envisioned was built on settler colonialism and the wide-scale displace-
ment and murder of Native American populations. The government
would use war, removal, containment, and even more coercive pressure in its westward expansion. As the legal historian Stuart Banner
describes, there was a continuum between buying Native American
land using legal contracts and taking that land through militarized
conquest. But from the start the contracts were always created under legal institutions favorable to white settlers, and as time went
on those contracts blurred into and became indistinguishable from
conquest. The land on the frontier was only "free" when it was taken,
with force, from the people already living there.[3]

Yet the Homestead Act has something to teach us about our
era of massive inequality in wealth and power in America. Here
was a period where people understood that inequality of wealth
and capital, in the form of land, meant inequality of power in our
everyday lives and a real lack of freedom. Americans debated how
the distribution of their wealth would create the kind of society
they would inhabit. This vision could be more egalitarian and free,
or it could be regressive and unfree. Would the public domain,
the lands owned by the federal government, help expand slavery?
Would it be bought and sold by large, rich estates? Or would it be
broadly distributed in limited quantities to workers and settlers?
The push for free homesteads redefined economic freedom and
was an unapologetic demand to keep something away from the
market, a demand that drew on an ideological foundation laid by
a generation of thinkers and activists.

There's a reason so many early reformers focused on land as their issue. Land was one of the major sources of capital and wealth in the early United States, and access to land structured not just families but society itself. The federal government also owned a lot of land. In the first decades of the country, states ceded 233 million acres to the federal government beyond their own borders. This was radically expanded by the Louisiana Purchase of 1803, which gave the federal government an additional 523 million acres of land. Throughout the first half of the nineteenth century, between purchases and conquest, the federal government absorbed almost a billion acres of land.[4]

How to distribute all this land was one of the central questions of American politics from 1803 through the Civil War. The default decision was to use the market to raise revenues. The federal government was deeply in debt, and it needed money. Selling all this land for profit was the obvious choice. From the Louisiana Purchase to the start of the Civil War, public land sales would account for around 10 percent of federal revenues. Though not a large source of funds on their own, these sales helped supplement the revenues from trade tariffs, which contributed the vast majority of tax revenue.[5]

From the beginning, however, there was also pushback against treating land like any other thing for sale. Land was a source of wealth, yet nobody created it. Inequality in this wealth would cause problems on both ends of the distribution. Those too poor to access land they could own would be subject to the whims and domination of landowners. Meanwhile the rents and profits of landowners could be invested in more land, creating large concentrations of land and power among the already wealthy. These landowners could use their wealth to turn politics to their own ends, as the South would do as it fought to expand slavery west into the public lands.

You can see this argument in the writings of the influential Revolutionary Era writer Thomas Paine. In his 1796 pamphlet

Agrarian Justice, Paine argued that anyone developing and cultivating land "owes to the community a ground-rent," a term he coined to describe the unique obligations when it came to land. Landowners owe everyone a payment because land isn't a commodity like any other, as it is not created by anyone. "Man did not make the earth," and as such "he had no right to locate as his property in perpetuity any part of it."[6] In Paine's telling, early hunters and shepherds had no sense of property in land. It was only when people started farming that property in land came into being, as it was no longer possible to differentiate between the land and the investments people put into that land. But no matter how much people invested and innovated with what could be done on land, from erecting buildings to raising crops, they never could create the land itself. By taking from this collective pool of resources nobody created, landowners owed the public a cash payment.

Paine feared the growing power of concentrated landowners. He thought excluding people from land ownership would create poverty and dependency, precluding them from developing themselves fully as free citizens. Paine also believed that landowners owed a collective debt for obtaining the land in the first place, and that those revenues should be used to provide universal economic security. He proposed taxing the inheritance of land in order to fund both a retirement pension and a cash grant to citizens when they reach adulthood, an early example of a program like Social Security.

Some thought this argument didn't go far enough, and that only direct public ownership would stop the abuses of landowners. The English radical Thomas Spence thought that Paine's plan of allowing for private landowners and simply taxing them made it so that people would "sell their birth-right for a mess of porridge, by accepting of a paltry consideration in lieu of their rights." Spence was worried that this cash grant would act like a bribe, allowing the rich to pay off the poor and then abuse the whole system. Spence saw this system as one where the "rich would abolish all hospitals, charitable funds, and parochial provision for the poor, telling them, that they now have all that their great advocate, Paine, demands."[7]

But arguments about the land issue didn't just stop with insisting on the obligation rich landowners had to everyone else. They also included ensuring that everyone also had land for themselves. Thomas Jefferson saw land as special because it created a certain kind of citizen that was worth nurturing. He wrote to James Madison in 1785 that "[w]henever there are in any country uncultivated lands and unemployed poor, it is clear that the laws of property have been so far extended as to violate natural right. The earth is given as a common stock for man to labor and live on." In Jefferson's *Notes on the State of Virginia*, he wrote that "those who labour in the earth are the chosen people of God."[8]

As cities grew after the Revolution, the demand for free land became louder. One voice in this chorus was Thomas Skidmore. Born into a struggling family in Newton, Connecticut, in 1790, Skidmore wandered up and down the East Coast as a tutor after leaving home. He eventually moved to New York City in 1819 and became a machinist. Difficult and sarcastic, he was self-taught when it came to politics and economics, absorbing all the political philosophy of the period.[9]

Skidmore's one major work, *The Rights of Man to Property*, was published in 1829. The thesis of the book is in its extended subtitle: *Being a proposition to make it equal among the adults of the present generation, and to provide for its equal transmission to every individual of each succeeding generation on arriving at the age of maturity*. In it, Skidmore makes the argument for the mass redistribution of private property, especially land.

The title is a take on Thomas Jefferson's statement in the Declaration of Independence that our Creator gave man "certain unalienable Rights, that among these are Life, Liberty and the pursuit of Happiness." Skidmore argues that without a right to owning property, the other rights are meaningless. Property, in his view, was necessary to pursue happiness in our society, and to get property one had to risk both their life and liberty. "Do we not every day, see multitudes, in order to acquire property, in the very pursuit of that happiness which Mr. Jefferson classes among the unalienable rights of man, obliged to sacrifice both liberty and health and often ultimately life, into the bargain?" [10]

Skidmore showed the radical potential of land reform and the threat of a land monopoly. It would be one thing if property was already fairly divided, but land was unequally owned, and the resulting inequality was carried across generations. According to Skidmore, the world was rapidly becoming divided between "two distinct classes" of "those who own the world, and those who own no part of it." This is exactly the worry that the newly urbanized workers in New York City would have felt at the time. Life expectancy fell for workers living in cities, driven by disease, fires, pollution, and violence. These urban workers had grown up with Jeffersonian ideas that widespread democracy was built upon property ownership, and many feared becoming lifelong wage laborers, which they identified with dependency and unfreedom. [11]

The core of Skidmore's book is a twenty-point plan for a new constitution for the state of New York, one that actually embraced the radical implications of equality of opportunity. It included a proposal for a General Division that would carry out a mass redistribution through one giant auction of all property. As a first step, Skidmore envisioned a debt jubilee in which all private debts would be canceled. The state would then claim and assess all property, take the total value, and divide that value among adult citizens as a recorded credit. Those citizens would, in turn, bid on the stock of property with this credit. Property would thus be more or less equalized. At death, a citizen's property would go back to the state, where it would be distributed among new people, instead of the state using its powers to extend wealth and privilege across generations. Skidmore believed inequalities that flowed from his plan, such as from some people working more or producing better goods than others, were justified. The real danger stemmed from already existing inequalities and from an unequal distribution of inherited wealth across generations.[12]

This wasn't just a thought experiment; it became a short-lived political platform. Skidmore was writing his book at the same time as he was building one of the first labor parties. A recession made 1829 a difficult time for workers in New York. In response to rumors that employers were about to lengthen the working day one hour to eleven hours per day, a group of journeymen workers held a public meeting about a potential mass strike. Skidmore was there and became a leader of this movement, pushing the workers to call for a series of resolutions including a radical one stating that "all men hold their property by the consent of the great mass of the community, and no other title." A few days later, between five and six thousand people showed up to protest, and thus started the short-lived Working Men's Party. Their platform, strongly influenced by Skidmore, called for a ten-hour day, free public education, an end to debtors' prisons, and ways for workers to recover wages when firms went into bankruptcy. Skidmore successfully pushed to get two additional planks added to the Working Men's Party: a denouncement of private property in wealth and an end to its hereditary inheritance.[13]

That fall, the Working Men's Party, running on this remarkable platform, fielded candidates for state office. They did surprisingly well, winning 31 percent of the vote in New York City. One member was elected to state office; Skidmore himself came within twenty-three votes of being elected to the State Assembly. But shortly after the election, betrayals from within destroyed the party. Some other, less influential leaders wanted nothing to do with radical land redistribution and successfully conspired to push Skidmore out at a meeting, packing the audience and preventing him from speaking. Infighting caused the party to collapse shortly after.[14]

Mass political agitation on land reform would have to wait

until the creation of the National Reform Association by the newspaper publisher and activist George Henry Evans. Evans was born in Bromyard, Herefordshire, England, in 1805. At fifteen, he moved with his family to what would become Binghamton, New York. An avid reader, Evans absorbed the thinkers and writers of the American Revolution, and shared with Skidmore a fascination with the writings of Thomas Paine. In 1824, at the age of nineteen, Evans started his own newspaper, the *Museum and Independent Corrector.* After moving to New York, he created the *Working Man's Advocate*, one of the country's first major pro-labor newspapers and which was originally the paper for the Working Men's Party, with which he was also involved. He kept the newspaper in print until it was bankrupted in the 1837 depression.[15]

In 1844, Evans worked with other organizers, including those protesting against landlords in upstate New York, to create a plan for land reform. They converged on three core demands. The first was freedom of the public lands, which would require free homesteads for settlers. Second, a homestead exemption, which would prevent homes from being collected for the payment of debt in bankruptcy. Finally, a limitation on the number of acres any one person could own. The first two would protect the individual by ensuring they had a baseline to survive, as well as make their right to land inalienable, even against the worst economic difficulties. The last would foster equality and protect the individual from the threat of powerful inequality in land ownership. These three ideas were the core agenda of their new organization, which they named the National Reform Association.[16]

National Reform soon became a full-fledged political movement. Though it was built out of the New York labor movement, it spread rapidly across states and became a formidable lobbying machine. The organization collected dues, prepared memos, and drafted legislation. It educated the public through newspapers, pamphlets, and meetings, both local and large scale ones organized by workers. Evans restarted his *Working Man's Advocate*, which became the newspaper of the movement. Members of the organization signed an "agrarian pledge" to only vote for candidates who agreed with the National Reform principles.[17]

The *National Reform Almanac* for 1848 reported that fifty National Reform auxiliaries existed across twenty states. They were responsible for the mass volume of petitions swarming Congress, which had at least 64,000 signatures on 533 petitions between 1845 and 1855. In 1849, the number of petitions for land reform was second only to petitions for cheap postage. One of the three planks that Evans set out, the exemption of homes from the collection of debts, produced an immediate string of victories, with eighteen states passing a version of it between 1847 and 1852. The exemption proved popular because it helped protect the security of the household from financial collapse, the business cycle, and other vagaries of the market.[18]

In October 1845, Greeley's *Tribune* printed the text of the National Reform's pamphlet "Vote Yourself a Farm" with instructions on how to order more "at the rate of ten copies for a cent" in order to pass out to additional people. The text had been available before as a handbill, but Greeley's support gave it a much wider audience. The pamphlet opens with a remarkable proposition: "Are you an American citizen? Then you are a joint-owner of the public lands. Why not take enough of your property to provide yourself a home? Why not vote yourself a farm?"[19]

There are two clear demands in the document: set a limit on the amount of land anyone can own or inherit, and make the public lands free only to settlers, not speculators. Those settlers could, in turn, sell their improvements to anyone else who did not own any land. The "Vote Yourself a Farm" pamphlet explicitly called on people as equal citizens to claim they were owed a portion of the national wealth as a common heritage.

The language of "Vote Yourself a Farm" was not only framed in terms of freedom but also addressed many different kinds of people on their own terms. If you were religious, "assert that the land is the Lord's, because He made it. Resist then the blasphemers who exact money for his Work." If you were less religious and instead viewed yourself as "endowed with reason," you were to argue that "your right to life hereby includes the right to a place to live." If you were "a party follower," then "you have long enough employed your vote to benefit scheming office-seekers; use it for once to benefit yourself—Vote yourself a farm." It's a set of talking points, but also an argument about how wealth should be distributed in a free society. The enemies are clear: scheming office-seekers who don't care about your actual interest, blasphemers who take money for God's work, the "aristocracy" of mass landholders, a "hoggish monopoly" sitting on the product of labor, and the "hoary iniquities of Norman land pirates" that passed for then-current land law. By using this kind of language, the pamphlet established a villain for workers to oppose.[20]

This debate about how free land formed the foundation for a free society extended through the work so many thinkers, from Jefferson's early championing of yeoman farmers and Paine's social obligations, to the labor-infused radicalism of Skidmore's political party and the mobilization of the National Reform Association. Each had their own focus. Yet there was a core set of arguments about freedom and land that appeared over and over again, no matter the context. All the homestead advocates were adamant that they weren't promoting a form of charity. They advocated for homesteading as a means of creating a more equal citizenship, rather than a way of simply compensating the losers of society.

Mass industrialization, and the way it would change the entire economy and the country, was still too far in the future to see. Yet even then there was a class enemy common to all the labor reform arguments, with reformers deploying many of the same arguments against what they called the "land monopoly." They argued landowners used the government to ensure that they had the best pick of lands available. The owners also wanted to speculate, which meant they kept land that could be productive to a community unsettled and undeveloped. It was only after the work of others had been done to create and build up those communities that speculators would then be willing to sell at a hefty profit. By hoarding all the productive capital in an area, landowners forced men into waged labor, where they were subject to the abuses of bosses to survive. As George Washington Julian, who would go on to help create the Republican Party, argued, "Land monopoly brings into the country a surplus laboring population, whom it first deprives of their natural right to the soil, and then prescribes the terms upon which it will give them food and shelter."[21]

These arguments needed someone to popularize them, and Horace Greeley took up the challenge. Horace Greeley was born on a farm near Amherst, New Hampshire, in 1811. His father had lost the family farm due to debts when he was a young child. He excelled in school; by age thirteen his schoolmaster sent him home, admitting there was nothing left to teach young Horace. He arrived in New York in 1831 and started his own short-lived *New-Yorker* newspaper, which would collapse in the Panic of 1837. The Panic, which was blamed on Democratic economic policies, gave a boost to the Whig Party, whose New York leaders took the young Greeley under their wing. Greeley became an editor of the Whig newspaper *The Jeffersonian* in 1838, and in 1841, he founded the *New-York Tribune*.

Greeley's causes mattered because he was one of the nation's most prominent voices in the middle of the nineteenth century. He was the publisher and editor of the *New-York Tribune*, which, within fifteen years of its founding, boasted an audience of nearly 280,000 readers who subscribed to either its daily, weekly, or semi-weekly edition. This made it one of the most influential papers in the world. As a result, even those who disagreed with Greeley had to engage with him, using his ideas as a foil for their own.[22]

Greeley was a modernizer. As a leading Whig, Greeley didn't get lost in the conservatism of his party, but instead described

himself as "a mediator, an interpreter, a reconciler, between Conservatism and Radicalism." One can see this role when it came to
his view on the economy and workers. Greeley believed that there
was a shared interest among all parties in the economy, especially
when it came to bosses and workers. He refused to see labor and
capital as having opposing interests. Greeley supported labor but
hated class conflict. He endorsed arbitration, worker cooperatives,
and the ten-hour workday, but was against strikes. Like many in
his era, Greeley believed that waged labor would weaken the character of those who worked. Greeley went further and supported
aggressive government policies, such as the tariff, that he believed
would help people become self-sufficient.[23]

His idea of shared interest and self-sufficiency among all parties was at its most developed when it came to leading the campaign for land reform and free homesteads, as he saw land as the
solution to labor unrest within the growing market economy.
Greeley came to the Homestead Movement through Evans.
Though hesitant at first, Greeley embraced the National Reform
agenda, and put his significant influence fully behind popular-
izing it throughout the country. Within a year Greeley declared
that fifty newspapers had endorsed land reform, building on his
arguments for free land, which reflected his distaste for class
conflict. Businesses would, in Greeley's mind, also benefit from
free land. "Every smoke that rises in [the] Great West," he wrote,
"marks a new customer to the counting rooms and warehouses of
New York." He didn't create the phrase "Go West, young man,"
but he did popularize it. Greeley described free public lands as
"the great regulator of the relations of Labor and Capital, the
safety valve of our industrial and social engine." This safety valve
metaphor became key for Greeley. He saw land ownership as a
method for countering economic depressions, giving workers an
opportunity when unemployment increased. In his mind, both
the freedom of public lands and limitations on landholding were
"vitally necessary to the ultimate emancipation of labor from

thralldom and misery." Greeley believed that this safety valve would help support those being left behind in the growing cities. He briefly served in Congress in 1848 and introduced a homestead bill on his second day. When asked why someone from New York would be pushing so hard for free land in the West, he responded that he "represented more landless men than any other member" in Congress.[24]

All the politics regarding land changed in 1846 with the start of the Mexican War. James K. Polk, president from 1845 to 1849, carried out more land acquisition than any other president in our history, greater than even Jefferson and the Louisiana Purchase. Polk bought Oregon and the northwest part of the country and waged a war against Mexico to take the southwest. By the time Polk forced the Mexican government to hand over what is now California, New Mexico, Arizona, and Texas, his own Democratic Party was mad that the U.S. didn't seize all of Mexico. At this point the South saw slavery not as its own peculiar institution, but instead the main economic system that ought to dominate politics across the Western Hemisphere. Cotton-producing slavery expanded through the 1850s, taking advantage of expanding financial markets and its own control of American foreign policy. Whether valuing its own economy centered on "King Cotton," or the sugar from Cuba and the coffee from Brazil also created by slaves, the South saw the future of the hemisphere as one based on slave labor, one that was its own to control.[25]

The Missouri Compromise of 1820 had governed how slavery would extend into the Louisiana Purchase, but this newly acquired territory changed the question of slavery. Pennsylvania Democrat David Wilmot introduced a provision to block slavery from expansion into these new lands, which succeeded in the House but failed in the Senate. Suddenly Northerners, both Democrats and Whigs, saw the South as trying to seize land for the expansion of slavery. The South, in turn, saw the North as trying to kill the

South's entire political and economic way of life. Politics was splitting along sectional lines.

The Mexican War radicalized Greeley on the expansion of
slavery. He opposed the war from the beginning, writing in the
Tribune that it was "most unjust and rapacious" and "instigated
wholly . . . by a determination to uphold and fortify Slavery."
Greeley supported the Wilmot Proviso as "a solemn declaration of the United North against the further extension of Slavery under the protection of our Flag." Abolitionists noticed this
change at the time. Charles Sumner noted that "the *Tribune* has
spoken at last" on the topic of slavery.[26]

Whether Western lands would be accessible in the form of free
homesteads or whether it would be used to expand slavery became
central to debates about freedom in the 1850s. One figure who
wrestled with this issue was George Washington Julian, a former
Whig who was elected to the House as a Free Soil representative
from Indiana in 1850. His first House speech, in January 1851,
endorsed a homestead bill by Andrew Johnson, a Democrat from
Tennessee. On the floor of the House, Julian explained why land
reform was common sense: land reformers, he said, "advocate no
leveling policy, designed to strip the rich of their possessions by
any sudden act of legislation. They simply demand that, in laying the foundations of empire in the yet unpeopled regions of the
great West, Congress shall give its sanction to the natural right of
the landless citizen of the country to a home upon its soil."

Yet to the dismay of Johnson and moderate land reformers,
Julian used the speech to taunt the authors of the Great Compromise of 1850, which was designed to provide a balanced spread
of slavery into the West. He argued that homesteads could bring
about the end of slavery itself, claiming that "the adoption of the
policy for which I am contending will be a much better 'settlement' of the slavery question" than the Compromise of 1850.
"The freedom of the public lands," he continued, "is therefore an
anti-slavery measure." Julian believed homesteads would weaken

the ideology of the Slave Power by showing that men had rights to a home and the fruits of their own labor, and that the labor itself had virtue.[27]

Before the 1850s, the South had a mixed view of homesteading and opening up the lands of the West. By 1852, however, the South was opposed to it. There were many practical reasons for this opposition: the South was nervous about declining relative population; it couldn't easily attract new people, and much of its industrious free population was leaving for states such as Indiana, Illinois, Wisconsin, Iowa, and Minnesota. More important, the South correctly saw homesteading as opposed to its interest in expanding slavery. Southerners were worried about how little influence the ideology of slaveholding would have over homesteaders in new territories. Those leaving slaveholding states for free ones had little connection with slaveholding and would abandon the ideology once they were gone. Abraham Lincoln's family, which moved from the slave state of Kentucky to the free state of Indiana when he was seven, is one such example.[28]

The passing of the Fugitive Slave Act in 1850 made many Northerners worried that slavery would come to dominate all national politics. Greeley denounced the law, calling it a "gross and unpardonable exercise of tyrannical power" and that it turned Northern states into "accomplices and bailiffs of the slaveholder for a paltry share of his unjust gains." But the final issue that radicalized Greeley and other Northerners, forcing them to create their own new political party, was the Kansas-Nebraska Act of 1854. Designed by Democrat Stephen Douglas, this law would allow Kansas and Nebraska to be admitted as either slave or free states, depending on how local citizens voted. In effect, it meant that slavery could extend anywhere in the West, breaking the Missouri Compromise that limited slavery from extending to the Northwest. Greeley immediately wrote in the *Tribune* that "this Nebraska movement of Douglas and his backers" was "one of measureless treachery and infamy." As fighting broke out in Kansas between proslavery and antislavery forces, Greeley teamed with Frederick Law Olmsted, who would go on to be the famous landscape architect of New York's Central Park and Prospect Park, to purchase a howitzer cannon and send it there to help those opposed to the expansion of slavery. (The howitzer arrived in time in Lawrence, Kansas, to fight off attacks from proslavery forces.) Greeley wrote that this was where the line would be drawn: "The one question on which all earnest opponents of the Slave Power are united and determined is the Kansas Question." [29]

The Republican Party was founded in the midst of this conflict, with people like Julian and Greeley among its initial members. It was immediately competitive and came within reach of the presidency in 1856. The Republicans' core focus was preventing the expansion of slavery into any new territories. Their agenda also combined the Whig priorities Greeley championed for internal improvement, including tariffs and railroad development as well as free homesteads. [30]

The slaveholding South maintained control of the Senate and the presidency between 1852 and 1860. Three homestead bills made it through the House in that time, and all were blocked in the Senate. A homestead bill made it through the House and Senate in early 1860, only to be vetoed by Democratic president James Buchanan. The *New-York Tribune* ran a line-by-line refutation of Buchanan's veto statement, with Greeley posing an obvious rhetorical question to his readers: "Does anybody suppose that Abraham Lincoln would ever veto such a bill?" Lincoln would win the presidency that year. [31]

The Homestead Act passed on May 20, 1862. It provided for any adult citizen or person intending to become a citizen to claim 160 acres of surveyed government land. The claimants would have to improve the land by building a dwelling, and after five years they would be entitled to the land for free, minus a small registration fee. The land could not be used for the satisfaction of settlers' debts, and the public domain would no longer be used as collateral for the debt of the United States.

The Homestead Act had significant flaws. It didn't provide enough safeguards against speculation, as land speculators would pay people to create dummy applications and sit on the best land until they could sell it. The government was also separately giving away huge grants of land to railroads, which meant settlers would be left with the choice of taking what lands remained or purchasing the better lands at inflated prices. Homesteads also failed to create the safety valve Greeley had hoped. The journey to the West was too expensive and serious for people to undertake lightly. During recessions, workers couldn't amass the capital they needed to travel west and secure a homestead, which limited the policy's effectiveness at counteracting unemployment; and those with enough capital to reach their homesteads and get started still struggled to find stability, because one bad farming season could mean the difference between success and failure. For every family that succeeded in gaining a homestead, another left the land or sold their rights.[32]

But even with all the problems, it still provided a floor of opportunity for all those who were able to use it. It was a massive transfer of wealth, one of the largest in American history, to everyday people to provide for their families. Over the next seventy-six years, 3 million people applied for homesteads and nearly 1.5 million got them. That was a transfer of around 246 million acres of land, or 16 percent of the public domain. To give a sense of the scale, this is around 90 percent of the size of Texas and California combined. One estimate finds that 46 million Americans are descendants of those who received land under the original Homestead Act. And all of it was free, given from the public domain to citizens willing to cultivate the land.[33]

The Homestead Act shows how people were motivated and organized by a belief in the wide distribution of opportunity and wealth as well as who the nation's wealth should serve and what kind of country we should create. It also shows how the concept of a baseline of resources and wealth necessary for survival outside the market animated ideas and politics throughout our history. Yet there's also a limitation here, one that can be seen by looking at land policy in the South during Reconstruction, and what became of Horace Greeley.

In the aftermath of the Civil War, the freed slaves had what W.E.B. Du Bois described as a "land hunger" for their own property, which they viewed as an "absolutely fundamental and essential thing to any real emancipation of the slaves." There was a chance that this hope would be met. In order to provide for the newly emancipated slaves following him as he marched through the Southeast, General William Tecumseh Sherman issued Special Field Order No. 15 on January 16, 1865, setting aside the Sea Islands and the area south of Charleston for the newly freed. Each family would receive forty acres, and the army would help them with acquiring mules. (This is very likely the origin of the phrase "40 Acres and a Mule.") By June of 1865 there were forty thousand freedmen settled on 400,000 acres of land in what had been one of the richest areas of the slaveholding class. The Freedmen's Bureau, an administrative agency tasked with assisting the newly freed slaves, came to control more than 850,000 acres of abandoned land in the South. General O. O. Howard, the Bureau's chief, issued Circular 13 in July of 1865, which would start carving these possessions into forty-acre plots to be given to the freedmen. These measures didn't last. After the assassination of Lincoln, Vice President Andrew Johnson took over. He would quickly end both orders, returning all the lands to their former Confederate owners.[34]

Congress passed a Southern Homestead Act in 1866, opening up 46 million acres to the program. Throughout the Civil War, George Washington Julian had argued that the North would need to break up large landholdings in the South and turn them over

to homesteads if they hoped to break up the power of the plant-
ers and turn the slave economy into one of free labor. That effort
failed, yet Julian held out hope that his Southern Homestead Act
would work to help create self-sufficiency among the freed people.
However, because of local violent terror by whites and the lack of
capital for newly freed slaves, very few freedmen were able to take
advantage of Southern homesteads. Much of the land simply went
to business interests for resource extraction. Though the Homestead Act would survive until the 1970s, the Southern Homestead
Act was repealed after just ten years. Only 28,000 people would
receive land, with fewer than 5,500 freed people being able to take
part in the promise of free homesteading.[35]

Horace Greeley started as a supporter of Reconstruction. In
1866 he wrote, "If we shall close this long controversy with the
negro still a serf," then "we shall be a beaten bankrupt party, and
shall have richly deserved our fate." Yet he resisted the idea of seiz-
ing the land of former slaveholders and redistributing them to
freedmen, stating "we shall realize that inevitable evils of confiscation are too great to justify an experiment of this character." Greeley instead imported his idea of homesteads to the South. He told
a black audience to "[b]ecome land-owners, all of you, so soon as
you may," as it will "give you a deeper feeling of independence and
of self-respect, and do not wait to obtain a home by confiscation"
of slaveholding lands through the government. Though Greeley
had been worried about the power of concentrated land ownership for decades, and even though he was one of the most vocal
critics of the Slave Power, he could not bring himself to support
land redistribution from slaveholders. Taking land from Native
Americans in the West, however, gave him no such pause.[36]

Greeley, like many Republicans of the time, believed that mass
prosperity for workers in the North and South would result from
the end of slavery, creating a country of free workers no longer
having to compete with slave labor. But the process of industrialization only intensified after the Civil War, increasing the wealth

of the capitalist class but also creating poverty as well as class conflict. Between 1863 and 1873 there were 249 strikes within New
York alone. By 1872 labor unrest was so much the norm that a
fundamental conflict between capital and workers was increasingly seen as the ordinary state of things.

Those like Greeley who believed in a natural harmony of interest in the economy became worried about extensive labor unrest,
and saw Reconstruction as aiding that upheaval. They linked the
demand for political and civil rights for the freedmen in the South
with the demand for labor rights in the North. It turned them
against the continuation of Reconstruction. Greeley argued that
the freedmen should "root, hog or die" on their own rather than
expect more from the government. The *Tribune*, once a proud op-
ponent of the Slave Power, began publishing influential agitprop
against black rule in Southern state governments with article titles
like "A State in Ruins."[37]

By 1872, these alienated Republicans bolted to form their
own party, the new Liberal Republicans, and, to the surprise of
all, chose Greeley as their nominee for president. The Democrats,
knowing they couldn't successfully run their own candidate, endorsed Greeley. It was an awkward campaign given that Greeley
had spent decades describing Democrats as "murderers, adulterers,
drunkards, cowards, liars, thieves." Greeley tried to cover up those
slurs by saying, "I never said all Democrats were saloon keepers.
What I said was that all saloonkeepers were Democrats." Greeley
was crushed by Ulysses S. Grant in the election, winning only six
out of thirty-seven states. He died weeks later. Though defeated
here, his platform ultimately won the long game, with Reconstruction abandoned and the Republican Party turned into a pro-
business party in subsequent decades.[38]

In this turn against Reconstruction we see how the American
idea of freedom is a living, evolving thing. Before, Greeley believed that simply ending slavery and providing a background of
free labor policies would be enough to ensure that people could be

self-sufficient, independent, and removed from the arbitrary domination of others. It led Greeley to promote ideas that were genuine and remarkable in creating this freedom, with free homesteads among the most important. But the challenge of Reconstruction showed Greeley that this wouldn't be sufficient in a new era. New times require new definitions of freedom, and new methods of how the government must suppress markets. This forced him to a make a choice: freedom could either come from a commitment to civil rights and labor rights against white supremacy and industrialization, or it could come from a laissez-faire abandonment of both in favor of economic freedom. He made the wrong choice.

2

FREE TIME

Frank Wigeman started off 1884 with some bad news. On New Year's Day, Wigeman showed up to his job at Godcharles & Company, a Pennsylvania nail mill where he had been working since the previous year, to learn that his wages were being cut. Godcharles had been paying its workers in scrip, a form of currency that could only be exchanged for cash at the store that the company ran. Such company stores, often in isolated locations, charged higher rates than the prices that people could get elsewhere. Paying workers in scrip had also recently been made illegal in 1881, through the passing of a new state law designed to protect workers. Wigeman sued for the $87.67 he should have been paid in cash.[1]

This law stood out for two reasons. The first was that it was designed to protect workers from abusive practices. While not uncommon, it was combined with another key feature: it couldn't be contracted away. Labor contracts were governed by a harsh, even feudal, set of court-enforced default rules. Employees couldn't receive back pay if they didn't complete their contracts, other employers couldn't try to hire away already employed workers, employees assumed all the risks of injury, and employers had full control over employees' actions. While these default assumptions could be changed, employers tended to hold the power in these negotiations.

This meant efforts to limit the length of the working day by changing the default rules governing contracts would run into the lack of power workers had. Employers would simply require workers to waive these suggestions. In 1868, for instance, Pennsylvania passed a law that set an eight-hour workday as the default. But this law would function just as a suggestion, as it had no authority to actually prevent longer working days. It merely stated what would govern labor contracts if nothing else did. If any contract stipulated something else, that would govern the contract. When miners in Schuylkill County, Pennsylvania, had attempted to stop working after eight hours, as per the law, employers instead wanted a longer day. Workers went on strike to try to get the law to work for their benefit, but ultimately failed to secure the eight-hour workday. The dynamic played out the same way in Illinois and Massachusetts, where state-proposed background limits on working-hours caused strikes, yet employers were successful in forcing workers to negotiate around them, leaving the laws toothless.[2]

But the 1881 law was different, as it explicitly outlawed payment to workers in scrips to the company store. The politicians and labor organizations advocating for the law understood it was controversial, as opponents would quickly argue that the government had no right or ability to alter private labor contracts that people chose to enter. The proponents spent a decade carefully constructing arguments addressing both the practical and legal objections. They argued that the unequal power between bosses and workers made the contracts not freely chosen. Advocates also argued that courts shouldn't enforce labor contracts that were influenced by the "weakness of parties, infringement on the civil rights of the citizen, [or were] oppressive and against public policy," and that contracts "which take away the free rights of citizens are oppressive and . . . not just and should not be protected by law."[3]

The case went all the way to the Pennsylvania Supreme Court, which sided with the company in *Godcharles v. Wigeman* (1886). Worse, Wigeman not only lost, but the Court killed the 1881 law entirely, setting into motion a war the courts would wage against economic regulations for the next fifty years. There were several other state-level cases that would invalidate economic laws during the 1880s on the basis of the idea of "freedom of contract." In 1886, the Illinois court struck down a requirement that mine owners install and use weighing scales to determine miners' wages on the idea that it interfered with the ability of workers to bargain over working conditions. But the short, 335-word opinion, written by Judge Isaac Gordon, set the stakes most clearly. To Gordon, the anti-scrip law was "an infringement alike of the rights of the employer and the employe[e]; more than this, it is an insulting attempt to put the laborer under legislative tutelage, which is not only degrading to his manhood, but subversive to his rights as a citizen of the United States." Gordon understood this to be a debate about freedom. As he concluded, a worker "may sell his labor for what he thinks best, whether money or goods, just as his employer may sell his iron or coal, and any and every law that proposes to prevent him from so doing is an infringement of his constitutional privileges, and consequently vicious and void." The logic of the case spread widely in the following decades, shutting down state efforts to pass similar laws limiting scrip or otherwise strengthening the relative bargaining position of workers.[4]

That contracts were a foundational form of freedom, and government should never interfere with markets, would have been a complete surprise to workers and judges alike in the early 1800s. Local and state laws throughout the first half of the nineteenth century regularly structured markets toward addressing concerns of the overall community. Cities and states would commonly regulate products, create licensing, and oversee public marketplaces to ensure a balance between competing parties. As Roger Taney argued before the Supreme Court in 1827, the law never understood there to be a natural right to sell, else a person "may offer for sale large quantities of gunpowder in the heart of a city, and thus endanger the lives of the citizens" or "offer hides, fish, and articles of that description, in places offensive and inconvenient to the public, and dangerous to the health of the citizens; he may hold an auction at his own warehouse, and refuse to pay any tax to the State; he may sell at retail; he may sell as a hawker and pedlar." This kind of absolute right of property had to be created.[5]

That the government never was involved in the actions between workers and bosses, those who labor and those who own capital, is a libertarian fantasy. The state has always structured markets, and during the late 1800s the government and courts intervened in important ways to boost the power of bosses and owners while limiting and stymying the actions of workers. The state did this in service of a then brand new idea of what freedom meant in the market economy, an idea that once again has taken control in our own time.

The workplace has been one of the central battlegrounds in the debate over freedom. In the workplace, we subject ourselves to a kind of private government. On the clock, bosses tell us how to act and what to do, even controlling basic bodily autonomy like when we are allowed to use the bathroom. Bosses are also able to exert a significant amount of control over our lives outside the workplace, dictating to us what we are allowed to say and surveilling our political actions. Public governments can imprison us for breaking their rules; private governments have an equally vast level of power because they can fire us, which has serious consequences, depriving us of the basic necessities and resources we need to live. Unlike our democratic form of public government, there isn't a presumption of fairness, accountability, or even regularity in the private sector. Private government can therefore function as a kind of despotic state in miniature. The ability of employees to simply leave their jobs is no check to this despotic tendency. People know this, which is why for centuries Americans have demanded more than the power to walk out the door.[6]

One demand workers have made in the battle over the nature of the workplace is for shorter working hours, most notably in the Eight-Hour Day workers' movement. Workers demanded a limit on working hours for additional leisure time, and also for the idea that it would limit unemployment in recessions and bolster productivity to encourage economic growth. But workers also went beyond this to demand a space and time free from the marketplace. Workers understood that if they didn't have free time, they couldn't have the kinds of relationships and commitments they needed to lead free and full lives. Time, like labor, is a fictitious commodity, something that we can't store or separate from the actual lives of the people who experience it. Workers understood their time as something they had to sell in order to survive. Yet the severity with which bosses and workplaces could colonize that time meant that all the other things time was needed for suffered.[7]

This is a story almost as old as America itself. In addition to demanding land reform and free homesteads, urban workers in the 1830s also demanded shorter working hours. In May 1835, a group of carpenters, masons, and stonecutters in Boston wrote and released the "Ten-Hour Circular," a short document demanding a ten-hour workday. The arguments were as clear as they were righteous. "The God of the Universe has given us time, health, and strength. We utterly deny the right of any man to dictate to us how much of it we shall sell." This system was "odious, cruel, unjust and tyrannical" as long hours turned workers into depleted husks rather than citizens engaging in the otherwise noble act of doing labor. The circular's description of bosses forcing a worker "to exhaust his physical and mental powers by excessive toil, until he has no desire to eat and sleep, and in many cases he has no power to do either" resonated with workers, especially those who were newly encountering waged labor.

The authors of the circular called upon workers to recognize their Natural Rights, which bosses violated through their exercise of control over them. Citizens left in this worn-out state could not be "friends to the country or the Rights of Man," nor could they meet their "duties to perform as American Citizens and members of society." The circular's authors also understood that excessive

hours disrespected workers as the creators of value in the economy. "We are willing to bear our portion of the burthens, and perform our part of the services of social life, if we can be treated as
men and not as beasts of burthen." Finally, they tied their struggle
against excessive hours to the memory of the American Revolution itself, writing that "we claim by the blood of our fathers, shed
on our battle-fields, in the War of the Revolution, the rights of
American Freemen, and no earthly power shall resist our righteous claims with impunity."[8]

The document's publication was a success, leading to a wave of
protests and strikes. In Boston, reading and debating the circular
inspired people to maintain a strike for a ten-hour day over the
next six months. Though it failed, others actions across the Northeast succeeded. When the printed circular made its way to Philadelphia in June 1835, the energy it created caused what is likely the
nation's first general strike. What started with handloom weavers
demanding a ten-hour day quickly spread across all the industries
of Philadelphia, with bricklayers, plasterers, masons, cigar makers,
city employees, bakers, saddlers, and printers all joining in rapid
succession. House painters joined the strike, claiming the "present
system of labor as oppressive and unjust" and "destructive of social happiness, and degrading to the name of freemen." Within a
week and a half, more than twenty trades were on strike. A parade
was organized by the workers, where they carried banners reading "From 6 to 6, ten hours work and two hours for meals." The
city's first ten-hour law passed as a result, setting the standard for
public employees, and many private employers backed down from
demanding longer hours. In Baltimore, strikes were successful
in granting the ten-hour day to city mechanics. There were similar outcomes for shipbuilders on strike for shorter hours in New
York.[9]

One thing that was clear from this wave of strikes, and that
would stick with the nascent labor movement over the next century, was that time was becoming a kind of currency in the new

American economy. Demands for time could unify workers facing very different working circumstances. Workers across many varied industries and skill levels all had different demands over wages and workplaces and, for better or worse, didn't see themselves all in the same situation when it came to how to organize. Yet all still wanted time for rest, for their families, and for their communities. Time became a mechanism for which to coordinate the demands of workers. That cigar makers and bricklayers could both see a better world through the guarantee of more time helped bind them both in a collective enterprise. Instead of asking for wages industry by industry, firm by firm, they could use time as a measuring device to determine a fair working condition across the entire economy. Because employers wanted to capture more and more of it for themselves, time became a universal measure of, and a battlefield over, the idea of freedom.[10]

During the Civil War, the shortage of labor in the North caused by military mobilization gave labor a power it hadn't experienced before. Lincoln, having famously said in his first inaugural that "[c]apital is only the fruit of labor, and could never have existed if labor had not first existed," ran an administration that was generally not hostile to labor groups, giving them breathing space to organize. Between 1863 and 1864, trade unions more than tripled in number, from 79 to 270, with a record number of 200,000 organized workers. Labor newspapers began to expand, with *Fincher's Trades' Review*, the newspaper of the machinists and blacksmiths, being the largest and an important leader in the fight for shorter working hours. The editor of *Fincher's Trades' Review* argued that "Labor is equality. Labor is dignity. Labor is power. It is able to regulate its hours."[11]

Republicans turned against Reconstruction in part because it became associated with greater labor agitation. But a small number of people saw that gaining shorter working hours was an important extension of fighting slavery. One of the most important thinkers writing about the eight-hour workday, Ira Steward, tied his cause to the spirit of abolition. To Steward, the eight-hour workday "mean[t] anti-pauperism, anti-aristocracy, anti-monopoly, anti-slavery." Steward believed that it was necessary to complete the legacy of antislavery by liberating American workers not just from chattel slavery but "wage slavery" as well. Steward was born in 1831 and raised in Massachusetts. Working twelve hours a day as an apprentice machinist before the Civil War converted him to the cause of shorter working hours. He was deeply involved in the Machinists' and Blacksmiths' International Union and was a leader of the Grand Eight-Hour League of Massachusetts, a role he shared with the abolitionist Wendell Phillips. He was a tireless proponent of shorter working hours, writing pamphlets, testifying before legislatures, and addressing workers themselves.[12]

Steward was one of first people who tried to understand what democracy and freedom for workers would look like in an industrial society. He argued for a living wage, a term he likely created, and fewer working hours. He also pushed the labor movement in new directions. He believed that high wages and shorter working hours weren't just good for workers themselves, but for the economy as a whole. High wages would create more demand for goods, which in turn would create more production. Shorter hours meant that the amount of work could be spread further among more people, helping temper the unemployment that comes with a changing economy. Shorter hours also meant that productivity could increase, since employers would look for ways to invest to make workers create more, and this would in turn increase wages. This would lead to a virtuous cycle that would leave everyone better off.[13]

This view also put workers and consumers, instead of bosses and owners, at the center of who is creating value in the economy. To Steward, since workers "consume the most," they "furnish the most employment," and increasing their pay and lessening their work hours play a role in establishing a high employment rate.

Otherwise economies could become stuck in major depressions, ones that individuals would be powerless to change on their own.[14]

Steward also saw consumerism as a way to achieve an industrialized democracy. Mass enjoyment of the prosperity that an industrial economy creates was necessary to keep the engine running; for Steward, "consumerism" meant the ability of workers to buy the things they need through their own fair share of what they were creating. He saw it as a method for harnessing and deploying working-class power as well as stabilizing the economy. He attacked those who used the concepts of thrift and self-denial to discipline the working-class. The "charge of extravagance" against working people "is made to sustain the claim that wages ought not to be any higher." Consumerism wasn't just about individuals satisfying their own desires and preferences, but a way for workers to claim a share of the economy that they produced for themselves.

Steward had no problems criticizing the mass culture of his time. He deplored those who "sell rum, print dime novels, race horses or play base ball for a living," as they made workers "not sufficiently ambitious to agitate for anything." A mass culture distracted by frivolous things meant workers would "attend the circus, but never go to labor meetings; and are generally ready to take the strikers' vacant places." As astute as Steward was about many things, he missed that the growing working-class culture was far richer than this. Workers built a culture to gain control over their time and neighborhoods, to keep their traditions and communities, and ease the experience of the often brutal working conditions they faced. Shorter working hours contribute to freedom by creating the time and cultural space necessary for civil society to thrive.[15]

Demand continued to grow for an economy that gave more to workers while also clearing time for them, their families, and their communities. When asked what labor wanted in 1898, Samuel

Gompers, the leader of the American Federation of Labor, simply responded: "More! More today and more tomorrow; and then . . . more and more." "More" wasn't about a specific wage, or a specific policy. It was about ensuring that workers received more of what they produced, instead of watching a surplus be funneled off to those at the very top of the income distribution. The demand for "more" could be a way to coordinate across lines that divided the working class.

As the historian Rosanne Currarino describes, this politics of more extended beyond the workplace to a vision of society as a whole. Gompers said labor demanded "[m]ore leisure, more rest, more opportunity . . . for going to the parks, of having better homes, of reading books, of creating more desires." "More" was a way of organizing society, to ensure that prosperity was broadly shared and would create an abundance of both social life as well as working life. Gompers demanded "more of the good things that go to make up life; better homes, better surroundings, higher education, higher aspirations, nobler thoughts, more human feelings, all the human instincts that go to make up a manhood that shall be free and independent and loving and noble and true and sympathetic." It also provided an opposition to work against, as when Gompers stated: "What does labor want? We want more schoolhouses and less jails; more books and less arsenals; more learning and less vice; more leisure and less greed; more justice and less revenge; in fact, more of the opportunities to cultivate our better natures."[16]

Time was one of the essential components of this politics of more, and limitations on the number of hours worked became one of its rallying calls. By setting a maximum amount of work performed through an eight-hour workday, the politics of more became capable of describing a broader prosperity than just that of wages. The 1870s protest song "Eight Hours" starts with this demand:

We mean to make things over;
We're tired of toil for naught;
We may have enough to live on,
But never an hour for thought.
We want to feel the sunshine,
We want to smell the flowers;
We are sure that God has willed it,
And we mean to have eight hours.[17]

An eight-hour workday was one of the central demands of workers through the late nineteenth century. In 1884 the Federation of Organized Trades and Labor Unions issued a resolution that "eight hours shall constitute a legal day's work from and after May 1, 1886." The call turned out to be far more successful in motivating people than the Federation had imagined, with a wave of labor energy hitting the streets that year. Workers marched with the slogan "Eight hours for work, eight hours for rest, eight hours for what we will!" The year 1886 saw strikes break out across the nation. These strikes took place during an economic expansion where workers wanted their share of the new prosperity through better pay, shorter hours, and more say within their workplaces. They were encouraged by local organizers from the Knights of Labor, who were channeling all the energy around a shorter working day into action. Though there were many strikes in the early 1880s, the number more than doubled in 1886. Even before May of that year, there were already a quarter of a million workers involved in the demand for shorter hours. By the second week of May, that number had expanded to 340,000 workers, with 190,000 of them on strike. Half a million workers participated in 1,400 strikes at almost 10,000 establishments over the course of that year, more than double the previous year. An estimated 200,000 workers won shorter working hours as a result of their demands.[18]

Workers would face opposition in every possible way during their campaigns across the late 1800s for control over the hours

they worked. Presidents would call out the military to break
strikes on behalf of owners. Bosses would deploy squads to break
up and even fire upon workers. But one group was able to go far
beyond this, both in the power they wielded and their willingness
to deploy state violence to back a conflicting theory of freedom:
the courts and the judges who sat on them.[19]

Between 1880 and 1910, 28 million people moved to urban areas, with 12 million arriving between 1900 and 1910 alone. This
represented a major shift in the population as a whole. In 1880
just 28 percent of the population lived in urban areas. By 1910,
that number had risen to 46 percent. An increasingly urbanized
country changed many aspects of daily life, including causing a
major shift in the production and purchasing of food. Many of
the tenements that people were living in didn't have ovens, and
even when they did it was often difficult to cook given the over-
crowded conditions. One outcome of this was the growth of the
baking industry.[20]

Today, we may think of baking as an artisanal enterprise, bringing to mind that fresh bread stall at our local farmer's market.
But the business of bread was serious and part of the industrial
changes during this period. Crackers weren't snacks but nonper-
ishable food staples that could survive long travels. Large business
trusts merged to dominate the cracker industry, with the National
Biscuit Company controlling 70 percent of the market. In cities,
bakeries were often small and locally run, but workers there faced
difficult and dangerous working conditions. Almost all baking
ovens were in the basements of tenements, because they could
hold the weight of the ovens and the supplies. These basements
often had sewers made of brick and clay, which would leak and
smell. They lacked sunlight and airflow. This created the conditions for communicable diseases to spread. Though the main killers today are things like heart disease and cancer, at that time the
most common cause of death was contagious diseases. The most

common killers in 1900 were pneumonia and tuberculosis; many people worried, with good reason, that what caused the latter were cramped and dirty working conditions in tenement basements.[21]

In addition to unsanitary conditions, the work itself was difficult. Moving heavy bags of flour in the narrow basement spaces for low pay wasn't even the worst part. The biggest grievance was the number of hours. A strike by New York bakers in 1881 demanded a reduction in hours to just a 12-hour workday. One estimate had bakers working 74-hour weeks in 1895; some places had much longer hours, with some reports of even 114-hour weeks. As one worker in New York described it, "the bakers had been robbed of daylight, robbed of everything that makes life sweet and desirable, and left to work almost incessantly, day and night." Family life, much less engagement in a broader civil society, was impossible under these working conditions.[22]

In response to this abysmal situation, New York passed the New York Bakeshop Act in 1895. The new legislation regulated the conditions of baking workshops and put the maximum number of hours at ten hours a day or sixty hours a week. Before the act was passed, many labor laws had acted as default templates, rules that would only be binding if nothing else were put into place, and were easily waived away by the conditions demanded by employers. As one labor group lamented in 1867, "Eight Hour laws have been passed by the legislatures of six states, but for all practical intents and purposes they might as well have never been placed on the statue books, and can only be described as frauds on the labouring class." The Bakeshop Act was designed not to fail on these terms. Like the scrip laws in Pennsylvania, it had an enforcement mechanism built into it. There were criminal penalties for not obeying it and, to ensure that the rules were followed, the law created a team of state factory inspectors to carry out enforcement.[23]

In April 1901, Joseph Lochner, a small bakeshop owner from Utica, New York, hired one of his bakers, Aman Schmitter, to work for more than sixty hours in a week. Lochner was charged later with a misdemeanor under the New York Bakeshop Act, a charge he had faced before. At his trial a year later Lochner did not plead guilty or innocent, or offer any defense. The judge found him guilty and required him to pay fifty dollars or spend fifty days in jail. Lochner would appeal the decision all the way up to the Supreme Court of the United States, which heard it in 1905.[24]

The Supreme Court had already overturned many pieces of economic legislation. The Court, at that point, had recently stopped an income tax, weakened antitrust enforcement, and upheld labor injunctions that made it easier to stop strikes. Yet it wasn't clear that it would do anything with the case. Many thought that the Supreme Court would find that this kind of labor law would fall well within the boundary of states' police powers, or the ability of states to regulate the health and safety of their citizens.[25]

It did not arrive at that decision, in a case that has become infamous in the American legal canon. In *Lochner v. New York*, the Supreme Court of the United States overturned the maximum-hours restrictions of the law on the basis that people have a freedom to contract. Justice Rufus Peckham, writing for the 5–4 majority, said that the Bakeshop Act "necessarily interferes with the right of contract between the employer and employees, concerning the number of hours which the latter may labor in the bakery of the employer." Peckham continued: "There is no contention that bakers as a class are not equal in intelligence and capacity to men in other trades or manual occupations, or that they are not able to assert their rights and care for themselves without the protecting arm of the state."[26]

Peckham used the Fourteenth Amendment to justify this attack. In the aftermath of the Civil War, Radical Republicans in Congress led the way in passing two amendments that overhauled the relationship between the federal government, the states, and citizens, in order to ensure freedom would exist for the newly freed people. The goal was to use the federal government to prevent individual states from depriving "any person of life, liberty, or property, without due process of law," as well as ensuring that the "right of citizens of the United States to vote shall not be denied or abridged by the United States or by any State on account of race, color, or previous condition of servitude," guarantees that were written respectively in the Fourteenth and Fifteenth Amendments. While the Bill of Rights focused on preventing Congress from taking certain actions that affected citizens, these Reconstruction amendments each ended with the promise that "[t]he Congress shall have power to enforce this article" using "appropriate legislation." As with minimum-wage laws, Radical Republicans understood that these rights needed enforcement beyond just the letter of the law. It was a second founding of the country, with the power to enforce principles of equality built into the Constitution.

It is the saddest irony that the Supreme Court used these Reconstruction amendments to attack labor legislation, which they were never designed to do, while they also abandoned using them to preserve civil rights for blacks in the South. Two years before the *Lochner* decision, during the 1903 case *Giles v. Harris*, the Court found that new voting restrictions under Jim Crow, designed to prevent blacks from voting, would not violate the Fifteenth amendment. The Supreme Court perverted the Reconstruction amendments, using them as a weapon against labor at the same time it disavowed their purpose in challenging white supremacy.[27]

The *Lochner* decision was so poorly decided, it's worth teasing out the multiple ways in which it was wrong. Two in particular stand out, each emphasized in one of the two dissenting opinions. In the first dissent, Justice John Marshall Harlan argued that the law was constitutional under the police powers, and that the Court had overstepped its bounds by creating a presumption that state laws regulating the economy would be unconstitutional. Harlan noted that the police power gave states the ability to regulate public health, safety, and good order, and that regulating working hours fit well within that boundary. In the passage of the law, a reasonable case was presented that working hours directly contributed to the health and safety of workers. As Harlan wrote, "[M]ore than ten hours' steady work each day . . . may endanger the health, and shorten the lives of the workmen [. . . and] that ought to be the end of this case." Whether or not a maximum-hours law was a good idea, it wasn't the job of the Court to second-guess the content of laws passed by the legislative branch and the states.[28]

Harlan noted in his dissent that this decision would "involve consequences of a far-reaching and mischievous character," as it would "seriously cripple the inherent power of the States to care for the lives, health and wellbeing of their citizens." By substituting the mercurial personalities and prejudices of a handful of people for an actual legislative agenda it created a cloud of uncertainty of what would pass the Court's test. In *Lochner*, the majority opinion argued, "To the common understanding, the trade of a baker has never been regarded as an unhealthy one." (To which Samuel Gompers responded: "[I]f the majority of the court who signed the opinion had visited modern bakeries in this state, and had seen the conditions that prevail, even under the ten-hour law, they would have believed that it was within the police powers of this state to regulate the hours.") While the Court believed bakers didn't deserve protections, in the 1917 case *Bunting v. Oregon*, it upheld a ten-hour workday for workers in mills, factories, and manufacturing. It was now a guessing game as to which occupations the Supreme Court believed should be subject to labor market protections.[29]

It was also up in the air when it came to how the Supreme Court viewed groups of people. In 1908, the Court ruled in *Muller v. Oregon* that a maximum-hour law could be enacted for women, in order "to preserve the strength and vigor of the race." Fifteen years later, in the 1923 case *Adkins v. Children's Hospital*, it struck down a minimum-wage law for women, on the argument that women could now vote and thus didn't need any labor market protections. There could be giant swings in the justices' actions depending on when you caught them, with more aggressive decisions against regulations before 1911 and again after 1923. This was no way to try to tackle the new and widespread problems of an industrial society.[30]

This ambiguity was weaponized by people who wanted to not only strike down economic laws but also prevent them in the first place. Defenders of the *Lochner* decision argue that the Supreme Court didn't strike down a significant amount of economic bills during this time. But what these decisions did was chill and warp the imagination and actions of those looking for ways to push back against social problems. Judicial review lead to a permanent and incoherent threat hanging over each and every law. This limited and distorted the possibilities and ambitions of what could be done, something that would weaken solutions up to and through the New Deal.[31]

But there's a deeper criticism of what the courts were doing, and that is shown in the second dissent in the *Lochner* case, by Justice Oliver Wendell Holmes Jr. In his briefly worded argument, Holmes wrote that the Constitution "is not intended to embody a particular economic theory, whether of paternalism and the organic relation of the citizen to the State or of laissez faire," and that the decision in the case was based "upon an economic theory which a large part of the country does not entertain." As he infamously put it, "The Fourteenth Amendment does not enact Mr. Herbert Spencer's Social Statics," referring to an economics text embodying the conservative laissez-faire ideas of the time.

Holmes was pointing out that a truly neutral market is a lie. Take something as simple as property. Our commonsense understanding, and the one that the courts deployed, was that you own your property as a vertical relationship of you over it. But property is really a horizontal relationship between people based on social rules, mutual coercion, and reciprocal duties. I own my house not because I have a special relationship with the bricks and wood, but because I can exclude other people from using it. We can say it is my property because other people have a duty not to enter, and I have the power to use it as I want without others being able to prevent that. The state and its institutions cannot be neutral in this, because they are the ones that define and enforce how the limits of that exclusion works. Reference to liberty cannot solve the question either, since an extension of economic liberty for some comes as a result of restricting the liberty of others. Instead of one, static thing, property rights should be envisioned as a bundle, each with different types of rights, privileges, powers, and duties that can be weighed in any number of ways. The ability to enter into contracts to change property is simply individuals telling the state to enforce these social obligations and networks of coercion in a different manner.[32]

The government interferes in decisions for the benefit of some at the expense of others all the time. Holmes pointed to limitations on usury, lotteries, and stock market speculation and the prohibition of certain activities on Sundays, as well as compulsory vaccination laws. All of these imposed some limitation on the ability of people to contract, and all of them had been debated in public forums. Beyond the laws Holmes mentioned, the state had taken any number of actions that benefited the owners of capital, including incorporation, limiting the liability of shareholders, creating laws for bankruptcy, and enforcing contracts. The courts had no problem with this, as they also had no problem with using antitrust laws against unions or issuing injunctions that prevented workers from striking. The only time that courts would call foul was when laws provided better protections for workers. Their willingness to use a very specific understanding of economics to override law not only oversteps boundaries, it also writes a preferential view of economics into the Constitution itself.[33]

Holmes's dissent in *Lochner* argued that there ought to be a democratic process for establishing how to set up such a system. Holmes himself likely had conservative economic views, and probably thought that efforts by working people to make their lives better through legislation were not likely to achieve very much. But he understood it was an open question, and he detested the certainty that came with the judiciary putting its own pet theories about the economy into practice. A constitution, Holmes wrote, "is made for people of fundamentally differing views" to experiment and try to find answers. Holmes was influenced by the new school of thought known as Pragmatism, which tied the validity of a statement to its usefulness, and contended that the search for truth ought to be modeled on a kind of experimentation and evolutionary understanding. So too should the definition of freedom in an industrial economy.[34]

The dream of an American economy built around small-scale land ownership, so important to political movements in the 1850s, quickly fell apart as industrialization took over the country. The transition to wage labor changed the lives of American workers to the point where they no longer had any control over their hours. And they resisted, articulating how their own freedom was tied to being able to control their own time, from being with their families to serving as active members in their communities. Free time was understood to be a checking mechanism on the market. Fewer working hours could mean more stable employment, which was especially important as recessions and the advent of technology devastated jobs. It could also mean higher wages, which in turn would generate higher productivity, fight the effects of recessions, and give workers a claim on all the wealth they created. It was a demand for more—more of the good things in life. Workers built movements around this idea. They also ran into brutal opposition, and not just from the businesses themselves. A notion of property and markets as freedom, invented and enforced by the courts, put severe limitations on what could be accomplished democratically.

This was bad enough for workers in their place of employment. But what about those who couldn't work? What about those who couldn't find jobs, or who found themselves too old, sick, or disabled to participate in waged labor? What about those who were severely injured by the dangerous work of the time? This was no less an assault on freedom, but in order to tackle it a whole new form of protection had to be created: social insurance.

3

FREE LIFE

On October 22, 1915, a self-assured insurance actuary named Isaac Max Rubinow announced to a convention of his peers gathered at the Hotel Astor in New York City that they should get ready for social insurance to sweep the United States. Social insurance is a public program designed as a hedge against the economic risks of a modern society. Rubinow would later identify these risks as "accident, illness, old age, loss of a job," describing them as "the four horsemen that ride roughshod over lives and fortunes of millions of wage workers of every modern industrial community." More than just an economic safeguard, he understood social insurance as a basis for freedom. No one could be free if their lives could be destroyed by economic forces beyond their individual control. Social insurance provided freedom through security.

The insurance experts gathered at the convention believed it was only a matter of time until the risks of the modern economy, risks Rubinow and the nearly forty fellow actuaries in attendance had so carefully articulated, catalogued, and quantified, were addressed by the government. Rubinow declared that the trends "for more liberal and equitable scales of compensation, for elimination of the vicious elective system, for compulsory insurance of some kind or other, for better systems of public control of adjustments, and finally for public control of rate making, are unmistakable." As he told the same group earlier in the year, "social insurance is both necessary and inevitable."

At that time Rubinow was not only one of the leading authorities on social insurance in the United States, he was also one of the leading practitioners, pushing the young field in new directions. At that October convention, he was giving his presidential address to the Casualty Actuarial and Statistical Society of America, which was made up of experts looking to not just study the new field of insurance but also change policy as well. A dozen papers followed his talk that day, ranging from burglary insurance to probability curves and the valuation of death benefits. No matter how technical the subject, the excitement that things were changing was evident in the room. Rubinow opened the meeting with news of the laws that were being debated and passed around the country. They had every reason to believe that universal health care and a widespread system of social insurance would pass in short order.[1]

But then progress stopped. Rubinow retreated from the public stage and had to wait nearly two decades before the United States established basic national public insurance against unemployment and poverty in old age. A century later, the project remains incomplete. Yet Rubinow and his generation of reformers were right to be excited; they were creating a new definition of freedom and security. To them, their statistical models accounting for the high prevalence at the time of accidents, poverty, and death weren't just describing bad luck or a lack of individual initiative. These epidemics were a new kind of unfreedom created by the modern economy, and the project of these reformers was to try to address this unfreedom in a culture that didn't want to hear the answer. They not only made the economic case that private markets and voluntary society, left alone, would consistently fail to solve the problem. They went further and showed how their new concept, social insurance, was necessary to rejuvenate what freedom meant for the country.

We are constantly rediscovering the case for social insurance. That the market can't provide genuine security against poverty, sickness, old age, and disability is something that is understood but not readily accepted, as we keep looking to the market and local communities to solve it. Yet the arguments for public insurance were more or less understood over a century ago, and it is a revelation to see how much they still speak to our current moment. Those writers, thinkers, and activists investigated and described how the new industrial economy of the early 1900s was failing people when they were most vulnerable. The answers they found still stand today.

The United States rapidly urbanized between 1880 and 1920. People who moved from farms to become wage workers in cities saw not only their living and working arrangements transformed, but also their baseline level of security. Living on a farm provided access to shelter and usually enough food to survive, but these basics could no longer be guaranteed when it came to cities and waged labor. Losing all or most of one's current and future income because of sickness, an accident, or a layoff suddenly threatened families in a new and sweeping manner.[2]

The idea of poverty itself changed as a result. In the late nineteenth century Americans held conflicting, almost paradoxical, views on poverty. On one hand, Americans thought poverty was unnecessary, since the raw abundance of the country meant there was more than enough to go around. They took pride in their vast nation and the sense that it uniquely offered opportunity for everyone. On the other hand, they believed poverty was inevitable, indeed even something that was necessary and good for society. Poverty acted as a motivating force for the rich and poor alike. It allowed the rich to be inspired to acts of charity for the community, and it forced the poor to learn from their desperation and pushed them toward, patience, thrift, and hard work. Popular stories like those of Horatio Alger described how the adversity of poverty lead people to eventual success.[3]

Yet ever so slowly, especially starting around 1890, those near the front lines in addressing poverty began seeing its causes and consequences through a different lens. Rather than seeing personal failing leading to poverty, they began to view poverty as the result of social ills. This view redefined poverty as a problem of insecurity and insufficiency rather than dependency and immorality. Poverty did not inspire greatness; rather, it trapped people and limited their possibilities. You can see this change in a Russell Sage Foundation monograph about children in poverty from 1914, which argued that "[poverty] does not kill perhaps but it stunts," and it "takes the form of a slow, chronic contest against everlasting odds" in which "the tenement child runs his race, but it is always a handicap." Poverty was not worthwhile or necessary for social balance; rather, it reflected a failure of society to provide work and income to its most vulnerable.[4]

This different way of understanding poverty among scholars, students, and social workers changed two important, interconnected sets of assumptions. The first was shifting the definition of poverty from a moral condition to a more clinical definition based on low income, which in turn means insecure access to food, clothing, and housing. As the social worker Robert Hunter argued, families lived in poverty when they "may be able to get a bare sustenance but they are not able to obtain those necessaries which will permit them to maintain a state of physical efficiency," and as a result are "underfed, underclothed, and poorly housed." The new understanding blurred the line between the deserving and undeserving poor, a line that put the poor at a distance from the rest of society. Hunter argued that even the "more fortunate of the laborers are but a few weeks from actual distress when the machines are stopped." Poverty was a condition of not being able to secure a certain level of income through waged work.[5]

Armed with this insight, researchers found poverty to be far more widespread, persistent, and less contingent on personal characteristics than commonly believed. Estimates varied depending on researchers' criteria for what constituted minimal income, but according to a reasonable definition based on the income of a family with three children, around 30 to 50 million American were poor. Another estimate put the number of workers living in poverty at around 40 percent. Poverty researchers at the time found that only between 12 and 25 percent of those considered poor faced such circumstances for, in their terms, "undeserving" reasons of personal conduct. The vast majority were poor because of irregular access to wages.[6]

These findings led to a second new idea, which was tying poverty to the dangerous conditions of work itself. If the ability to escape poverty wasn't about someone's moral worth but instead whether they could secure consistent waged labor, then the terms and conditions of that labor became core to understanding how poverty persisted. If people are injured, if they get sick, if they become too old, then poverty can happen even to the most virtuous and hardworking person. Focusing on injury in particular was important, as an epidemic of death and injury characterized the workplace in the industrialized United States. In the early 1900s, one in a thousand workers would die in an accident each year, and about 2 percent of the workforce would die or be disabled for more than a month as a result of a work accident. Railroads and coal mine workers, in particular, faced shockingly high death rates. In 1890, railroad workers, trainmen, brakemen, and coal miners faced death rates between 215 and 1,100 per 100,000 workers per year. To put that in today's context, the most dangerous job in the United States in 2015, logging, had a fatal injury rate of 132 per 100,000 workers. The growing ranks of people working in these new industrial positions faced death rates roughly two to eight times higher that of the most dangerous job that exists now. Experts found at the time that the work was much more dangerous than in Europe, with fatality rates in coal mines two to four times higher depending on the country.[7]

This is the world from which emerged the idea of social insurance in the United States, and Isaac Max Rubinow was one of the key leaders in introducing it to Americans. Born in 1875 to wealthy Jewish textile merchants in Russia, his family fled to New York City from Moscow in 1893 due to rising persecution. Rubinow stayed in contact with Russia for years, serving as an American correspondent to Russian newspapers. Though Rubinow wasn't raised as an orthodox Jew, he had a deep appreciation for Jewish traditions of mutual assistance, especially associations that attempted to provide insurance for those who fell ill. His knowledge of such traditions made the idea of some sort of public benefit fund seem possible.

Rubinow studied at New York University Medical College, and practiced medicine in poor areas of New York City from 1899 to 1903. In this role he saw that poverty and poor health locked his patients into a self-reinforcing cycle. He'd often give his poor patients money rather than charge them. He returned to graduate school at Columbia University, devouring economics and statistics, and then left medicine to go into government work. There he led a comprehensive study on the variety of European workmen's insurance laws, with the final report clocking in at over three thousand pages. In 1911, he moved back to New York to work as a statistician in order to be at the front lines of the social insurance movement. He continued publishing scholarly articles on workmen's insurance, and pioneered new techniques of how to assess and predict risks to workers.

Rubinow joined leading Progressive Era groups like the American Association for Labor Legislation, and became a contributing editor to the *Survey*, the leading journal for debate among the new field of social work. He lectured on social insurance at the New York School of Philanthropy, providing what was probably the first such course offered on the subject in the United States. By 1912, he was at the intellectual front of the new social insurance movement and looking for how to accelerate it further.[8]

As someone confidently using his expert knowledge of the new methods of statistics and social science to make the case for public reforms, Rubinow embodied the Progressive Era reformer. But he was also an immigrant and a socialist. He said he stood for "reforming, remaking, radically changing our social institutions." As for his Progressive Era colleagues, Rubinow noted that "they are afraid of a change" and that "a new patch on an old hole—that is as far as their social vision goes." This blend of experiences gave Rubinow a unique ability to combine his knowledge of international experiments with a broader political vision, an approach he would use over the next three decades.[9]

As interest in social insurance surged across the United States, the movement needed a blueprint for where to go. Rubinow accomplished this with his 1913 textbook, *Social Insurance: With Special Reference to American Conditions*, which became the standard for the movement. It was so definitive that in the early 1930s, when newer textbooks emerged in reaction to the Great Depression, they referenced it as their inspiration. Rubinow's unique career path, from doctor to government researcher to private statistician, enabled him to craft such a volume. It was compiled from his lecture notes, and applied the detailed, encyclopedic knowledge of European social insurance laws he gained from government work. It also incorporated all the leading private-sector models of insurance and risk management, many of which he had created himself.[10]

Rubinow's first challenge was simply to define social insurance for American audiences unfamiliar with the term. Social insurance, he wrote, is the "effort of the organized state to come to the assistance of the wage-earner and furnish him something he individually is quite unable to obtain for himself." It is insurance against the "impairment of the capacity for work, and, with this, of the earning power" of individuals. This impairment could be temporary or permanent; each would cause severe poverty.[11]

The innovative way Rubinow introduced the topic helped define the terms of debate. At over five hundred pages, the book catalogs every possible type of insurance experiment in both the

United States and across Europe. But Rubinow's presentation also helped inaugurate a major conceptual shift. Rather than go through examples country by country, Rubinow instead introduced each section by the type of risk to be managed. The sections were, in order: insurance against industrial accidents, insurance against sickness, insurance against old age, invalidity, and death, and finally insurance against unemployment. This created a taxonomy of the kinds of risks common in an industrialized society, including temporary impairment, such as sickness, accident, child-bearing, and mass unemployment in the labor market. But it also included permanent impairment, such as invalidity and old age. Once the categories of risk were clear, then examples could be introduced on the best ways to tackle them.[12]

By looking at how ordinary events, from getting hurt or growing old, stopped people from earning wages, Rubinow explained how poverty perpetuates itself. By listing the risks that can cause this poverty, be it a sudden illness or having a child, Rubinow set an affirmative agenda for what kinds of risks must be addressed. By looking at the way poverty comes from a break in the ability to secure paid work, policy makers began to analyze how each risk contributes to insecurity and devised tools to combat it. At the time, it was revolutionary.

Rubinow could draw from the European experience because European nations were so ahead of the United States on matters of social insurance. Old-age pensions, health insurance, and workmen's compensation were established in the 1880s in Germany. Britain adopted these as well by 1911. Around a dozen other Western countries, including Belgium, Denmark, France, Italy, New Zealand, and Sweden, would adopt social insurance programs before the United States did in the 1930s.[13]

Historians debate the many reasons the United States lagged behind Europe before the Great Depression. Compared with Europe, it lacked a strong working-class party or socialist movement, and it also had a relatively weak federal state with a bureaucracy to advocate for social spending. Another issue was the conservative courts' attack on reform, with reformers uncertain as to which programs that protected workers would be allowed to survive.[14]

Yet one of the most important obstacles to public social insurance was the American ideal of voluntarism, or the notion that freedom could be maintained only through voluntary civic life. Voluntarism is the belief that social and political problems are best solved by individuals working together in voluntary groups, rather than through the government's involvement. This idea was one of the bedrocks of American political thought throughout this period. These voluntary groups function in a political space between businesses seeking profits and governments seeking to rule and enact laws. These were the vast network of charitable groups, voluntary associations, clubs, lodges, and other little platoons that made up American social life at the time. They also evolved into professionalized fraternal groups, who, in between their membership rituals and ceremonies, tried to provide a semblance of social insurance.

Voluntarism can be seen as one manifestation of how the American liberal tradition of freedom and liberty translated into everyday governance. It allowed for limited government, since people and communities themselves would assume the responsibility to exercise power and figure out solutions. This, in turn, emphasized liberty, since citizens could define and pursue their own interests by creating the groups necessary for them to carry out these projects. In the eyes of their advocates, voluntary societies could provide support among people while also playing a paternalistic role of discipline and management, but one that wasn't backed by the state. It allowed for collective solutions without imposing restrictive government actions from a distance.[15]

This view of voluntarism was a distinctly American form of collective action and was noted for its uniqueness among foreign visitors. The French aristocrat and politician Alexis de Tocqueville

noted in his 1840 *Democracy in America* that "[i]n America . . .
I frequently admired the boundless skill of Americans in setting
large numbers of people a common goal and inducing them to
strive toward that goal voluntarily." Tocqueville argued that voluntary associations were not just a check on state tyranny but were
also able to accomplish goals that Europeans looked to the state
to carry out. "Wherever there is a new undertaking, at the head of
which you would expect to see in France the government and in
England some great lord, in the United States you are sure to find
an association." [16]

The reach of voluntary societies was vast. According to one
estimate, a third of all adult males were members of a fraternal
society in 1910. Although it would be logical to assume fraternal
organizations at that time were composed mostly of white men,
in fact women, blacks, and immigrants also created their own
organizations for mutual aid. The Ladies of the Maccabees was
founded in 1892 as the auxiliary of a life insurance society. It became the largest fraternal organization run by women, with its
membership passing two hundred thousand by 1920. The United
Order of True Reformers was started in Kentucky in 1872 as a
small black affiliate of an all-white fraternal association. By 1910 it
had fifty thousand members in over twenty states, allowed women
to join, and its work was praised by both Booker T. Washington
and W.E.B. Du Bois. Numerous voluntary societies were created
by immigrants and ethnic communities and would use their resources to help newly arrived immigrants acclimate in brand new
cities. [17]

This period before the New Deal is romanticized among conservatives today, who not only believe that these groups were at
the forefront of addressing public issues, but that the government,
especially the federal government, was largely absent from playing
any major role in the economy. Yet this story of a stateless economy
in the late nineteenth and early twentieth centuries is another libertarian fantasy. The federal government played a leading role in

the creation and expansion of the market economy. New York, for instance, passed the world's first law creating a process for incorporation. Trade policy included tariffs designed to protect and expand domestic industry. The federal government spearheaded efforts to secure nationwide communications and transportation networks. These programs were often done through a mix of private and public efforts, with the government often delegating authority to private entities to carry them out. But that didn't make them any less public. As Tocqueville also wrote about America, "government authority seems anxiously bent on keeping out of sight." [18]

Efforts to address poverty and provide social insurance throughout the nineteenth century also featured this delegated mix of public and private efforts. From colonial times through the early 1800s, providing relief was a legal responsibility for towns, counties, and parishes. A local community would have a responsibility to offer relief for those who were settled and lived there. But as American society became more mobile and unsettled, this became more difficult to do. This informal, local system was replaced with the construction of poorhouses, which were purposely designed to be harsh in order to discourage people from living there. These horrific institutions became the default support system for orphans, the mentally ill, and the elderly who were without income or family to support them.[19]

Also at this time, well before the New Deal, there were attempts at providing various social insurance programs, the most notable of which created pensions for Civil War veterans. At its height in 1910, this de facto disability and old-age pension system delivered benefits to more than 25 percent of all American men over sixty-five, accounting for a quarter of the federal government's expenditures. In addition, between 1911 and 1920, forty states passed laws establishing "mothers' pensions" for single women with children. These programs provided payments for needy widowed mothers to help them provide for their children.[20]

As the nation grew and the need for a formal system of social insurance became more apparent, voluntary societies tried to take on this difficult task. However, in total they could only provide a thin, small amount of insurance, usually no more than money to cover funerals and burials for their members. Yet, even as they failed to carry out their self-appointed role, these same groups successfully led resistance to reform. As historian Roy Lubove notes, voluntarism created "socio-economic no-man's-lands; voluntary institutions failed to respond to mass needs, but thwarted governmental efforts to do so." [21]

Voluntary organizations were joined by a new private insurance industry, which understood the strategic importance of pushing the idea of voluntarism as a stand-in for government solutions to social insurance. At the second annual National Fraternal Congress of America, one insurance company executive, addressing the gathering, argued that those in voluntary fraternities and the insurance industry shared a common agenda of "resisting the onward march of a paternalistic theory which means the destruction of your business and mine." Government action on social insurance is a "paternalism that is trying to inject itself into the body politic of this country and take away enterprise, destroy individual initiative, tear down American ideals, and make us like some of the countries that we do not care to pattern after." [22]

Public social insurance advocates faced two problems. They had to make a technical, economic case for why private markets and charity would never be capable of solving the problem of economic insecurity. But they also had to make a moral and political case for how compulsory government insurance wouldn't conflict with the American tradition of voluntary associations and freedom. The technically minded social scientists and statisticians in Rubinow's camp were uncomfortable, and often frustrated, with arguing notions of philosophy and fairness. But private markets and charity would continue to fail at this task if these arguments couldn't be addressed.

In *Social Insurance,* Rubinow succinctly made the case against private insurance: "The voluntary system is slow in extending. It never extends far enough. It is not satisfactory as to services furnished. It places too big a share of the burden upon the wage-working class." Private insurance couldn't cover everyone. Since that meant a smaller-scale system and less risk sharing, it was even more expensive than it needed to be. As a result, the costs of insurance that fell on individuals was still too high. Those who needed the insurance the most were least capable of paying and likely to face discrimination by private insurers, who would ultimately cover too few people. Private markets would always end up failing to meet the vast need for economic security.[23]

And private charity wouldn't be able to make up the difference. Charitable donations retrench at exactly the moment they are most needed, as during a recession. Charity also has a hard time covering entire geographic regions, instead clustering wherever wealth is there to support it. It also doesn't line up well with what society actually needs, but instead focuses on whatever rich donors believe is worthwhile. When it comes to social insurance, private, voluntary charity predictably fails in ways no less severe than the market.[24]

Only compulsory, universal public insurance could make sure there was no way for people to be lost when they were most in need. By spreading the costs wide through compulsory payments, especially on the rich through progressive taxation, everyone would have access to insurance, and the burden that fell on everyday people would be lower.

Rubinow tackled the question of freedom and social insurance along three lines. First, he pointed out the absurdity and cheap moralism of much of the debate. Those arguing against public programs would often say that insuring someone's risks leads them to a state of moral degeneracy: being insured means they'll simply take more risks and that they will not look out for themselves. As one economist at the time wrote in the *Survey,* "The ultimate

test of a pension system must be not the degree of comfort bestowed upon the aged poor . . . but its effects upon the character"
of those insured. Rubinow deployed his sarcastic wit in service of
his counterargument: if "freedom from anxiety as to the future
must be demoralizing," then the character of the rich, who have
no such worries, must already be destroyed. If being able to meet
human needs must necessarily weaken ours spirits to an equal degree, then all of human progress had been immoral.[25]

Second, he and others argued that the idea that people can
self-insure is not only bad psychology, but also misconstrues the
American spirit. Rubinow argued, correctly, that most young
people do not act according to what they imagine they will be doing in their old age. If the threat of poverty in old age is meant
to force young people to behave morally well, Rubinow and his
peers argued, it is one of the least effective mechanisms one can
imagine. As Henry Seager, the political economist and president
of the American Association for Labor Legislation, said in a 1908
speech, "It is not fear that makes men prudent and thrifty, but
hope." Statistics can easily predict the number of people who will
get old, sick, or injured in a year—but most people believe that
they can simply overcome those odds. Rubinow and his colleagues
recognized this miscalculation as fundamental to the American
character. Indeed, the typical American has "an innate optimism"
and by belief in their personal ability and luck, and feels they can
simply overcome any specific accident or misfortune. Yet the reality is otherwise.[26]

But the reformers' ultimate argument was a response to the
way that the economy had been transformed in the late nineteenth and early twentieth centuries. They had to convince the
public that new tools were necessary to ensure that people had
genuine freedom in the industrial age. Poverty in old age, for instance, was never a historical problem of economic insecurity in
the same way it was under industrial capitalism. In older farming communities, Rubinow wrote, "the authority of the patriarch

is paramount and lasts longer than his productive powers. When no longer able to lead a plow, he is still looked up to for advice. The family is one large consumption unit, its members all prosper or starve together." Yet under modern capitalism, the moment an older person's abilities fell "below the minimum level of productivity set by the employer" they became totally disabled, unable to earn any income. This couldn't be avoided by better individual precautions, as aging "is a problem radically different from that of accidents, in that it is not an abnormal occurrence, but a normal stage of human life." Modern hygiene and sanitation, moreover, prolonged human life, but they made the issue of poverty in old age even worse.[27]

Though advocates for social insurance were in broad agreement, there was one fundamental difference that split them. To many social insurance experts in the 1920s, notably the Wisconsin economist John Commons, social insurance would correct what we would now call a negative externality. This is a situation where an entity, usually a business, doesn't cover all the costs of its actions. Think of a business that pollutes and leaves it to others to clean up. Externalities don't always have to be negative; positive ones include the way education and clean air benefit everyone, even those who don't pay for it directly. One way to counter a negative externality is to tax it, in order to force the business in question to pay the full price of its actions.

Many social insurance experts began to make the argument that the goal of social insurance was to correct for a cost individual businesses were creating for workers and society. For example, the British economist A.C. Pigou, who was pioneering these same ideas during this time, used factory employment of expectant and recent mothers as an example of a negative externality. Work by mothers immediately before and after childbirth "often carries with it . . . grave injury to the health of their children." These mothers are forced to choose between poverty and factory work, each of which poses its own harm to the infant, unless social insurance is available. Or take the case of a factory worker who is injured by their employer's negligence. The costs of that injured worker extend far beyond the factory to families, communities, and society as a whole. Employers were imposing costs on others without compensating them.[28]

Using this framework, a Wisconsin School of experts (named for a set of ideas circulating at the University of Wisconsin) argued that social insurance should force firms to internalize the costs they impose on society. The emphasis was on prevention: if firms were forced to face those costs, they would try to prevent them from occurring in the first place. If companies had to pay when workers got hurt, they would then invest in preventing those injuries. Social insurance laws would use market forces as a way to prevent industrial accidents, unemployment, and sickness. In practice, this meant targeting firms, and assuming that once the market was made to work better through taxing bad behavior, many of these risks would disappear.[29]

Rubinow disagreed. He acknowledged the need for businesses to minimize the harms they do to their workers and society. But when it came to social insurance, he contended that risk was going to be a consistent feature of a modern economy. The goal of social insurance should be income maintenance and the prevention of destitution. No matter how much you tried to focus on prevention, there would always be an element of need because risk would always be present. Businesses fail. Injuries happen. Better to have a system that was clear and adequate rather than one that assumed you could make the problem go away. The goal of social insurance, he wrote, was to maintain the "standard of living of the neediest and productive classes" and "prevent destitution among them." This makes social insurance "true class legislation" that can "readjust the distribution of the national product more equitably."[30]

The difference between these two approaches is clearer when you look at the case of unemployment insurance, which split the social insurance movement in half when the subject was finally debated during the Great Depression. In 1932, the state of Wisconsin would pass unemployment insurance modeled on the idea of prevention. It created company-specific reserve funds that would collect money through taxes and pay out unemployment insurance to workers on a firm-by-firm basis. Employers were only responsible for their own employees. Commons applauded it for fitting "the public policy of a capitalistic nation which uses the profit motive to prevent unemployment."

In response, a commission studying unemployment insurance in Ohio, following Rubinow's thought, pushed for statewide insurance that would have a general, pooled, insurance fund with more generous benefits for unemployed workers. The argument from Rubinow was that individual firms can't insure against economy-wide risks; they can't maintain their unemployment funds in the face of recessions; and some level of unemployment will always be present in a modern economy—so the public must ensure there's a minimum level of redistributive spending. Rubinow saw that the idea of markets simply working themselves out with some public guidance was yet another fantasy. The real question was whether we as a society were willing to make up for the defects that accompany a market system. Unemployment insurance wasn't about trying to ensure that individual businesses didn't impose costs on their workers. It was something for society itself to provide, to ensure against the risks of the economy as a whole.[31]

These principles regarding unemployment and other forms of social insurance would have to wait until the Great Depression to have a chance to be enacted as federal laws, because, after an initial period of promise, the movement stalled and completely disappeared by the 1920s. There are many reasons why. The entry of the United States into the First World War against Germany made Americans suspicious of policies that originated on enemy territory. Suddenly the international successes of social insurance became a liability. "Made in Germany" became an attack against health insurance bills floated in the 1910s. Employers, commercial insurance companies, and doctors all deployed their growing political strength to shut down experiments into social insurance. Labor organizations like the American Federation of Labor were skeptical and ultimately opposed to government insurance until the Great Depression, believing this benefit should be worked out in contracts between unions and employers. Yet underneath these waves of powerful opposition was the idea that social insurance wasn't necessary: we could just take care of it ourselves, in our communities, without the help of the government.[32]

American society had evolved a variety of temporary mechanisms for trying to manage persistent economic risks. From poorhouses and pensions for soldiers, to voluntary society and private insurance, Americans tried to find ways to handle the risks of a modern economy without adopting a full social insurance mechanism. The threat of paternalism and obligatory programs conflicted with a sense of freedom that derived from voluntary, small-scale efforts. Yet civil society did not, and could not, provide a serious response capable of matching the insecurity of modern capitalism.

I.M. Rubinow and his allies fought to define freedom in a new way—for an era when people couldn't count on being able to secure incomes, no matter what they did. Rubinow saw that the public as a whole could insure itself against these modern risks, and as such enable citizens to lead more secure and free lives, where they weren't subject to market forces beyond their control. They fought, but failed, to undermine the patchwork, voluntary system that had prevailed since the earliest days of the country. It would take the Great Depression to force these already weak mechanisms into immediate collapse, a shattering event that finally spurred a new national discussion about economic security and its fundamental relationship to American freedom.

4

FREE SECURITY

In early 1935, Secretary of Labor Frances Perkins met with President Franklin Roosevelt to discuss the direction of the New Deal. They had successfully stabilized the country, overhauled the financial sector, removed the gold standard, and passed a wave of economic reforms. Yet two of the key things they wanted to do remained. They still needed to create a national system of social insurance and a means to ensure workers had power in their workplaces. The Great Depression was a crisis that demanded a solution to these problems, and there was progress being made. The Committee on Economic Security, a group of experts Perkins was leading, was preparing to release its report describing a system of social insurance that could encompass a federal solution to unemployment and old-age economic insecurity. While workers were organizing under a thin set of provisions put into early New Deal reforms, Congress was also working on a bill that would formalize a right to join a union. Yet they all still faced two challenges that had stopped reform for decades: the country's reluctance to embrace public social insurance, and a hostile Supreme Court. For the latter there was a plan. Roosevelt would tell Perkins at their meeting that "[w]hat that Court needs is some Roosevelt appointments. Then we might get a good decision out of them."[1]

These battles required a new idea of freedom that limited and constrained markets, one that would eventually be articulated in two of the major achievements of the New Deal: the Wagner Act, which assured the right of workers to organize, and Social

Security. These achievements helped fulfill the workers' vision of freedom *inside* the workplace, and a societal vision of freedom *outside* whatever security people could muster from the marketplace. These landmarks were the culmination of decades of mass organizing and fighting. They were designed so that they could empower people to defend this idea of freedom and expand it through their own efforts. But first they had to be passed into law.

Well before she was the first female member of a presidential cabinet, Frances Perkins was building a career as an advocate for working people in New York. While majoring in physics at Mount Holyoke College, in Massachusetts, she took a class where she used the new tools of social science to do surveys of the working conditions in factories around Worcester. She saw how industrial accidents and irregular hours destroyed families and created poverty. After reading Jacob Riis's *How the Other Half Lives*, a study of the tenements of New York City, and being inspired by seeing Florence Kelley of the National Consumers' League speak, she devoted herself to addressing the problem of urban and industrial poverty. After college she ended up working for the National Consumers' League in New York, an advocacy group dedicated to ending child labor and the terrible working conditions in sweatshops, where she got to work closely with Kelley. Part of Perkins's work involved investigating the squalor of New York's cellar bakeries, which had been at the center of the *Lochner v. New York* case.[2]

Perkins's life changed forever on March 25, 1911. While having tea in Manhattan near Washington Square Park she was a witness to one of the defining industrial accidents of the time. At the other end of the park, a fire had broken out at the Triangle Shirtwaist Factory. Racing toward the smoke, Perkins saw women jumping to their death from the roof to escape the fire. A total of 146 people from the largely female workforce died. Perkins was appointed to a special commission to investigate and suggest better and safer working conditions. She worked alongside Robert

Wagner, who would become an important U.S. senator during the New Deal, and Governor Al Smith. She became involved in New York reform politics, gradually moving up the ranks in terms of projects and responsibilities. The horror of the Triangle fire changed the lives of those who investigated it, and motivated them to try to end the conditions that created it. It would stick with them for the rest of their lives. Thirty years later Wagner won a bet by successfully recalling the exact date and time of the fire; Perkins would attend a special fiftieth memorial commemoration held at the site.[3]

While working in New York politics, Perkins became allied with Franklin Delano Roosevelt. She had met him briefly much earlier, in 1910, when he was a young, arrogant state senator. Roosevelt was initially indifferent on reform, and mostly interested in name-dropping his family connection to Theodore Roosevelt. He then ran for vice president of the United States in 1920, alongside James Cox of Ohio, and lost. Shortly afterward, Roosevelt was stricken with polio. Physically disabled below the waist, his contemporaries believed his political career was over. Yet Roosevelt wanted to rebuild; he ran for New York governor in 1928 and won. Perkins noted that he had changed in response to his disability. "I would like to think he would have done the things he did even without his paralysis, but knowing the streak of vanity and insincerity that there was in him, I don't think he would have unless somebody had dealt him a blow between the eyes," she later observed. This time, Roosevelt would lead with a much more progressive economic agenda.[4]

As governor, there was only so much he could do to stem unemployment during the early years of the Great Depression. Roosevelt had to deal with both a Republican Congress and the expectation that the government could not and should not do anything to respond to mass unemployment. He was able to create a work relief program, paid for with progressive taxation, arguing that "it is the duty of those who have benefited by our industrial and economic system to come to the front in such a grave emergency and assist in relieving those who under the same industrial and economic order are the losers and sufferers." He sent Perkins to England to study how to implement an unemployment insurance system, something that would become important a few years later.[5]

Roosevelt used his time as governor to start building his argument and agenda for freedom through economic security, a project that would culminate in the New Deal. Speaking before the New York State Federation of Labor in 1930, Roosevelt demanded "an honest law guaranteeing an eight-hour day and a forty-eight-hour week for women and children in industry." He wanted it declared "by law that the labor of a human being is not a commodity or an article of commerce." He also wanted "some form of old-age security against want," and noted that "[m]ost of the civilized countries of the world have undertaken a Government-supervised program to alleviate the distress of fluctuating unemployment." In his 1931 annual message to the legislature of New York, Roosevelt stated that the "American aged do not want charity, but rather old age comforts to which they are rightfully entitled by their own thrift and foresight in the form of insurance." The Great Depression was going to give him a chance to take these arguments to the entire nation, because the entire existing system of economic security was collapsing.[6]

Running for president in 1932, Roosevelt argued that prioritizing property rights, business interests, and the market was detrimental to human freedom. At his nominating address, Roosevelt said, "Our Republican leaders tell us economic laws—sacred, inviolable, unchangeable—cause panics which no one could prevent. But while they prate of economic laws, men and women are starving. We must lay hold of the fact that economic laws are not made by nature. They are made by human beings." Later, at a speech given at the Commonwealth Club in San Francisco, he noted how all property rights are a creation of the government: "[E]ven Jefferson realized that the exercise of the property rights might so interfere with the rights of the individual that the Government, without whose assistance the property rights could not exist, must intervene, not to destroy individualism, but to protect it." Property should exist to serve people, not the other way around. Roosevelt won the election. He would have a chance to implement his new ideas because the old system was breaking down all around everyone.[7]

Back in December 1928, as he was leaving office, President Calvin Coolidge had written in his State of the Union address that the country should "regard the present with satisfaction and anticipate the future with optimism." A year later the stock market crashed, and the overall economy fell 12.6 percent in 1930, with over 26,000 businesses failing and unemployment rising above 11 percent. The freefall continued, with unemployment reaching 20 percent by 1932.[8]

The first president to face this crisis was Herbert Hoover. Hoover's entire career was a testament to the power of voluntarism, and he considered the actions taken by voluntary groups and civic associations to be the highest expression of the tradition of American individualism. His philosophy was to try to harness the voluntary energy of business and civic groups, using the government to coax people toward private action rather than carry out duties directly. Hoover had experienced tremendous success with this approach over his career. During World War I, he ran the U.S. Food Administration. In that capacity he urged Americans to eat less meat and self-ration in service of the troops as part of his approach to ensuring the food supply of the country and war effort would hold up. In a different role, he led aid and relief to the Belgian people, where he also called upon support from charity and voluntary aid. Serving as commerce secretary under President Coolidge during the 1920s, Hoover continued this voluntarist approach of encouraging people toward private action on everything from unemployment to disaster relief to industry regulation.[9]

As president, Hoover believed there should be a response to the Depression, but that it was necessary for the private and civil sectors to do this work. As Hoover said in 1931, the government's response must encourage the American people to "maintain the spirit of charity and mutual self-help through voluntary giving." He was ideologically locked between addressing the obvious need for action and insisting that only the private sector should respond. The more he pressured charity and voluntary groups to make up the slack in the economy, the more they resisted. Their local, temporary, and targeted support were no match for the national, persistent, and widespread misery of the Depression. Hoover attempted to favor, in the words of historian Ellis Hawley, a "nonstatist alternative to atomistic individualism, the romantic images of voluntarism as more truly democratic than any government action, and the optimistic assessments of the private sector's capacity for beneficial government action." Yet in adhering to this idea, he failed the country.[10]

The collapse of voluntarism as a governing philosophy was matched by the collapse of the everyday voluntary organizations that had structured everyday life. But this didn't start with the Great Depression, as voluntary societies were already struggling well before then. Fraternal societies were experiencing slower membership growth during the 1920s. Tales of embezzlement and corruption among leaders and management scared off new members from trusting them with their money. New mass media technologies such as movies and radio programs became an alternative source of entertainment. Immigrant organizations saw fewer new members as a result of tighter restrictions on immigration. These limits were also reflected in the inability of voluntary societies to provide social insurance outside of burial insurance. Between 1920 and 1930, only 2.4 percent of benefits paid by fraternal societies went to old-age funds, while between 80 and 90 percent of them went to death benefits.[11]

The Great Depression obliterated what was left of these institutions. From benefit societies to building and loan associations, fraternal insurance policies, and banks, all experienced serious rates of failure during the first years of the economic collapse. As unemployment became widespread and long term, people rapidly depleted their savings and the immediate networks they could rely on for support. Once that happened, private charities and civic groups faced a massive demand for aid. But these same groups couldn't solicit new donations.

These failures did more than discredit specific institutions. As the historian Lizabeth Cohen found, the Depression represented "not simply the loss of a job, a home, or insurance" but also "called into question the sustaining institutions of the 1920s." As the New Deal provided banking insurance, stopped foreclosures on the houses of workers, and employed people who couldn't find work, the government demonstrated to workers that it could fill the gaps that the market left. In turn, workers understood that as citizens they had a rightful claim to these benefits.[12]

During the initial fights over social insurance, a frustrated I.M. Rubinow would criticize fellow progressives for putting charity above state action. In 1913 he wrote that the "progressive social worker must learn to understand that a sickness insurance law" would do more to reduce poverty "than a dozen organizations for scientific philanthropy with their investigations, their sermons on thrift, and their constant feverish hunt for liberal contributions." By 1933 Rubinow could confidently state that the "great American bubble of private philanthropy as a basis for social justice— one might say the great American substitute for social policy—has finally been burst."[13]

People at this point couldn't turn to private insurance to fill in the gap. Private old-age pensions weren't providing a true level of security or freedom. In 1925 an estimated 2.8 million workers were covered by employer or private pensions; coverage had grown from nearly no workers in 1905 to a little over 5 percent of workers. But these private pensions were small and had escape clauses stipulating they were voluntary gifts, not formal contracts or obligations. One study at the time found less than 10 percent of those who believed they were covered ended up with any actual benefit.

These failed experiments with private insurance and voluntary societies, institutions hostile to public social insurance, ironically paved the way for a possible government solution. By showing a model of what people could aspire to get, yet failing to deliver it at any scale and with any reliability, private insurance opened an opportunity for government action. Social insurance advocates used the existence of private insurance companies to argue that the next, obvious conclusion was for the government to run these programs. As Rubinow wrote in the 1930s, the social insurance movement was influenced "both by what private insurance could and did do, and by what it couldn't and didn't do." Yet getting from these failures to something else required much more—it required movements.[14]

On June 8, 1934, President Roosevelt addressed Congress. He congratulated members on the progress that had already been made, but pointed to what needed to come next. Citizens "want some safeguard against misfortunes which cannot be wholly eliminated in this man-made world of ours." Roosevelt argued that in the era in which they lived "the complexities of great communities and of organized industry make less real these simple means of security." Instead, what was needed now was "the active interest of the nation as a whole through government in order to encourage a greater security for each individual who composes it." The policies he was proposing could build on lessons "available from states, from industries and from many nations of the civilized world." The bill he was imagining needed to be comprehensive because the "various types of social insurance are interrelated." Roosevelt argued that social insurance would restore the freedom that had been lost under the changing economy. This kind of security "does not indicate a change in values. It is rather a return to values lost in the course of our economic development and expansion."[15]

In July 1934, Roosevelt appointed the Committee on Economic Security, helmed by Labor Secretary Frances Perkins, to come up with plans for a social insurance bill. "You want to make it simple—very simple," was Roosevelt's advice. Roosevelt also wanted it to be clear. Roosevelt made sure the taxes funding the program came from payrolls rather than a general fund to allow workers themselves to justify their claims over their own public pensions. As Roosevelt responded to criticism from economists that this would fall too heavily on workers, "I guess you're right on the economics [but the taxes] are politics all the way through. We put those payroll contributions there so as to give the contributors a legal, moral, and political right to collect their pensions and their unemployment benefits. With those taxes in there, no damn politician can ever scrap my social security program."[16]

Perkins promoted the bill publicly in the language of freedom. She wrote in one editorial that individuals cannot "possibly save enough out of their earnings to provide for their old age or to tide them over the 'rainy day' due to unemployment, accident, illness, or some similar hazard which spells temporary or permanent loss of earnings." Without public social insurance, this "life is passed in a constant ferment of fear and insecurity. When that condition applies, not merely to an individual, but to a major section of the population, it becomes a matter of national policy to remedy and to prevent it." She referred to social insurance as an invention, "another great forward step in that liberation of humanity" that must be deployed to continue to ensure that people lead free lives.[17]

Social Security passed in part because the elderly themselves demanded it. Advocacy groups known as Townsend Clubs, started by an elderly doctor named Richard Townsend in 1934, spread rapidly across the country. Within three years there were an estimated seven thousand Townsend Clubs and 3.5 million members, their newspaper boasting a circulation of two million. Their demand, referred to as the Townsend Plan, was simple: every person over sixty who was retired would receive $200 a month. They were vocal in letting their representatives know their demand as well. The political threat this movement posed is what helped the Roosevelt administration ensure that funding for old-age pensions stayed in the Social Security bill as it navigated the Senate.[18]

The movement struck observers as having an "old-time American religion" feel to it. There was also a lot of complaining about the "wildness" of young people; the *New York Times* described how advocates believed the plan would boost spending and thus "make jobs for the young people and take them out of their cigarette-smoking, whisky-drinking, roadside-petting hell of idleness."[19] There was an insular quality to it as well, with no reference to the idea that many other countries had already figured out how to do old-age pensions. One pamphlet stated that after the Townsend Plan passed, our "country will show the way to other nations." There was also an amateur quality to the policy advocacy. Professionals attacked the plan as lacking realistic numbers. In response, when questioned during House testimony on how the financing would work, Townsend responded, "I'm not in the least interested in the cost of the plan."[20]

Yet it was successful. As the bill worked its way through Congress, there was a real question over whether the Senate Finance Committee would remove the old-age pensions in Social Security. Edwin Witte, executive director of the Committee on Economic Security, was called to make the case for it to several senators. Witte said if they didn't pass it, "the probable alternative was a modified Townsend plan." That was enough to get the necessary votes. Wilbur Cohen, an architect of both Social Security and later Medicare, noted in 1986, "I think the more radical Townsend Plan helped us get a solid program like Social Security," as "having a radical idea on the agenda proved helpful in building a moderate-center coalition." [21]

One reason that this movement was so successful was that it spoke to a distinct and profound unfreedom that the elderly living in poverty faced in their old age. The specter of the poorhouse and the indignity of relying on charity came up over and over again in the movement's political materials. As one particular pamphlet stated, "One need only to visit the alms houses and poor houses of the United States, one need only talk to the old men and women who are there, to see what a mess we have made of things under the present order." Once their plan was in place, the elderly would be "no longer paralyzed with the fear of the poorhouse and dread of having to receive charity." Townsend described how he found that his patients were increasingly falling into rapid decline from the despair they felt as they "found themselves not only helpless but a burden to their financially embarrassed relatives." Nobody knew better how poverty made people unfree, and how little control individuals had over random misfortunes, than the elderly themselves. [22]

At the same time a revolution in social insurance was taking place, another was happening within the workplace. The path to the Wagner Act started with the National Industrial Recovery Act (NIRA) of 1933, a law designed to get industries to cooperate among themselves by creating industry codes of conduct for competition. Unfortunately, for those who were hoping this would lead to some social accountability, large companies dominated the code-writing process that determined prices and productions. The Act was terminated at the hands of the Supreme Court in May 1935. Nevertheless, the industry codes did include maximum hours and minimum wages, and the law wiped out child labor and other sweatshop practices in some industries. Advocates for labor laws pointed out that industry functioned perfectly well with those regulations in place. It demonstrated that industry and nationwide labor policy could coexist.

One particular section of the law, seemingly a minor after-
thought, acted as a fuse, ready to ignite workers across the country. Section 7(a) provided a process for unionization. Labor leaders
took advantage of this to start organizing workers. John L. Lewis,
the president of the United Mine Workers of America, started an
organizing drive among coal workers whose message stated that
"the President wants you to join a union." These efforts, in turn,
mobilized broader actions. A major strike wave broke out in 1934,
ranging from farmworkers in California and New Jersey to workers waging a general strike in the city of San Francisco to textile
workers across most of the entire country. In all, there were over
1,800 strikes, with 1.47 million workers involved, a little over half
of the country's total workforce during that year. These strikes
met violent resistance from bosses. Yet they continued, as millions
saw that the president and his administration were committed to
bringing some sort of democracy into their workplace.[23]

The reality was more complicated. After the NIRA was killed
by the Supreme Court there was a need for a new process for workers to unionize. In its place was the National Labor Relations Act,
often called the Wagner Act, which passed in July 1935. Senator
Robert Wagner of New York had been introducing this legislation
for years, but momentum coming out of the big midterm wins
for the New Deal in 1934 gave it strength. Wagner had worked
with Frances Perkins in the aftermath of the Triangle Shirtwaist
Factory fire almost twenty-five years earlier, when he chaired the
New York State Factory Investigating Committee. Now they were
working together to create a mechanism for workers to unionize
across the country. Except Perkins and Roosevelt weren't on the
leading edge of the labor movement: neither supported the Wagner Act as it was moving through the Senate. Perkins and Roosevelt's priority was trying to provide for workers through laws and
public programs, rather than by directly supporting unionization.
As the bill worked its way through Congress, Roosevelt, eyeing his
upcoming 1936 election, suddenly changed gears, supporting the

bill as part of a "Second Hundred Days" that included a push for high levels of progressive taxation and an overhaul of the corporate structure of public-utility holding companies.

Roosevelt signed the Wagner Act on July 5, 1935. The law affirmed the right of workers to form a union and provided a mechanism for doing so. It prevented bosses from engaging in unfair, anti-union practices, while also ensuring the right to strike as well. It changed the balance within the workplace by giving workers a mechanism outside the market to determine the way they were governed. The Wagner Act was followed up by the Fair Labor Standards Act of 1938. This law took the labor-friendly portions of the NIRA and formalized them, creating the first national minimum-wage and maximum-hours laws. For the first time, the country had a law dedicated to enforcing a 40-cent-an-hour minimum wage and a forty-hour workweek. Businesses could hardly say it would kill the economy, since these parts were at least partially in place during the early parts of the recovery under the NIRA.[24]

As law professor Rebecca E. Zietlow has explained, Wagner also deployed the language of freedom to move his bill. Without collective bargaining, "there would be slavery by contract." He argued that it was inconsistent with the country's legacy to put so-called economic rights above the freedom and well-being of citizens: "The fathers of our Nation did not regard freedom of contract as an abstract end. They valued it as a means of insuring equal opportunities, which cannot be attained where contracts are dictated by the stronger party." Wagner would argue that the purpose of the act was "to make the worker a free man." Other supporters of labor reform used this language as well. Democratic senator Arthur Walsh of New Jersey argued that "any injunction or any law that prevents a man from striking, is a law of servitude, and that is the principle we have to keep in mind. It is the difference between freedom and servitude." Democratic representative Vito Marcantonio of New York asked, "Unless Congress protects the workers what liberty have they? Liberty to be enslaved, liberty to be crucified under the spread-out system, liberty to be worked to death under the speed-up system, the liberty to work at charity wages, the liberty to work long hours." Linking the promise of Reconstruction with labor rights, Democratic representative Charles V. Truax of Ohio argued that "as Lincoln freed the blacks in the South, so the Wagner-Connery bill frees the industrial slaves of this country from the further tyranny and oppression of their overlords of wealth."[25]

The law amplified a wave of labor activity across the nation. In the aftermath of the Wagner Act, a major unionization campaign was launched by the Congress of Industrial Organizations (CIO). Massive sit-down strikes broke out in Flint, Michigan, a town dominated by the auto industry that employed around 80 percent of the workforce. General Motors was the largest firm in the city, and it was also the world's largest manufacturing company. GM acted just like an authoritarian government toward its workers, surveilling them for any sign of disobedience. It spent a million dollars to hire hundreds of spies, informants, and wiretappers to infiltrate spaces where workers gathered in private, and stifle even the possibility of labor organizing. A government commission that investigated this system concluded the firm had "the most colossal supersystem of spies yet devised in any American corporation." As one worker described it, GM had the town "so well propagandized to their own good that one don't even dare talk here," and that one "couldn't belong to a union and breathe it to a soul. That soul would probably be a spy." Foremen could fire or penalize workers at their arbitrary whim, including those found to be sympathetic to unions.[26]

On December 30, 1936, workers organizing with the United Auto Workers (UAW) sat down in GM's Fisher Body Plant No. 1 and stayed sitting. Here was an example of workers claiming the physical right to occupy private corporate property and interfere with production. Their demand was that GM recognize the union. The UAW ignored court injunctions to leave the property, and withstood attacks from police, including tear gas. The protesters were so successful in continuing their sit-down strike, they even were able to expand and take over another Chevrolet plant on February 1. The company stood down after forty-four days and, on February 11, agreed to recognize the UAW as the representative of its workers.

This victory rippled across the entire country. The UAW expanded rapidly, gaining more than two hundred thousand members by the end of the year. Seeing the power of workers organizing, U.S. Steel recognized the Steel Workers Organizing Committee on March 2 and included a pay raise and guarantee of a forty-hour work week. The victory inspired other actions across the country, with millions sitting down on strike, walking off the job, or joining unions during 1937. By August the CIO would have 3.4 million members.

In Flint, one of the main reasons the movement was so successful is that the government stopped interfering against labor on the side of capital, as it had almost always done in the past. Frank Murphy, the governor of Michigan, was a New Deal advocate who refused to send in the National Guard to fight the workers. Roosevelt and Perkins decided to remain neutral publicly, while privately pressuring GM to recognize the union. These decisions on how to enforce markets—by the government—made all the difference to the freedom of these workers.[27]

That opening gave workers a once-in-a-generation chance to change the country's entire economy. The only thing remaining was to ensure that the law empowering the workers' struggle would survive a challenge in the Supreme Court. Between 1933 and 1936 the Court had struck down laws at ten times historical rates, creating "new doctrine now faster than I can absorb it," in the words of the usually dissenting Justice Harlan Fiske Stone. It attacked federal and state laws, creating what Roosevelt called a " 'no-man's-land' where no Government—State or Federal—can function." After Roosevelt's nearly unprecedented landslide re-election in 1936, he announced a court overhaul, allowing him to appoint new judges for every justice over seventy years old who refused to retire.[28]

Roosevelt made multiple mistakes in the process. He didn't run on fighting the Supreme Court at all in 1936. He didn't prepare his own party, with many of his allies in Congress learning about the court overhaul from the news. Yet despite the unpopularity and failure of his proposal, Roosevelt ultimately won his political goals. When the Court voted to uphold the Wagner Act, Chief Justice Charles Evans Hughes wrote that labor organizing was "a fundamental right" that was "often an essential condition of in-dustrial peace" and the conduct of interstate commerce. One of the lawyers of the National Labor Relations Board noted, with shock, that the opinion read as if "the law had always been this way, that there had never really been any dispute about it."[29]

Overnight, one of the central obstacles of reform disappeared. The actions of the Supreme Court had limited and warped reform for decades. It was unpredictable and arbitrary in what it would allow, and as a result forced reformers into half-measures and piecemeal solutions. It had invented doctrine to keep the Ameri-can government malformed and undeveloped. It forced its own theory of freedom down Congress's throat. This was now all over. Though it's impossible to know what actually changed the Court's mind, it ultimately stood down in the wake of Roosevelt's massive campaign and reelection.[30]

The progress of the New Deal was limited by white supremacy, es-pecially through political power exercised by Southern Democrats in their defense of Jim Crow. These Democrats supported policy as long as it wouldn't endanger white supremacy in their states. This meant that the South wanted to control its funding locally. When it came to poverty assistance in the form of Social Security, for instance, Committee on Economic Security executive director

Edwin Witte noted that the "Southern members did not want to give authority to anyone in Washington to deny aid to any state because it discriminated against Negroes." Southern members also worried labor laws would weaken Jim Crow, by allowing black workers to obtain the same wages as white workers. As Florida representative James Mark Wilcox said, "[t]here has always been a difference in the wage scale of white and colored labor. So long as Florida people are permitted to handle the matter, the delicate and perplexing problem can be adjusted." But "when we turn over to a federal bureau or board the power to fix wages," he argued, "it will prescribe the same wage for the Negro that it prescribes for the white man." Both Social Security and the Wagner Act didn't apply to 9.4 million domestic and agricultural workers, who were largely in the South and disproportionately black and female.[31]

Yet, as the political scientist Eric Schickler shows, even with these exclusions the New Deal started a long-term process of re-aligning the Democratic Party and economic liberalism with civil rights. As opposed to the approaches of more racially exclusion-ary unions, the CIO used the Wagner Act to organize workers of color. But their efforts went beyond organizing labor. For its 1938 scorecard evaluating the voting record of politicians, the CIO's lobbying and political operation included how legislators voted on anti-lynching bills, in addition to bills dealing with traditional labor concerns like strikes, wages, and hours. Immediately after issuing the scorecard, the CIO added opposition to the poll tax to its list of priorities for elected officials. This went beyond potential political opportunities, as it reflected the ideals of the CIO leader-ship. As its leader John Brophy asserted, "behind every lynching is the figure of the labor exploiter, the man or the corporation who would deny labor its fundamental rights."[32]

Supporters of civil rights took notice. The NAACP's magazine, *The Crisis*, wrote that "Negro workers ought to flock to the C.I.O. unhesitatingly," and that they had "nothing to lose and everything to gain by affiliation with the C.I.O." Black newspapers like the

Chicago Defender started to report on the CIO and described it as aligning with their own issues. Opponents of civil rights also took notice. The Imperial Wizard of the Ku Klux Klan said, "The Klan will not sit idly by and allow the CIO to destroy our social order, nor shall the CIO flout law and promote social disorder without swift punishment." The KKK unleashed a campaign of cross burnings, kidnappings, and beatings against CIO labor organizers in the South. Reporting on the violence, *The Crisis* wrote, "[Y]ou can tell a man by the kind of enemies he makes," and for making its enemies, "the C.I.O. is certainly an unparalleled blessing in our land." [33]

At the same time, the traditional allegiance of black voters to the Republican Party was being undone. There was a massive outreach campaign by Democrats to black voters in the North designed to build on the limited, but real, success New Deal programs had in black communities. One noteworthy event in that effort was a September 1936 "Emancipation Day" rally. Madison Square Garden was packed with fourteen thousand African Americans, and the proceedings were broadcasted to twenty-six different meetings across the Northeast. Cab Calloway and many other musical acts performed, and Senator Robert Wagner received a standing ovation for his promise to pass anti-lynching legislation. R.R. Wright, a bishop in the African Methodist Episcopal Church, said that they were there to "carry forward the real spirit of Abraham Lincoln by supporting the social and economic programs of the great President, Franklin D. Roosevelt." A message from the president was read that said "in the truest sense freedom cannot be bestowed. It must be achieved; and that there must be constant vigilance if it is to be maintained." An administration official, Donald Richberg, attacked their conservative opponents for "preserving the liberty of a few men to wring their bread from the sweat of other men's faces," adding that when workers are "compelled by necessity to live in one kind of place and to work for one kind of employer, with no choice except to pay the rent demanded and to accept the wages offered—or else to starve—then the liberty of the property owner contains the power to enslave the worker. And that sort of liberty is intolerable and cannot be preserved by a democratic government." [34]

The year 1936 saw African Americans vote overwhelmingly for President Roosevelt after decades of supporting the Republicans. One editorial in *The Nation* magazine at the time presciently observed this switch happening and listed five contributing factors. First were the efforts by the CIO—estimated at the time to have one hundred thousand black members—to break down the color line among workers. Second were the jobs provided by the Works Progress Administration, whose regulations successfully prevented discrimination by race. Third was the spectacle of the racist senator Ellison "Cotton Ed" Smith of South Carolina bolting from that year's Democratic convention after the Reverend Marshall Shepard prayed over the gathering and Congressman Arthur Mitchell seconded the Roosevelt nomination. When both of these black men were given positions of importance in the convention, to the dismay of racist Southern Democrats, it highlighted changing roles within the party. Fourth was the work of Eleanor Roosevelt with the black community, especially her role as host of an event for black women from the National Industrial Training School for Women and Girls on the White House lawn. Fifth and last was the realization that, while Franklin Roosevelt wasn't doing anything on civil rights and anti-lynching bills, neither were the Republicans, who were taking their voters for granted. [35]

Though African American voters did not become partisan Democrats at that moment, this election signaled that their votes were up for grabs. This meant that enterprising Northern local and state officials in the Democratic Party could began to court them, and that an agenda of freedom through economic rights and civil rights started to emerge from the bottom up. As Schickler notes, "By the time of World War II, the liberal coalition identified civil rights as a critical front in the battle for economic and social progress, and its members understood that defeating southern defenders of Jim Crow was essential for liberalism's future." Meanwhile Republicans, no longer able to take black voters for granted, had to debate whether to try to win them back or begin bringing racist and conservative voters into their fold. The business community and economic conservatives, key groups for Republicans, fought laws preventing discrimination in the workplace. As those laws became linked to civil rights, it pushed conservatives and Republicans even further away from African American voters.[36]

The Social Security Act and National Labor Relations Act weren't just policies solving economic problems. They declared a new concept of freedom, one that was defined by suppressing the market.

Because of the NLRA and the movement it inspired, the freedom workers enjoyed in the workplace was no longer limited to whatever meager gains they could bargain on their own, or secure if they threatened to leave. A level of democracy was brought into the workplace, giving workers the power to organize among themselves, to strike, and to have some safeguards and protections against their bosses' retaliation. Social Security attacked the unfreedom of poverty that accompanied unemployment and old age by exorcising the idea that only the market and local communities had the responsibility for managing these problems. Instead, the public itself would provide these solutions.

The NLRA and Social Security also provided a path for people themselves to expand on both of these achievements. Roughly 12 percent of workers were in a union by the late 1930s. This number doubled during World War II, and reached a peak of around 30 percent of all workers by 1955. These unions boosted wages and gave workers a say in their workplaces. They also disproportionately benefited people of color, who were more likely to be in a union and gained a larger wage boost for doing so in the years between the 1940s and 1970s.[37]

Social Security expanded its reach in similar ways. In 1939 it added benefits for family survivors, expanding its scope from the worker to the family and providing itself as a true form of insurance in old age. In 1950 domestic and agricultural workers were added to the program, fixing the earlier shameful exclusion. The program has gone through roughly thirty major legislative changes since it passed. Later changes adjusted for inflation and added a formal disability program. Today, between 10 and 15 million elderly people, roughly 30 or 40 percent of all elderly, are lifted out of poverty by Social Security. More than half of the elderly rely on the program for more than half of their income in retirement. With people of color facing higher poverty rates, and with women living longer than men, Social Security in particular now benefits these vulnerable populations. It has proven itself a versatile tool for dealing with changing economic times.[38]

Instead of crowding out charity and civil society, social insurance allowed those entities to evolve and go beyond their previous limitations. The Family Welfare Association of America had been one of the opponents of federal action before the New Deal. Yet in 1934, one of their leaders, Linton Swift, wrote "there is now a general recognition of the primary responsibility of local, state, and national government for the relief of unemployment and similar types of need." The voluntary private sector, he explained, would "meet human needs not yet recognized by a majority of the public as vital or meriting community support." In 1935, the National Catholic Welfare Conference switched from opposing government action toward accepting that the state has a role to play. "Social justice," one if its leaders wrote, requires "wages and hours which will insure continuous employment, a decent livelihood and adequate security for all workers." Charity benefited from social insurance taking care of the broad risks of a market economy, as organizations' funds could now support services in a narrow but meaningful way. Meanwhile there was a renaissance in civil society. After 1940, membership in chapter-based, religious, and other organizations increased dramatically, and stayed at high levels for decades.[39]

I.M. Rubinow died on September 1, 1936, living just long enough to see his life's work culminate in the passage of the Social Security Act. Because of policy fights he had with many close to the administration, as well as his connection to socialism, he wasn't formally consulted in the process, before or after, though he very much wanted to be. He had been fighting lung cancer over the previous year when he died, and though it took its toll on him he continued to argue for social insurance where he could. Rubinow was critical of the shortcomings of the bill, but he correctly believed it would be able to evolve and grow with the times. Even as his facilities started to decline, Rubinow spent the last weeks of his life poring over arguments for the constitutionality of the program from his hospital bed. Shortly before Rubinow died, Franklin Roosevelt sent him a copy of Rubinow's own recent book, *The Quest for Security*, signed by the president, with an inscription noting that "this reversal of the usual process is because of the interest I have had in reading your book." Though he was sadly isolated from the circle carrying out his life's project, it was an oblique and small acknowledgment for a lifetime of work that was thankless and frustrating, but that generated a measure of success beyond what Rubinow himself would get to see.[40]

5

FREE CARE

"[A]ll Americans able to work and seeking work have the right to a useful and remunerative job. . . . [I]t is essential that continuing full employment be maintained in the United States." So stated the Full Employment Bill that Democratic senator James Murray of Montana introduced in January 1945. This legislation was one of the last major battles of the New Deal era, and forced the debate about economic management onto the floor of Congress. The bill was a mix of wartime planning and the culmination of New Deal ideas about economic liberty. Language such as the "right to a useful and remunerative job" comes straight from the Economic Bill of Rights, also called the Second Bill of Rights, that Franklin Delano Roosevelt proposed in his 1944 State of the Union address. Other liberals joined in this argument, including Senator Robert Wagner, who argued that the right to a job was "synonymous with the inalienable right to live." Here was the idea that economic rights are no less essential than other kinds of liberal rights, like freedom of speech. As Roosevelt said, individual freedom couldn't exist "without economic security and independence."

The bill was also a statement about who would maintain responsibility for the stability of the economy as a whole in the aftermath of the Great Depression. The legislation called for agencies to predict the number of jobs needed as well as the number of jobs the private sector would create in the near future. If there was a gap between the two, the president would have the ability to create public jobs. At issue was who would ultimately determine the final number of jobs in the economy: the private sector, often with government incentives and subsidies, or the public sector. President Roosevelt died while the bill was being debated, and his successor President Truman continued the push for its passage. A watered-down version ultimately passed as the Employment Act of 1946, with the references to "full employment," a phrase that wouldn't appear in the final text, replaced with "maximum employment." [1]

One group of working people was left out of this debate over the right to a useful and remunerative job: women working in the home. Even in the original version of the bill, after declaring that all Americans have the right to good jobs, it clarifies: "It is the policy of the United States to assure the existence at all times of sufficient employment opportunities to enable all Americans, who have finished their schooling and who do not have full-time housekeeping responsibilities, freely to exercise this right." In one of the few times the question of women working outside the home came up during the yearlong debate, Senator Murray contended that "it was not expected that this bill was intended to take the housewives out of the homes and put them into industry or other employment." Another senator who supported the full-employment policy agreed with Murray, explaining that the bill would not set an expectation that the government would try to employ people who "ought to be at home helping to raise families" and "that we were not undertaking by a Government program to break up the family." [2]

The New Deal ripped opened the nominally private sphere of the workplace and extended, however tenuously, a set of laws, programs, institutions, and expectations for how work would be governed in a more democratic manner. From the passage of Social Security to the enactment of working hours laws, workers gained a new definition of freedom that wasn't solely that of the freedom to get whatever they could in the marketplace. Yet, as the historian

Emilie Stoltzfus argues, that other nominally private sphere, the household, received no comparable rethinking or extension of public support. Even at the height of New Deal liberalism, and the debate about what full employment would mean after the war, the legislative focus was on how to empower a male worker with a wife at home.[3]

While the men in Congress were debating whether or not women should be able to work, President Truman faced a wave of activism by women demanding a place at the postwar economic table. Many national educational, health, and welfare organizations were pressuring the White House to keep wartime day care centers open. These centers were a temporary war measure designed to make sure that women with children were able to work in the wartime economy. These programs had significant support among women using them, who saw them as essential for being able to engage freely in the labor market. With the war over, the government moved quickly to cut funding and end the programs. The pressure convinced Truman to keep them open, but only as a six-month temporary measure during the reconversion of the war economy back to peacetime. This opened a window where women could fight to protect this public support for working mothers from being dismantled.[4]

Capitalism relies on work that is carried out in homes, communities, and families. This unpaid care work of having and raising children, nurturing young people, and sustaining adults is essential for society to flourish. The background work of building and maintaining communities enables society itself to thrive and to reproduce itself over time. This usually gendered division of labor is seen as a private family matter existing within the household, yet it is necessary for the other entire world of markets and capitalism to function. These activities don't command market wages, though the market economy and waged labor can't exist without them.[5]

For some, this question of social reproduction, of how to

make sure that the unpaid work of maintaining communities is sustained, can be answered by simply affirming traditional, patriarchal family structures. For such conservative thinkers, the extension of the marketplace into the family is seen as bad insomuch as it undermines the authority of men in their homes. Often those who fight for freedom from the market fall into a trap of defending this kind of patriarchy, romanticizing any set of social protections that could provide an alternative to market dependency.[6]

Yet there are alternatives to protecting and supporting care work that do not rely on social norms that restrict women's freedom. As the political theorist Nancy Fraser reminds us, the goal isn't just protection from market dependency, but also emancipation from unjust domination. Public programs designed to help families can play this role in empowering women to make the choices they want in their families and lives. In the aftermath of World War II, women took the lead in fighting for such programs.[7]

The United States did not leave it to the market to win World War II. The government set prices, administered a massive wartime buildup, and directed investment. One thing the nation's leadership paid close attention to was the size of the available workforce. So much work had to be done and the government had drafted and deployed millions of workers to be troops overseas. With America at war, the nation needed women to work outside their homes.[8]

Such a demand would involve an enormous shift in society, as married women did not work very often during the Great Depression. In the 1930s, roughly 90 percent of all women married, but only about 15 percent of married women were in the labor force by 1940. One 1936 Gallup poll found that over 80 percent of people believed that wives shouldn't work outside the home if they were married to men with jobs, with three out of four women agreeing. It was common for bosses to first fire the women who were married when handling layoffs and downsizing. This was the case for both public-sector jobs—for teachers and others—as well as private-sector ones.[9]

This changed with the war. The number of women in the labor force jumped by over half, and the percent of all women who were employed grew from 27.6 to 37 percent of all women between 1940 and 1945. This represented over 6.5 million new workers, with the number of working women increasing from 12 million to 18.6 million. Of these new female workers, around 75 percent were married. These headline numbers also downplay the number of women who were experiencing paid work for the first time. As women were likely to move in and out of the labor force throughout the year, estimates have 50 percent of all women employed at some point in 1944. The kinds of work that women could do changed as well, as the war undermined the sex segregation policies and practices in industries and other fields that kept women in low-paying service jobs and domestic work. Women went from working 22 percent of jobs in manufacturing to 33 percent, and doubled their share of jobs in government, from 19 percent to 38 percent.[10]

There were many reasons women took these jobs, from a sense of patriotism to the need to make up for the lost income of enlisted husbands. Yet many of these women found a new kind of satisfaction in the workplace. Having colleagues who were working on projects, learning and exercising knowledge and skills, gave them a different experience of the world and of independence outside the home. One working mother explained that "companionship of working with others is vastly more stimulating and rewarding than housework," and, regarding the alternative, noted the "narrowing effect that staying at home full time exerts upon my outlook in life."[11]

Caring for children outside the home was seen as a private, voluntary matter well into the early twentieth century. Charitable institutions, settlement homes, and community organizations provided a thin layer of services for poor women. The Great

Depression did little to change this ad hoc system. The Works Progress Administration did create emergency nursery schools, but this was mostly intended as a jobs program for unemployed teachers and others working in youth services, rather than a comprehensive program for the care of children. Though these emergency nurseries served between 44,000 and 72,000 poor children, depending on the year, the main rationale and funding for that program ceased with the end of the Great Depression.[12]

There was a strong bias against having mothers work during mobilization. Chairman Paul McNutt of the War Manpower Commission stated "no women responsible for the care of young children should be encouraged or compelled to seek employment" in the war effort unless absolutely necessary. However, the demand for workers forced this issue. The need for day care programs became directly linked to the war effort. As one lawmaker described it, "you cannot have a contented mother working in a war factory if she is worrying about her children, and you cannot have children running wild in the streets without a bad effect on the coming generation."[13]

Congress passed the Lanham Act as a mechanism to support the war effort with grants and loans, and under its broad authority the military authorized the funding of public day care centers. There were a number of bureaucratic hoops local communities would have to jump through in order for a day care center to receive public funds. To be approved, local communities had to demonstrate that war mobilization was responsible for an increase in women working and in the need for accessible day care. These applications were sent to the Federal Works Agency (FWA), which would grant the money assuming local communities would also cover 50 percent of the costs. Flat fees were charged to parents to use the centers. Yet even with all these required processes, this was still a national effort by the government to address support for children and families through federally funded public day cares. There was no eligibility threshold for parents as there was with welfare and charity agencies; anyone who wanted to use the programs could.[14]

The wartime public day care system started slowly and was underutilized as a result of the many obstacles it faced. The process was complicated by legislators' desire to limit the possibility of the program continuing after the war. It wasn't just Congress either. The influential National Catholic Welfare Conference demanded that all funding terminate immediately upon the end of the war. Many social worker organizations, such as the Child Welfare League of America, thought day cares were only appropriate as a form of supervised charity, one where poor mothers would be screened and counseled, with case files kept on their behavior. Members of these organizations would use their power in local communities to delay or stop applications for these public day cares.

It was also especially difficult to find places to host these day cares on such short notice, especially with many public buildings being used for the war effort. The facilities that communities could obtain were often second-best. Many of the day cares racially discriminated or otherwise made it harder for women of color to access them. Many parents were skeptical as well, especially with the idea of paying a fee for older children to have supervised care. There was also resistance from some employers too. When Mrs. Edsel Ford tried to have educational movies about nearby public day cares shown to the thousands of women working in a bomber plant, she was vetoed by their employer, Henry Ford.[15]

Yet despite these odds the day care centers continued to grow. At the height of the program, 3,102 centers provided care for close to 130,000 children. Overall, an estimated 600,000 children received care through these centers during World War II, at a government cost of $52 million. A survey conducted after the war found that, despite the initial skepticism of many parents, 81 percent had a "generally favorable" opinion of the program and 100 percent found that their "child enjoyed nursery school." One 2017 study found that areas that received more funding under the program had higher levels of female employment years afterward and that the children involved had better long-run outcomes related to educational achievement and employment.[16]

Though many day care clinics were improvisational, some devoted significant resources to ensuring they were the best clinic available for children of workers. The industrialist Henry Kaiser ran the Kaiser Shipyards, one of the major centers for wartime production, and took seriously his responsibility to the war effort and his workers. Kaiser aimed to make his factories the model for "the factory of the future," the kind that "should be equipped with child-care centers" and other essentials for workers. Kaiser brought in special architects to make sure the buildings were designed for the care and education of young children. Fifteen classrooms were arranged like spokes of a wheel around a central playground, with a special covering that allowed kids to play outside even when it was raining. The designs were remarkable enough to be featured in an issue of *Architectural Digest*. The architects designed the entire building from the child's point of view, including windows for a small child's eyes, furniture and bathroom fixtures for small children, and toys and plates specially designed with their needs in mind.

Kaiser proceeded with an aggressive hiring spree of the leading child education experts in the country to staff and advise the centers. He had, at first, considered just hiring day care operators from the general pool of workers, but was convinced to hire professionals. And when he learned what teachers staffing Lanham Act facilities were earning, Kaiser said, "You can't pay college graduates that! You won't hold them a week. All the administrative offices in the yards will steal them away from you." [17]

Kaiser Child Service Centers were revolutionary for workers. The facilities were open twenty-four hours a day and took children eighteen months to six years old. According to Miriam

Lowenberg, the Kaiser Centers' chief nutritionist, "[a] mother working in a shipyard with any problem relating to children may find here a place where she may seek help." The centers provided medical services, a sewing facility to help fix torn clothes, and drop-in clinics for emergencies. They even prepared take-out meals for parents when they picked up their children. Children dropped off for the morning shift got a hot breakfast. Parents getting off the night shift at 2 a.m. could find their sleeping children wrapped in a blanket, ready to be taken home. The centers served a thousand children at their peak in September 1944.[18]

The demands of wartime mobilization forced the federal government to respond rapidly to the problem of day care, not just in terms of funding but also designing a solution that was broadly accessible. There was significant bureaucratic infighting over who would carry out public day care responsibilities, largely between the Department of Education and the Federal Works Agency. The social worker bureaucracy and child care professionals wanted control, in part so they could target the program at only the most needy women. They wanted it positioned as an anti-poverty program, with case files and monitoring for those who used it, and managed with the general presumption that they shouldn't use it. But the military had absolutely no interest in stigmatizing potential workers, hiring case workers, or splitting the program's access into the deserving and undeserving. It wanted bombers and naval vessels, and was willing to arrange for anyone willing to make them to have the care infrastructure necessary to do it. The military had neither the time nor interest in playing amateur social worker, determining who was deserving and who was not. Given that mothers who needed support had to rely on a patchy and often humiliating network of charity and surveillance, this kind of universal and accessible program was a new and radical departure.

But the same political opening that contributed to these programs' success proved to be their undoing when the war ended. Very little administrative support built up around these programs, so there wasn't the internal government infrastructure to advocate for them. When Japan surrendered, the only remaining constituency who supported the care centers were the women using them. And these women weren't about to give up the newfound freedoms that the centers enabled without a fight.[19]

After the war ended, thousands of women sent letters, picketed, protested, lobbied, demonstrated, and coordinated media campaigns, all in the effort to keep the public day care programs open. Letters poured into Washington, DC. The FWA alone received petitions and letters from about six thousand people and groups in the short period after the war, and was hearing from an estimated five hundred people a day, calling for the day cares to remain open. Women using the day cares started organizing themselves, meeting in schools and churches, creating groups and debating political strategy. They led protests to get public attention. Advocates for maintaining the public day care system created groups in cities across the country, including Washington, DC, Chicago, Philadelphia, Detroit, and Richmond.[20]

Two groups of activists, one centered in Cleveland, Ohio, and the other spanning the state of California, are worth examining in detail here. The Day Care Committee was created in Cleveland in the immediate aftermath of the war. These women were able to quickly get over five hundred people at a high school auditorium to discuss ways to continue federal funding. They drafted a statement of principles endorsed by dozens of civic groups. A group of 150 women held a sit-in vigil in Cleveland's City Hall in February 1946 in a bid to force the mayor to continue the program's funding. They refused to vacate the building when officials said they would look into it, and were successful in getting the program extended for several months. In May, when the funding ran out, they occupied the building again, this time bringing their children as part of the protest. They succeeded in getting additional extensions until a judge ruled in a suit against the public day care system, deeming day care centers "an expenditure of public funds for a private purpose," and in early July ordered the city to cease all funding for the centers as soon as possible.[21]

In August 1945, hundreds of parents attended a meeting at a Los Angeles high school to discuss strategy to keep the day cares open. The meeting was supposed to be for local parents, but the interest in the programs was so intense that parents flocked from across and even beyond the city. They continued to organize in the following months, learning how to build political pressure. Parents would descend on the state capitol in Sacramento to advocate for keeping the funding for day care. This was a new experience, and the advocates had to learn on the fly how best to prepare materials and convince politicians to keep the program open. According to one story that circulated, two pro–day care delegates registered as an "agitator" instead of "advocate" when arriving at the capitol because they didn't know what the latter term meant. At a meeting of the state assembly's education committee, a male expert who argued against continuing the day cares was met, in the words of a reporter, "with feminine boos, hisses, and other exclamations of disapproval" from attending activists. Over the next several years a larger coalition would build in California, including parents, teachers, church groups, and women's clubs, all advocating for a permanent day care solution.[22]

Though the locations were different, each place faced the same difficulties. There were immediate problems, such as how to maintain funding. But the fundamental fight was over justifying why such a program should exist at all. One answer was that the day cares were necessary until all the men came home from abroad and life could return to normal. This bought them some time, as President Truman was willing to keep the programs open until 1946. But this argument could not justify a permanent program.[23]

The question of how to advocate for day care was tied up with how to advocate for the role women should have in the postwar economy. There were some women who articulated a comprehensive view of equality. One group organizing for a particular day care center in Cleveland stated their case clearly: "We believe that a democracy which professes no discrimination because of race, sex, or creed and in which co-education is prevalent has a responsibility to provide the service women need to enable them to express themselves in the way for which their talents, education and skills enable them, especially when this service contributes positively to the development of their children."[24]

The Columbus Day Care Committee chose not to use this language, focusing instead on women's economic need to work, especially in cases of poverty and single parenthood. Day care activists also emphasized the risk of juvenile delinquency and the dangers children faced with their parents at work. Such a change in messaging meant that the programs were now solutions for people in need, welfare programs for women in poverty. As the historian Emilie Stoltzfus writes, this argument "understood mothers' wage work as a problem to be solved, not a normal practice to support. In this way of thinking, publicly funded day care should be carefully doled out by professional social workers as a prescribed 'treatment' for dysfunctional families." This idea, and its consequences, became the norm in subsequent decades.[25]

California was the only state to maintain a public day care system after the war. After it became apparent that there would be no federal role, activists forced the state government to renew the program year by year until 1957, when it became permanent. California enjoyed many advantages compared with other states when it came to this campaign. The state grew quickly during the war, with its population increasing from 7 million to 9.5 million between 1940 and 1945. Many of these residents were women who were eager to work: half of the women using California wartime public day cares didn't have husbands serving in the military. These new workers weren't going anywhere, and they increased the need for a state-sponsored solution to the new demands they created.

The state's extensive war industry gave it the deepest experience with the wartime public day cares. California had over five hundred wartime child care centers, nearly 20 percent of all day cares nationwide, and at their peak they enrolled 25,000 children, a number three times larger than any other state. A deep network of progressive activists and children advocates saw this program as a stepping-stone to a broader universal program that could serve all Californians. California lawmakers were surprised that demand didn't fall as servicemen came back home; enrollment in the centers increased nearly 20 percent during 1946.[26]

There was one compromise that undermined the California program. The day cares were means tested, which limited eligibility to people based on their need. Advocates were opposed to this approach. As San Francisco League director Marion Turner asserted, "It is not legitimate to submit the problems of a home to an outsider," and "it's not possible to judge fairly family views." Parents viewed it as the government interfering in families' lives, and also pointed to the fact that options for child care were so underdeveloped that many working and middle-class families would also benefit from public day cares. They understood that means-testing programs splits off the broad support that universal programs can attain, and that having to prove eligibility is both cumbersome and degrading for those involved.

The advocates' predictions were correct, and the means test did exclude many families who would have taken advantage of the program. Two-parent families with monthly incomes over $275 and one-parent families with monthly incomes over $225 couldn't enroll their children. Of the four thousand application denials for being above the income threshold that occurred between 1952 and 1953, more than half of the families' reported incomes did not exceed the limit by more than $50. This shift changed the nature of the program and who used it. In 1946 more than 60 percent of children using the program had both parents working outside the home; in 1950 children of one-parent families became the majority of those using the program.[27]

But the California program still survived the aftermath of the war, making the state the exception to the rest of the nation. The wartime home front opened the possibility of the public supporting the work of raising families and providing programs and resources to working mothers as part of a normal functioning economy. This opened a wide range of freedom to women and families, and when politicians moved to end the funding and support, women organized and fought. However, this more radical vision was derailed by a newly assertive market vision of how to support families, one that took off in the 1950s.

In their 1937 tax return, Lillie Smith and her husband decided to deduct the cost of their nursemaid. Lillie had previously been taking care of their young child herself while her husband was working. When she decided to join the workforce as well, they needed a solution and hired help. They reasoned they could deduct the cost of this child care as a business expense, because it was necessary for Lillie to go to work. The only reason they got the help was to allow Lillie to work, and as such they believed their deduction would pass muster.

The deduction was denied, and the argument quickly came before the Board of Tax Appeals. The Board had two ways to consider this deduction. Deductions were allowed for "the ordinary and necessary expenses paid or incurred [for] carrying on any trade or business." If hiring a nursemaid was essential to carrying out economic activity, an expense that an entity like a business would face, it would stand. But deductions were not allowed "for personal, living, or family expenses." If caring for children was a personal decision and responsibility, outside the world of work, it would not count as a deduction. The Board had to decide where child-rearing stood in the division between public and private.

The Board chose private, ruling against the Smith family in *Smith v. Commissioner*. The 1939 decision stated, "We are not prepared to say that the care of children, like similar aspects of family and household life, is other than a personal concern." Care work and social reproduction were judged as existing in a private, domestic sphere of obligations. "The wife's services as custodian of the home and protector of its children are ordinarily rendered without monetary compensation. There results no taxable income from the performance of this service." The Board ruled that wives and mothers were not laborers, and their work was not work in an economic sense.[28]

In the postwar period this kind of argument would no longer be taken for granted. The expanding, consumer-driven economy and slow upward trajectory of women's employment during the 1950s forced the question into public debate. The columnist Sylvia Porter described how it was "grossly unfair" and "clearly an injustice" that working mothers could not deduct child care as part of "the production of her income." A *Redbook* editorial in 1953 argued that "it's the absolute responsibility of President Eisenhower and the Congress to change the tax laws so the working wife isn't penalized for working."[29]

Congress started introducing bills that would overrule *Smith* and allow for a deduction. In 1947, Democratic congressman Kenneth Keating of New York was the first to introduce a bill allowing women who paid for day care to deduct the expense from their taxes. Keating argued that women "should be able to deduct these [day care] expenses in the same way a businessman can deduct the ordinary expenses incidental to the conduct of his business." Within a few years, dozens of such bills would be introduced. There was opposition from those who, in the words of one legislator, believed "encourag[ing] mothers to work is an attack on the sanctity of motherhood and the generally accepted idea that her place is in the home." Proponents responded that women work out of necessity and for the benefit of their families, while also pointing out the often lavish expenses businesses were able to deduct. This idea of tax fairness started winning the public debate.[30]

A provision for the deduction for child care costs was included in the Internal Revenue Act of 1954, the first major overhaul of the tax code in decades. Congress allowed for a $600 deduction for child care, but it phased out at higher incomes. Once a family made more than $4,500 it was pulled back dollar for dollar, such that it was completely phased out for those making more than $5,100. To claim it you needed to itemize your deductions, which 72 percent of families, likely those with less income, didn't do in 1954. The gender dynamics were also questionable. Widows and women with disabled husbands weren't subject to the deduction phase-out and could claim it no matter how high their incomes were. Men who had never been married or whose wives couldn't work, however, couldn't get any deduction at all.

Rather than directly answer the question of whether child care was a business or personal expense directly, the structure of the deduction was designed to split the difference. For those women who were required to work by economic necessity, it would qualify as a business expense. For families where the wife could stay home, it was a personal decision. The intent was to help married working mothers, but only so much. In the words of one commentator, the design was such that a mother wouldn't "leave her children at home while she went out to earn money for a fur coat.' " The result was a fractured view, where the deduction tried to address the reality that care work needs to be compensated without acknowledging it, instead trying to patch around the contradiction.[31]

In lieu of a national program for day care, America opted in the postwar period for a set of tax incentives, cementing the idea that individual families would be responsible for their own support, with some encouraging funds from the government. A private child care industry began to form, and like all forms of private social insurance it was and remains unevenly accessible and far too expensive for a young family to handle on its own. The child care deduction would evolve and expand in subsequent decades, removing the unconstitutional gender limitations, becoming a broader benefit for the middle class, and converting into a tax credit in 1976. But no matter what form it took, handling child care costs through the tax code was a decision that replaced one potential system of social insurance with another.[32]

This decision submerged the problem of day care from the view of the broader public. It still represented spending on welfare and formed a kind of social insurance; the loss of tax revenue here was a real cost to the government, and as such it was spending money through the tax code. If you account for all the tax deductions, exclusions, and preferences, such as those for mortgage interest and employer-provided health care, the United States spends much more than is commonly assumed on social welfare. All together these expenditures add up to almost $1.5 trillion dollars a year now, a significant amount of social spending. But it is all in service to a specific, limited model of social insurance.[33]

There are many ways to build a welfare state. The sociologist Gøsta Esping-Andersen describes two such varieties on the basis of what kind of values they uphold and how they situate people with respect to the market. There is a social democratic model, one where programs are de-commodified and removed from market dependency, where economic security and goods are tied to rights everyone has as a citizen. Universal health care, available freely to all, is an example of a program in this kind of welfare state. Your ability to access it is independent of your income. These programs collapse the distinction between states and markets, instead focusing on the equality that strong public programs can create among citizens.

There are also market-based systems where benefits are tied to work and market income. These systems provide for people, provided that they also secure market wages. Tax benefits to provide extra income for housing, education, and health care are an example of this second model. These systems sometimes have more direct programs for poorer citizens, understood to be temporary, small, and difficult to use. This is to force people into the marketplace, rather than protect people from it. This inevitably reinforces inequality and leaves many behind.[34]

This second system of social insurance provided through the tax code not only forces market dependency, it also intensifies inequality. The benefits are usually tied to employment, with more for those with higher incomes. The more money you make, the more valuable is your ability to deduct spending, and as a result these programs give more to people who earn more. Those better off are also more likely to be sophisticated enough to take advantage of complicated tax structures. Tax incentives generally do not benefit people with low or unstable incomes. If you receive no income, then many tax credits do nothing for you. There's less pooling of risk, leaving more of it for individuals to manage. Among those who used the child care credit in 2014, for instance, the median income was $88,036, much higher than the $52,000 for all families with at least one child. Families with little-to-no income generally get no support for their children from it, with around 1 percent of the value of the child care credit going to households in the bottom fifth of the income distribution.[35]

This market-based form of social insurance also weakens public political action. It creates a hostile, incoherent form of politics, where the public is dependent on the state for these goods, but they have little ability to approach it as a public concern. They don't see that standing behind the curtain of these nominally private markets is a massive scaffolding of government action propping them up. These tax credits may not even be understood as a government program. One study found a majority of those who use the mortgage interest tax deduction, a tax-deferred savings account, or the child tax credit believed they weren't using a government program. The public programs that do exist only for the poor create a stigma against those who use them, and thus make it harder for them to expand to broader use or create any sense of social citizenship.[36]

This stigma is what defeated public day cares in the aftermath of World War II. From 1954 onward, when federal funding for public day cares was discussed, it was in the context of poverty policy and tax credits. The result was the continuation of the idea that, as the historian Sonya Michel describes it, "the presence of mothers in the workforce is presented not as a normal feature of advanced market economies but as a 'social problem' " that needs to be solved.[37] Yet there was an alternative vision, one that was articulated and fought for against overwhelming opposition. The women fighting to keep day cares open understood that society has an obligation to provide for its members in a way that expands, rather than limits, the freedom of its citizens. They argued that the work of caring for children is something that society should ensure is supported, as the market will fail to do so. The war forced into the debate the fact that capitalism is dependent on this labor of care work and social reproduction but will never compensate it fully. Yet the child care issue was just as quickly suppressed a decade later, papered over with a piecemeal solution of tax credits. We still live with this contradiction today.

6

FREE HEALTH

John Holloman was expecting to be disappointed, but he did not expect to be stood up. Dr. John L.S. "Mike" Holloman Jr. was the president-elect of the National Medical Association, a professional group of black doctors founded in 1895 in reaction to segregation within the American Medical Association. He was also the chair of the Medical Committee for Human Rights (MCHR), a group formed in 1964. Informally known as the medical wing of the civil rights movement, the MCHR was a group of physicians and health care workers dedicated to ending segregation and the substandard care black people faced in the United States. Holloman and the other members of his organizations had been doing everything from documenting segregated hospital facilities to providing frontline health care for civil rights activists when they suffered beatings by police.

Holloman was in Washington, DC, on December 16, 1965, for what should have been a tense meeting between leaders of the civil rights movement, including the NAACP Legal Defense and Education Fund, and the federal government. The meeting was to be hosted by Secretary John Gardner, the recently appointed head of the U.S. Department of Health, Education, and Welfare (HEW). It had been a year since the civil rights movement had pressured Congress into passing the Civil Rights Act, which desegregated facilities that provided public accommodations and received federal dollars, yet in that time there had been little success in desegregating Southern hospitals. The civil rights groups were there to find out if anyone at HEW was going to do anything about enforcing the law.

Secretary Gardner never arrived for the meeting. Angry, Holloman sent Gardner a telegram the press soon received as well, pointing out that Gardner had "met freely with the conservative elements of the health profession. We wonder if your failure to meet with us has racial implications and may be symptomatic of the reluctance of your department to come to grips with the discriminatory practices in health care." The civil rights leaders held a press conference the next day, where they argued that HEW had a unique opportunity to end segregation in health care and that it would blow this chance if it didn't take action. The bureaucratic response from HEW, that it would take "every reasonable step to assure" that hospitals "comply fully with the provisions of the Civil Rights Act" would not inspire confidence given the lack of success it had achieved thus far.[1]

There must have been a sense of exhaustion among the activists. For over a decade these groups had fought the brutality of health care under Jim Crow segregation. In the wake of the Supreme Court's ruling in *Brown v. Board of Education*, all they saw was disappointment and delay. Without a forceful push to desegregate hospitals, the providers would be left in the driver seat, and it was possible that hospitals would just ignore their obligations, slow-walk, break promises, and otherwise continue their wave of massive resistance to any action that would challenge Jim Crow. The activists could end up with a health care system just as segregated, without anyone there to force the change.

We'll never know what transpired on that day. Gardner was insistent that he missed the meeting as a result of a scheduling mix-up. Perhaps Gardner would have taken on their cause without the subsequent public embarrassment. But either way, a few weeks later Gardner started gearing up his staff for a major battle. He was going to declare war on Jim Crow health care in the South, and he was going to use the work of community activists and civil rights organizations as a weapon in that fight. This fight could be different, because he knew he had a secret weapon to deploy in order to dismantle white supremacy in the South: the recently passed single-payer health care system for the elderly, Medicare.[2]

To thrive and be free, all of us require a certain baseline, of which health forms a crucial part. Health is part of our freedom. We all get sick and injured, even more so as we get older, and we all need access to health care. But health isn't just about the absence of sickness, but about having the capability to choose and lead the healthy lives we want with dignity. How healthy we are is partially the result of the bodies we are born with, but it's also driven by the environments we live in, the information we have access to, and the resources available to us to access care. As a result, the conditions under which we can find that access is central to any politics of freedom.[3]

The ability of the market alone to provide health care fails in ways that are as predictable as they are absolute. There's a reason every modern country has a government program or mechanism for ensuring health care. Health insurance is the kind of market where people who sell insurance don't want to provide it for people who are already sick, and healthy people don't want to buy insurance until they are sick. This leads to people with preexisting conditions being excluded from insurance, and young people who think they are invincible going uninsured. Everyday people are bad at understanding the medical risks they face, and the costs of a serious medical condition are so dramatic and sudden it is impossible to save on one's own as a hedge against illness or injury.

Most countries outside of the United States have enacted either a single-payer system, where the government is the primary insurance provider for everyone, or else sets out very tight regulations on profit and payments between insurance companies and the medical community. The focus on the government as the insurance provider results from the fact that the government is capable of keeping costs in check by using the scale that comes with having everyone in a single program. Other countries have better or similar health care outcomes than the United States but manage to spend far less.[4]

Markets are great at distributing things based on people's willingness to pay. But there are some goods that should be distributed by need. The purpose of health care is to provide care for sick people; being sick is a necessary condition of getting care. No rational person seeks out expensive health care for fun or enjoyment, and sickness isn't something that is earned—but that falls upon us. Yet our society adds another necessary condition to receiving health care, which is having money.[5]

All of this was well understood by the early 1900s, when I.M. Rubinow was describing social insurance to a skeptical United States. But the history of health care in the United States shows us another reason to keep the market in check when it comes to our freedom: markets can perpetuate segregation and other unjust forms of exclusion. That was the case with the Southern hospital system under Jim Crow. Medicare played a key role in the destruction of the Jim Crow system in the South. But to understand how that happened, we need to see how health care evolved after the New Deal.

On September 6, 1945, just weeks after World War II ended, President Harry Truman called together a special session of Congress. Laying out his twenty-one-point plan for the reconversion of the economy from the war, he called for full employment and reiterated Roosevelt's Economic Bill of Rights. Within this proposal, tucked in at the very end was a call for national health care. "I shall shortly communicate with the Congress," Truman declared, "recommending a national health program to provide adequate medical care for all Americans and to protect them from financial loss and hardships resulting from illness and accident." This was the beginning of his Fair Deal, a continuation of Roosevelt's legacy. Liberals were impressed, but Republicans and conservative

Democrats who wanted to be done with reform were angry. "Not even President Roosevelt ever asked for as much in one setting," said one Republican senator. Others accused Truman of "out-dealing the New Deal."[6]

Two months later in a special message to Congress, Truman made the full case for single-payer health care. "Everyone should have ready access to all necessary medical, hospital and related services," he argued, and he recommended "solving the basic problem by distributing the costs through expansion of our existing compulsory social insurance system." This plan would have citizens "pay regularly into a common health fund, instead of paying sporadically and unevenly when they are sick."[7]

Truman's argument for the government's necessary role in health care still speaks to us today. Truman noted that the past reduction in mortality rates "have come principally from public health and other community services," and that "[i]n the past, the benefits of modern medical science have not been enjoyed by our citizens with any degree of equality. Nor are they today. Nor will they be in the future—unless government is bold enough to do something about it." Truman went on to describe how "families, fearful of expense, delay calling the doctor long beyond the time when medical care would do the most good." Truman noted that "sickness not only brings doctor bills; it also cuts off income." As with the push for Social Security within the New Deal, Truman was able to reference voluntary, private health insurance while also noting its essential insufficiency.

With the Cold War heating up, Truman went to great pains to argue that his plan "is not socialized medicine." The system would be decentralized in terms of medical administration but centralized in terms of payments to handle the risks. People would remain free to choose their medical services. But, as Truman noted, "[t]here would, however, be this all-important difference: whether or not patients get the services they need would not depend on how much they can afford to pay at the time."

Truman's push failed. The failure of his health care plan set the stage for how the health care debates would evolve until this day. Senator Robert Taft of Ohio declared, "I consider it socialism. It is to my mind the most socialistic measure this Congress has ever had before it," and said it came from the Soviet constitution. Whitaker and Baxter, a public relations firm hired by the American Medical Association, launched an education campaign alleging that Vladimir Lenin had once declared, "Socialized medicine is the keystone to the arch of the Socialist State." (The Library of Congress, when asked, could find no such quote.) This wasn't new, as the same tactics of referring to reform as socialism occurred during the New Deal. However, with the Great Depression in the background, and the Cold War rising, the specter of communism hung in the background and made this an effective attack line.[8]

The medical industry led an overwhelming campaign to stop single-payer health care. The American Medical Association deployed resources at a scale unheard of before, waging the most expensive lobbying campaign up to that point. In 1950, the AMA outspent a pro–single-payer group like the Committee for the Nation's Health on the order of sixty to one. It formed alliances with businesses, who wanted to fight government spending and public programs in general, and got them to sponsor ads about preserving American values. This campaign involved a massive multimedia push. Just before the congressional elections in 1950, the AMA, according to one estimate, was running ads in ten thousand newspapers, a buying spree that no doubt delighted editors and publishers. It also ran ads on 1,600 radio stations and in dozens of magazines.[9]

The AMA was successful in stopping single-payer health care because it stood at the center of two important networks, one economic and the other social. As private health insurance grew during this time period, the AMA was able to take advantage of the growing profits this industry was newly creating. It was at this time that pharmaceutical companies, in particular, looked to work with medical doctors to fight single-payer health care. Private insurance, especially insurance provided by employers, was becoming more and more common, thanks to the boost by a tax exemption created in World War II. But, beyond the profit motive, the importance of informal social networks that doctors inhabited shouldn't be overlooked. Elites from business and politics interacted with doctors in their most personal moments, and the advancements of medicine in this period gave doctors a significant amount of cultural prestige in their communities. These medical interests were as skilled in deploying this soft power as they were utilizing the harder power of dollars.[10]

Given these political and social currents, Republicans understood that they had a chance, at this historical moment, to provide an alternative to public health insurance by subsidizing private insurance through the tax code. They used the 1954 Tax Act, which also created the child care tax deduction, to lock in the employer deduction for health care. At that point, there was some ambiguity coming out of World War II over whether employer contributions to health care should be taxed. Republicans, recognizing the growing allure of a single-payer system, had a clear sense of what was at stake here. The Republican plan, as President Eisenhower described it, was to encourage "insurance and other plans adopted by employers to protect their employees against the risks of sickness . . . by removing the present uncertainties in the tax law." The *Wall Street Journal* applauded the Tax Act for being "a part answer to the false lures of socialized medicine." Not discussed was the likelihood this would become a huge source of government spending through the tax code in subsequent decades. Marion Folsom, Eisenhower's undersecretary of the treasury and later secretary of Health, Education, and Welfare, testified that they hadn't estimated how much it would cost but assumed it wouldn't be anything major.[11]

In addition to creating a private employer-based social insurance system through the tax code, the federal government was comfortable funding the construction of hospitals without putting any conditions on the private medical and insurance industries regarding their major decision-making powers. One of the most important ways in which federal funding was extended without any additional controls was with the Hospital Survey and Construction Act of 1946, often referred to as the Hill-Burton Act. This bill was designed to accelerate the construction of new hospitals, a sector that the Depression and the war had collapsed over the previous fifteen years. President Truman and others wanted the government to build out this sector to catch up with the growing postwar demand. Conservative members astutely saw that simply building new hospitals, independent of providing universal health care, would increase access, particularly in regions currently underserved.[12]

Hill-Burton required that funded hospitals promise not to discriminate on the basis of race. Yet Southern Democrats ensured that this funding wouldn't be used in such a manner to challenge Jim Crow in the South. First, they had a special measure added to the legislation that declared hospitals were private entities that couldn't be regulated by the federal government, only by the states. This not only shielded hospitals from public accountability, but also meant that they could discriminate against black doctors and other medical professionals in hiring and staffing. Another provision allowed federal funding for segregated hospitals and segregation by race within hospitals, as long as they were purportedly of equal quality of care, which they never were. This new funding stream continued and even deepened segregation in Southern health care; sixty-five of sixty-seven counties in Alabama used Hill-Burton money to build hospitals that were segregated, either within facilities or as facilities solely for people of color. A Social Security Administration official noted that "[t]hose of us who were involved in that bill took the position that if that was the price we had to pay for getting this legislation through, we would pay for it."[13]

This is exactly the kind of publicly funded discrimination that the landmark Supreme Court decision *Brown v. Board of Education* was designed to stop. Except a funny thing happened in the aftermath of that ruling: nothing.

Argued twice over two years, *Brown v. Board of Education* was finally decided unanimously by the Supreme Court in May 1954. In this ruling, the Court found that "separate but equal," the guiding idea for Jim Crow going back to the 1890s, was unconstitutional. The Court, in a follow-up ruling the next year, determined the applicable remedy for segregation in schools. Government officials should "take such proceedings and enter such orders and decrees consistent with this opinion as are necessary and proper to admit to public schools on a racially nondiscriminatory basis with all deliberate speed the parties to these cases." The idea of desegregation occurring with "all deliberate speed" was taken as the appropriate rule by both the courts and people following the case.[14]

The Court took this monumental action, then nothing changed. In 1955 a little over a tenth of a percent of black children, roughly 12 in 1,000, attended a school with whites in the South. Five years later that number was virtually unchanged, standing at 16 in 1,000. It wasn't until 1963 that the number would even hit 1 percent. The number did increase in the border states, from about 40 percent to 50 percent between 1956 and 1962, but even then, it still stood only at half. Looking at the statistics, one can't see *Brown* making a difference in the decade after its passage.[15]

It took the Civil Rights Act of 1964 to actually desegregate schools on the ground. The number of black children attending a school with whites in the South went from 2 percent the year the Act passed to 32 percent four years later, and 86 percent six years later. While the Supreme Court can be effective at holding back change and enforcing already existing power structures, it is actually very weak at creating new reform itself. It controls no funding and is dependent on elite power structures to carry out its decisions. What really creates change is popular mobilization and legislative changes.[16]

Brown should have applied to the wave of new public hospitals the federal government was funding in the late 1950s under Hill-Burton. Yet there was no mechanism by the Court to force action, and the business of white supremacy carried on as normal. The Department of Health, Education, and Welfare (HEW), responsible for carrying out the Hill-Burton funding of hospital construction, immediately concluded that *Brown* didn't have any consequences for the hospitals. The department also refused to investigate whether hospitals were actually equal or "of like quality," despite having the ability to do so. According to officials at HEW, "We are not intending to suggest at this time that we are required to be concerned with relative quality of segregated services," and unless it was "definitely established that segregation on the basis of race in public hospitals [was] unconstitutional, the Surgeon General [was] certainly under no statutory mandate to anticipate the outcome of court tests of that issue." Beginning in 1956, the NAACP started filing lawsuits against hospitals on the basis that "separate but equal" was unconstitutional under *Brown*. Many were dismissed or settled after hospitals made small, cosmetic changes. The hospitals' legal status as private institutions, even as their operation was possible only through a web of federal funding and tax exemptions, shielded them from the actions of civil rights activists.[17]

In the 1963 case *Simkins v. Moses H. Cone Memorial Hospital*, the Fourth Circuit Court of Appeals found that when it came to the Hill-Burton funding, "separate but equal" was unconstitutional under the Fourteenth Amendment. It ruled that federal funding made the hospitals not solely private but an "arm of the state." HEW responded by requiring nondiscrimination in new hospital requests. However, there was only so much that could be done, as it had no jurisdiction over the hospitals that had already been built with its funding. HEW couldn't force hospitals to re-pay old funds; it could only threaten new funding. As late as 1964, eleven Southern states required the segregation of white and black patients in hospitals, as well as segregated cafeterias, entrances, and training schools for nurses. These were backed by the threat of fines and even imprisonment.[18]

Into this fight came a wave of newly energized doctors and other medical professionals, all finding inspiration from the ongoing civil rights movement. One of the leaders was John L.S. Holloman Jr. Born in Washington, DC, in 1919, Holloman was the son of a Baptist preacher and the grandson of a slave. A friend gave him the nickname "Mike" to use instead of his initials, and also to capture his easygoing and friendly nature. Holloman went to a segregated grade school and later an integrated high school. He went to the all-black Virginia Union University, where he studied chemistry. He later attended medical school at the University of Michigan and graduated in 1943.

After graduating he applied to the nearby Dearborn Naval Station but was denied, receiving a letter saying that there were no positions for black commissioned officers in the Navy. He joined the Army Air Corp, serving in an all-black bomber group under Col. Benjamin O. Davis, one of the first black general officers in the armed forces. Holloman and his friends had a knack for names. They called their bomber group the "Spookwaffe" and their social group the Bilbo Breakfast Club, ironically named after the racist senator from Mississippi Theodore Bilbo, who called for sending American black people back to Africa. After the war, Holloman continued his studies at Cornell University before setting up his own medical practice in Harlem, where he would spend the rest of his life.

Holloman had a lifelong commitment to public, universal health care. As he said in an interview toward the end of his life, "Until we take the profit motive out of it and provide health care for all of our citizens, we are always going to have somebody who's left out because there are so many people on whom there is no profit to be made." Or more simply, in the words of an inscription on the back of the nameplate he used while serving as president of the New York City Health and Hospital Corporation in the 1970s, "Health Care Is a Right." [19]

In 1963, Holloman and several of his friends, in order to solidify their commitment to fighting discrimination in health care, created a group called the Medical Committee for Human Rights (MCHR), with Holloman agreeing to be temporary chair. At the same time, record protests were breaking out across the South as part of the civil rights movement. Many of these protesters faced intense violence and hostility, from both white citizens and police officers. Members of the MCHR decided that they would coordinate with civil rights leaders in the South to help provide frontline services for the protesters. [20]

When Martin Luther King Jr. led a march for voting rights across the Edmund Pettus Bridge from Selma to Montgomery, Alabama, the protesters faced a violent police response. Members of the MCHR, including Holloman, were there to respond, providing medical services to those that had been beaten. While there, Holloman met a white nurse named Patricia Ann Tatje, who was from Brooklyn and worked at Kings County Hospital. Though she would later describe her bus-driving father as similar to the conservative television character Archie Bunker, she became active with MCHR. While in Selma, she helped attend to Dr. King's feet, blistered from walking to the point he was limping. Holloman and Patricia kept in touch, and quickly fell in love when they moved back to New York. They married and had two children, a testament to the lifelong bonds created in the difficult struggle for civil rights. [21]

At the same time, two major political achievements had cleared Congress. President Lyndon Johnson used his knowledge of the Senate and political strategy to pass the Civil Rights Act of 1964, working with his allies to break a filibuster led by Southern

Democrats. Johnson ran for president that year on building a Great Society, with health care for the elderly and poor as one of the central tenets of his signature policy initiative. In the aftermath of Johnson's huge reelection win, Congress passed a major, sweeping set of public programs. Medicare, a single-payer system for the elderly, would be signed into law on July 30, 1965. The interconnection between these two laws was the opening the medical civil rights movement was looking for.

Trying to set up a major single-payer health care system, even one that would only provide insurance for the elderly as Medicare did, was a daunting task. From coverage baselines, to funding mechanisms for hospitals, to setting up a system to inform elderly people about their ability to use it, the launch of Medicare was a chaotic and fast-moving affair. A hundred offices had to be opened, with thousands of people hired, to make the program work. Congress accepted a window of only one year as the time for the entire program to go live and begin providing insurance on July 1, 1966. Though it would have made their lives easier, those implementing the program believed at the time that Congress wouldn't have accepted a two-year implementation because it wanted the benefits to promptly get to those who needed them.[22]

Outreach was one of the most important parts of setting up Medicare, and the numbers involved were staggering. Seventeen million people over the age of sixty-five had to be asked whether or not they would sign up for supplemental insurance as part of the program. Officials mailed out a series of punch cards for people to select their preference, which were then processed. In all, 19 million Medicare cards would be printed and mailed out. This outreach operation had to be completed within nine months, as the deadline for coverage was March 31, 1966.

Conservatives had tried to rally to defeat the passage of Medicare. In 1961 Ronald Reagan had recorded an album for the American Medical Association's political campaign against what would become Medicare. In the ten-minute recording, Reagan presents a public health insurance program for the elderly as a means for socialism to take hold in America. He concludes that if something like Medicare came to pass, "we are going to spend our sunset years telling our children and our children's children what it once was like in American when men were free." The American people disagreed. The response was overwhelmingly fast, as the elderly were excited to sign up for coverage. Government officials quickly recorded a 95 percent response rate over a short period of time. Medicare made its deadline, going live within one year, and it remains popular to this day.[23]

But these logistical problems paled in comparison to the political challenge of reconciling Medicare with the Civil Rights Act of 1964. This was the task that fell to John Gardner, who took over as secretary of HEW. Title VI of the Civil Rights Act prevented racial discrimination by any program or entity that received federal funds. Title VI was carefully designed so that government agencies could enforce it themselves, rather than having to wait for uncertain, piecemeal, and time-consuming lawsuits to work their way through the courts. The question of whether Medicare funding would go to segregated hospitals became an immediate flash point in the process of implementing it.

The problem wasn't just that segregated hospitals were already saying that they wouldn't change, though that was a problem: in the summer of 1965, as Medicare was in the process of being passed in Congress, many Southern hospitals were segregated even though the Civil Rights Act was already a year old. The United States Commission on Civil Rights found that two-thirds of the Southern hospitals in the sample they studied had continued segregated practices in their health care. These hospitals were selected because they received some federal funding, either through Hill-Burton or other related federally financed programs, and as such should have had to fully desegregate under Title VI. Yet they weren't desegregated. Selma Baptist Hospital in Selma, Alabama, for example, refused to accept any blacks at all, stating it had no plans on complying with the Civil Rights Act.[24]

The real issue was determining what threshold would be sufficient for hospitals to qualify to get Medicare funds and how the government would go about verifying it. Congress avoided providing answers to these obvious questions as Medicare was being debated, leaving them for the implementation of the program instead. As SSA commissioner Robert Ball remembered of Medicare as it moved through Congress, "We didn't want [Title VI enforcement] brought up legislatively. It would have been a big barrier to passage in the Senate, particularly if it had been clear that this was going to be applied. I think everyone knew it, but they didn't want to have to go on record about it." There were several things that could go wrong. The first would be a delay in the implementation of full desegregation. If Medicare funding went to hospitals that simply promised to start desegregating later, or were only partially desegregated at the time, then the main tool regulators had to force compliance would have already been spent. The second was the prospect of hospitals making false promises about being desegregated. How could checks be put into place to ensure compliance?[25]

The tight deadline for Medicare implementation created a game of chicken between segregated hospitals and the Johnson administration. Everyone knew that news coverage of senior citizens not getting care because hospitals lacked funding would be terrible for the new program. The hospitals also understood that if they could get the administration to budge on the strictness of desegregation requirements, say by splitting them into tiers to be implemented over many years, they could fight to keep delaying change indefinitely.

As the medical historian David Barton Smith describes, a crusade of reformers, civil rights activists, and health care experts aligned to carry out an almost impossible task. The first thing the administrators at HEW had to work out was the criterion regarding the pace of desegregation. They agreed that they wouldn't follow the "all deliberate speed" criterion that was used for schools in the wake of *Brown*. They would instead require full desegregation at the very beginning, no delays or gradual implementation, for hospitals to be certified and receive Medicare funding. Gardner put together a legal team to advise him on civil rights enforcement. Peter Libassi, who helped lead New York's investigations into discrimination and then worked on the Commission on Civil Rights, was brought on to help coordinate HEW's enforcement of Title VI. Libassi was the most knowledgeable expert on Title VI in Washington, DC, and only agreed to the job after Gardner confirmed to him that he'd be willing to cut federal funding for any place not complying with civil rights law. Libassi had a small team of civil rights experts who were also disillusioned by the stalled nature of voluntary desegregation. Among them was Derrick Bell, who had worked for the NAACP Legal Defense Fund and who would go on to be the founder of the legal school of thought known as critical race theory. They were seasoned in fights over desegregation and understood what had failed up to that point.[26]

The second matter to work out was creating a legion of bureaucrats capable of carrying this out. Gardner formed a special office to manage and execute the process of certifying desegregated hospitals, the Office of Equal Health Opportunity (OEHO), but it didn't get started until February 1966, giving them less than half a year before Medicare would launch. There was nowhere near the number of people assigned to the office to handle the task of certifying that the estimated four thousand hospitals in the country that were still segregated were no longer so under their criterion. Gardner made staffing a priority, and roughly one thousand people were reassigned on short notice to the OEHO to handle this task. Many were reassigned from other projects. But a large number volunteered once the word got out.[27]

On March 4, 1966, a special letter went out to all the hospitals in the country: "Dear Hospital Administrator: Title VI of the Civil Rights Act of 1964 prohibits discrimination on the basis of race, color or national origin [. . .] To be eligible to receive Federal assistance or participate in any Federally-assisted program a hospital must be in compliance." Included was a description of the clear yet comprehensive requirements necessary to be in compliance with Medicare. The hospital had to provide care on a nondiscriminatory basis "without regard to race, color or national origin." The hospital had a responsibility to take corrective action if "there is a significant variation between the racial composition of patients and the population service area." Training, recruitment, and staff privileges all had to be race-neutral. In order to ensure compliance, the letter noted that "[r]epresentatives from the Department of Health, Education, and Welfare Regional office will be visiting hospitals on a routine periodic basis to supplement this information and to be of further assistance in resolving any problems that may arise."[28]

The resistance from white southerners was fierce. A common tactic was for car rental agencies, working in cahoots with local police, to arrange for the visiting inspectors to use rental cars that had already been falsely reported stolen. If the inspector pushed too hard, they could be arrested for driving a stolen vehicle. OEHO managers would have to be on standby for quickly dealing with these and other trumped-up charges against their employees. Sometimes the threat of violence was more direct. One Mississippi hospital administrator told a government investigator, there to discuss desegregation, that "I called some of the boys in the KKK when you arrived. I didn't know you were going to be such a nice fellow, you better leave while you can." One federal manager in Baltimore found a cross burning in her front yard.[29]

Government investigators had one advantage though. They could rely on black people themselves, especially those in the medical community, to help turn them into agents for tearing down desegregation. HEW investigators would show up in a town and connect with the local NAACP or church group, who would in turn put the investigators in touch with black workers at hospitals and individuals who had received segregated care. These workers had to be careful, as state and local police would follow the investigators; black workers could be fired by their bosses if they were suspected of cooperating with federal HEW authorities. In a typical episode, a black employee told HEW investigators how to find the hidden, segregated break rooms for black employees. While on inspection tours, administrators would try to guide them away from such cramped, substandard work rooms—but the investigators would already have a map drawn for them by those who worked there.

Another anecdote, of two OEHO investigators who went to Louisiana, shows how this network could overcome the deception deployed against desegregation. Investigators examined a large hospital in Louisiana that stated it had desegregated as part of their application for Medicare. But things felt off to the investigators, such as the fact that the blood stored in a hospital refrigerator was labeled separately as "black" and "white." But they noted that the nursery was integrated, which was generally a good sign. After they left, doubts nagged at them. They decided to visit one of the black employees at her home, privately, to ask her about the situation at the hospital. She told them that during the inspection, her boss "came running down the hall and said, 'Mary, the Feds are coming, get those babies together.' As soon as y'all left she came in and re-separated the babies." That hospital failed its Medicare certification.[30]

John Holloman and the MCHR played a crucial role through their extensive documentation of the practice of segregation in hospitals. They coordinated with local nurses and doctors to compile all this information using a twenty-three-question form they created to catalog exactly how segregation worked. They conveyed this information by filing hundreds of complaints with HEW, information they used in their investigations. One HEW official later noted that of the five hundred documented cases of segregated hospitals that he saw, three hundred of them came just from the MCHR.

John Holloman himself worked as an HEW consultant. He was hired part-time to call black doctors from the network of Southern medical professionals that he had organized and put HEW investigators in contact with them. From this group, Holloman could identify where the problems were the worst and help HEW use this knowledge to deploy extra resources. When the investigators arrived, they could rely on the people that Holloman and others coordinated.[31]

The core reason why Medicare could ultimately force desegregation was that it controlled funding. Administrators and other executives understood that their business model wasn't sustainable in the post-Medicare world without having access to it. Take an example in Texas. Because it concerned Lyndon Johnson's home state, desegregation in Texas state hospitals was politically sensitive to the president. A black doctor who worked on civil rights in the U.S. Surgeon General's Office named Richard Smith was sent to Marshall County Hospital, Lady Bird Johnson's home county, to have a specially coordinated inspection. He was greeted by pickup trucks filled with men carrying rifles, a menacing group who said they'd be his unplanned escort to the hospital. The intimidation attempt didn't slow Smith. After a day of meetings, the hospital's administrator openly refused to cooperate with desegregation. Though surrounded by guns and resistance, the government had the ultimate weapon: "Fine," Smith said, "but you just tossed away $100 million in Medicare funding." A week later Smith got the call from the chairman of the hospital's board, who informed him that they fired that administrator and wanted to know what they had to do to desegregate and receive Medicare funding.[32]

But that didn't make change inevitable. There were real obstacles. In April, with three months left until the start date, only half of the hospitals in the country met their requirements, with the number half that in the South. Even in June, with weeks left, fewer than 40 percent of hospitals in Southern states had fully desegregated. There was a bluff being called, with hospitals trying to see if President Johnson would back down. There were worries that Medicare would not be able to deliver funding to many hospitals in these states, causing a public relations disaster at the launch where sick elderly people would be turned away from care. Staff floated proposals that included using army hospitals and emergency mobile medical facilities to handle areas without authorized Medicare hospitals. But a White House staff memorandum also suggested Johnson could allow "civil rights requirements be waived for an additional period" rather than see the Medicare launch become a disaster.[33]

Yet Johnson didn't budge. At a White House meeting with hospital leaders in mid-June he told them directly that the government wasn't going to back down and they should be aware of it. In his delivered remarks, Johnson said that when it came to compliance with the Civil Rights Act, "the Federal Government is not going to retreat from its clear responsibility" and "you are here today to help us make this reality clear to your communities." He added his own language on the spot: "I want you to know, we ain't gonna lock the barn door after the hoss has been stolen. We're gonna desegregate the hospitals." The night before Medicare launched, the president addressed the country, stating, "Tomorrow, for the first time, nearly every older American will receive hospital care—not as an act of charity, but as the insured right of a senior citizen [. . .] Medicare will succeed—if hospitals accept their responsibility under the law not to discriminate against any patient because of race." Johnson, across multiple venues, made it clear this was going to happen.[34]

They won. By July 21, less than half of a percent of hospitals weren't certified for Medicare. True to their word, those handful of hospitals that ignored the Civil Rights Act were denied funding. As Wilbur Cohen, a lifelong architect of social insurance in the United States, who worked on the launch of both Social Security and the Great Society, later reflected:

> On the day before Medicare went into effect, in every hospital in the South, over every drinking foundation, over every bathroom, over every cafeteria, there were signs reading "White" and "Colored" for separate but presumably equal facilities. On the day that Medicare went into effect in the South, all those signs and separate facilities began to come down. This I think was a singular achievement of Medicare. In one day Medicare and Medicaid broke the back of segregated health services.[35]

The effects were immediate and dramatic. Segregated health care was horrific for the black people who had to suffer under it. Infant mortality rates serve as a simple, but devastating, illustration. Up until that point, 40 black infants would die for every 1,000 born, rates that resemble countries like India or Iraq now. In 1965, black newborns were four times more likely to die of pneumonia and gastroenteritis than white newborns. These were two common causes of death among newborns that had become significantly easier to treat with medical advancements in administering antibiotics and fluids to babies. Those advancements lowered the rate of death for white babies, but you would never know these methods were even invented if you looked at the death rate for black babies. These life-saving improvements, and the expansion of Hill-Burton hospitals to carry them out, simply passed black families by. The desegregation of hospitals collapsed these rates, with the overall rate of black infant deaths falling by nearly half within a decade. The infant mortality rate in Mississippi fell by 25 percent in just the first year. This period of medical desegregation was the only convergence in black-white infant mortality rates since World War II.[36]

Universal public programs can create levels of access that the private sphere and marketplace will never match. Public programs can overcome and break persistent and widespread discrimination, especially against the most disadvantaged. Public programs can ensure that citizens have access to the fundamental supports they need to live free lives. Health and access to medical services are an obvious part of this support. Sickness can be a form of confinement, preventing us from living free lives. The market alone can't provide health care to everyone because it will quickly exclude those that need it the most. By ensuring health care is broadly available, independent of race, income, or preexisting conditions, the government can help ensure our freedom.

In the 1960s, the government used federal funding as a mechanism to break Jim Crow. President Obama used the same kind of funding mechanism to push an expansion of Medicaid with the Affordable Care Act. Under the passed law, states that wouldn't expand Medicaid to working-class people would jeopardize all their Medicaid funding. Losing this funding is something states wouldn't risk, and it was assumed all states would follow with expansion. When the Affordable Care Act came before the Supreme Court, it was this Medicaid funding requirement that Chief Justice John Roberts successfully stripped out of the law as a price to pay for it to survive. Millions, overwhelmingly in the South, remain excluded from health care as a result.[37]

7

FREE ECONOMY

It's impossible to say exactly when it started, but viewing the market and our dependency on it as something that needs to be checked has dropped out of our politics. Instead, we've watched as the market has extended further into our lives and even further into how we view ourselves and our society. The idea of "free markets" took over our language, and markets have come to be seen as both a foundation of our freedom and the place in which we experience the most freedom. Freedom means freedom for markets, but also freedom *through* markets and freedom as a kind of market. There are a lot of academic terms to describe this change over the last several decades, with "neoliberalism" being one of the most common. These terms are contested and debated, and sometimes they break out of the academy and into the public debates where they get fought over even more. But even without the scholarly background, the underlying change is something we all understand and feel in our everyday lives.

One way to understand neoliberalism is as a historical period, one where the economy was restructured to be far more favorable to bosses and owners, shifting power away from workers and citizens. Capitalism itself has always been changing since it began, always reshaping in response to workers, governments, technology, and laws. During the 1970s the United States faced a series of economic crises. The stagflation of high unemployment and high inflation destroyed the confidence liberal economists of the mid-century period had in steering the economy. The near bankruptcy of New York City was blamed on wasteful spending on big liberal programs, marking a turn toward limitations on what individuals could ask of the state. The beginning wave of deindustrialization started to shift the benefits of the economy away from manufacturing and toward finance. These crises planted the seeds for a whole new way of thinking about the economy.[1]

But describing it as a period also makes this change seem inevitable, something more like the weather than an actual movement based around an idea of freedom. What brought about this revolution was a successful intellectual and political movement, which used a set of ideas to take advantage of these crises. Those ideas were built over prior decades. Starting in the wake of the New Deal, business leaders, conservative intellectuals, and the wealthy built institutions and networks designed to challenge and dismantle the limits on the market created under Franklin Roosevelt and expanded in subsequent decades. Wealthy families and organizations such as the Liberty League started this network, but it would expand through conservative magazines and local organizations. Business leaders themselves would become more conservative and more aggressive against government efforts to check their power during the 1970s. The U.S. Chamber of Commerce went from 36,000 members in 1967 to 160,000 in 1980. The number of lobbyists increased nearly 1,000 percent over a decade, creating a small army to push the thinking of government officials toward free market ideas.[2]

With this movement as the background, the election of Ronald Reagan brought a New Deal in reverse. From the reduction of high progressive taxation, to the weakening of financial regulations on Wall Street, to the dismantling of labor unions, to the relaxation of antitrust restrictions on big business, efforts to suppress the markets were undone. Yet as the geographers Dale Peck and Adam Tickell have described, this kind of "roll-back" neoliberalism is usually accompanied by a "roll-out" version that actively seeks to create a new economy. This is a more subtle change that happened, one that had no less of an effect on how the economy works. One project of this rolling-out phase was stripping the notion of a public within the market itself out of the law, which had significant consequences for all.[3]

Before the 1980s, for over a century a series of laws, practices, and rules were put into place to ensure that there was a public component that checked the way the market worked. Three sets of these systems stand out: the public corporation, the public domain, and the public utility. The slow, evolutionary approach that embedded each within our country was rapidly overturned under Reagan in favor of a new regime that emphasized property as the only right, and property as the source of freedom. The architects of this change reconceived each of these worlds to be aligned with strong property rights, and excluded any broader public obligation. Property rights, in this view, would bring about the best economic results, but also the most freedom. The result has been massive inequality, abuse, stagnation, and unfreedom for everyday people. Understanding how the public corporation, the public domain, and the public utility changed, and where they were before, can help us understand the overhaul of the entire economy during the past several decades.

The dismantling of these three systems also reveals an important aspect of our neoliberal period. There's a common understanding that market fundamentalism embraces small government, but there's nothing small or anti-government about what changed here. The advocates of this new intellectual revolution were unapologetic about using the government and law to create their ideal vision of the economy and, in the words of historian Quinn Slobodian, "encase" property and markets in a shell that would protect them from democratic challenges of any kind. This also has nothing to do with a supposed conservative political temperament of being skeptical of change or interested in conserving what has been put into place over time. Within a very short time, this wave of conservative economics ripped up a hundred years of fencing around the market that protected people from it within a very short time period. This was tossed aside in order to build a new economy, based around property rights of owners as the fundamental freedom.[4]

The first overhaul dealt with the public understanding of what a public corporation is and who it should work for. A corporation is first and foremost a legal creation of the state. This was true at the beginning of our country, when in 1811 New York passed the world's first law creating a process for incorporating manufacturing companies as long as general minimum standards were met. Before, corporate charters were generally granted only by special appeal to the government. Since then and still today, the corporation gets a legal charter, and in exchange for that it gets powers, benefits, and responsibilities. It is a social being, invoking connections to places and people while being able to live beyond the life of its founders. It is a legal being as well, able to enter into contracts and own and convey property. It is also a dense network of relationships all under a single entity. There's the relationship between the firm and its workers, contracts paid out in wages exchanged for labor. The same is true with suppliers, who provide the raw materials that are turned into new products. Other stakeholders in this web include customers, banks that lend money, and the executives who run the corporation. The power balance between each of these relationships is determined by the legal environment as well as the economic one.[5]

The contract between shareholders and public firms has been at the center of the debate over who the corporation should benefit. In one sense it's just another set of contracts. Shareholders take on the risk of being the first to lose money when things go bad. If the firm ends up going bankrupt, shareholders are last in line and they often end up getting nothing. In exchange for taking on this risk, shareholders receive dividend payments and can elect the board of representatives of the firm.

Yet there is a prevailing notion that because shareholders bear these risks, they "own" the firm. This idea evolved out of the early corporation, where shareholders were the first to put money into the firm and were the ones who ran it. The linkage between ownership and shareholding was tight for early corporations. As shareholders became separated from running the business, a set of rules were put into place to limit the say they have over corporations in which they own stock. This limitation placed the corporation within a broader social context, and removed pressure that shareholders could put on the company.

The best description of what this looked like in practice came during the Great Depression from Adolf Berle, a Harvard economist, and Gardiner Means, a lawyer, diplomat, and influential member of President Franklin Roosevelt's "brain trust." In their 1932 book *The Modern Corporation and Private Property*, they established a new idea of how public companies worked. In their view, two major changes created the modern corporation. The first was industrialization, where independent labor came under the direct management of bosses. The second, which was equally important, was incorporation, where investors pooled their money, which came under the direct management of executives. They saw an investor not as an owner but as someone who so significantly "surrenders his wealth to those in control of the corporation that he has exchanged the position of independent owner for one in which he may become merely recipient of the wages of capital."[6]

Crunching the numbers, they found that the managers who ran corporations owned very few shares in the companies they ran. They also found that ownership of shares was very widely dispersed across a large number of people, with no one person or group owning even a notable number of shares. It was very rare for an entity to own even 10 percent of shares of a firm. This split meant that the corporate world consisted of "owners without appreciable control and the control without appreciable ownership."

The corporation had become a kind of "quasi-public" institution, where the shareholders are "passive" and no longer exert actual control or face any decision in management.[7]

This evolution changed who the company ultimately works for. In the traditional theory, owners and managers are the same. Profits are an inducement for those with wealth to risk it through investing, as well as an incentive for those carrying out the business to do the best job. However, this logic collapses with the separation of management and ownership. These two roles are carried out by two very different groups of people. Berle and Means write: "The prospect of additional profits [to capital] cannot act as a spur on the security holder to make him *operate* the enterprise with more vigor in a way to serve the wants of the community, since he is no longer in control. Such extra profits if given to the security holders would seem to perform no useful economic function." Past a point of a reasonable return on capital, extra profits to shareholders serve no economic function since they don't drive the business to be run better.[8]

Berle and Means argue that shareholders had slowly, over decades, given up their management of the firm due to the changing economic world. There were many steps along the way. The business judgment rule, which prevented shareholders from using judges to second-guess the actions of directors, was formally established by courts in 1919. As long as they were acting in reasonably good faith, executives could conduct the business of the firm as they saw fit. Shareholders slowly lost the ability to remove directors at will, a course of action that had started to disappear well before the New Deal. Stocks themselves evolved over this period, allowing for multiple classes of shares, and for the board of directors to create new shares, diluting old ones, without the permission of shareholders. Berle and Means believe that these "legal changes probably have merely recognized the underlying economic fact" that they were necessary for corporations to work well in a growing, modern economy.[9]

Though the changes were small and subtle, the conclusion was direct: "The owners of passive property, by surrendering control and responsibility over the active property, have surrendered the right that the corporation should be operated in their sole interest." But in whose interests should corporations be run? In a speculative passage, the authors argued for using the public interest to navigate a path between absolute control of the firm by shareholders and absolute control of the firm by the executives running it. Instead, there could be a balancing act between all those surrounding the firm. "Should the corporate leaders, for example, set forth a program comprising fair wages, security to employees, reasonable service to their public, and stabilization of business, all of which would divert a portion of the profits from the owners of passive property, and should the community generally accept such a scheme as a logical and human solution of industrial difficulties, the interests of passive property owners would have to give way." The evolution of the major corporations would develop "into a purely neutral technocracy, balancing a variety of claims by various groups in the community and assigning to each a portion of the income stream on the basis of public policy rather than private cupidity." It was in no way the case that corporations in the decades following the New Deal were sites of equality and openness to public concerns. But this idea created a legal infrastructure surrounding the fictitious thing that is a corporation that was open to the possibility of a balancing act between the dynamism of the market and the needs of the public.[10]

Nobody would talk about shareholders this way now. Now it is common to say that shareholders own the firm and that the managers of firms should only focus on increasing the share price for these shareholders. The consensus among academics is so tight that in the year 2000, one pair of legal scholars described the "End of History for Corporate Law," where all modern nations agreed on "a widespread normative consensus that corporate managers should act exclusively in the economic interests of shareholders."

This shareholder revolution, just like all revolutions, was based in an affirmative vision of freedom. This new ideal was not the freedom of managers to determine what is best for their business, or the freedom of the public and workers to make demands on how corporations exercise these actions; it was the freedom of shareholders to exercise their property rights according to their private wishes.[11]

You see it in the economist Milton Friedman's influential 1970 *New York Times Magazine* essay "The Social Responsibility of Business Is to Increase Its Profits," which called for reestablishing the corporation as simply the property of its shareholders. Friedman did not just argue that the idea that businesses have social responsibilities was "pure and unadulterated socialism" and that such ideas were "undermining the basis of a free society these past decades." He also had a very clear vision of what the modern corporation was: it was shareholders as "the owners of the business" with bosses as people directly hired by them to carry out their will. "In a free-enterprise, private-property system, a corporate executive is an employee of the owners of the business. He has direct responsibility to his employers." [12]

Freedom for shareholders to own corporations as their direct property overruled any other social or economic goal. For Friedman this right of shareholders must be respected not just by governments, but also by other shareholders. What if a majority of shareholders banded together and took it upon themselves to vote for social responsibility goals? In these cases stockholders are trying to get other stockholders "to contribute against their will to 'social' causes favored by activists" and must be resisted. A majority of shareholders couldn't even break the supremacy of shareholders over the firm.[13]

Friedman's idea that shareholders own corporations as their own property, and that corporate executives are employees of shareholders, has so won out in popular arguments that it's worth reflecting on why it is wrong. The CEO is an employee of the firm itself. The CEO's paycheck is paid out by the corporation, not a long list of widely dispersed shareholders, each having to sign the check themselves. CEOs don't interview with shareholders for their jobs. Shareholders hire the board, which in turn hires the CEO, but the board can consider any number of factors in that role. The CEO, through the business judgment rule and the legal framework of the mid-century period, had to take into account the interests of shareholders, but could also take into account many other obligations and responsibilities as needed by the firm.

Moreover, while shareholders have some legal powers and obligations, they lack most of what we would conceive of as real ownership rights. Shareholders don't control assets. Shareholders can't walk into the firms where they invest and start taking things off the shelf. They don't manage. They can't fire or hire everyday employees and bosses or tell workers how to do their jobs. They can't force the firm to do anything in their daily operations, be it buy or sell property, or open and close various business lines, or take on debts and other obligations. They also don't control funds. Shareholders aren't entitled to any or all of the profits of a firm. They receive dividends as decided by the board. Shareholders rarely even provide funding for firms, either individually or for the economy as a whole, where the scale of dividends and share buybacks is many times larger than funding from new shares. Firms instead finance projects largely through their own cash. This is all true whether there's many shareholders or just one. The whole point of limiting the liability shareholders face is because they have none of these rights that we associate with ownership.[14]

What Friedman needed was an intellectual framework that obligated executives to understand themselves as mere agents of shareholders. This framework was being hammered out in the seminar rooms of the newly insurgent "law and economics" movement. The first step was to weaken the notion that because shareholders were dispersed meant that they had only a tenuous connection to the firms themselves. In 1965, law professor Henry

Manne introduced the idea of a "market for corporate control." By selling and buying shares in firms, especially in the form of taking over firms and changing managements, shareholders could create a market for the control of corporations. This market was reflected in the share price. Management indifferent to shareholders would be punished by lower share prices. Manne was discussing the economics of mergers, and at this time federal agencies were still carrying out an active antitrust enforcement. Many economists thought at the time that the value that came from mergers came mostly from decreasing competition. Manne instead thought of them as a corrective, a check against a poorly performing company. He noted that mergers and takeovers, even hostile ones, constitute markets where shareholders can exercise control over management, and thus regain some of the power that they had lost.

This was not just a theory but a regulatory call to restructure the market to ensure that takeovers could be done much more easily. As Manne wrote, "Only the take-over scheme provides some assurance of competitive efficiency among corporate managers and thereby affords strong protection to the interests of vast numbers of small, non-controlling shareholders." Efforts to prevent takeovers lead to inefficient markets, and these inefficiencies are hostile to the market way of thinking. Even better, the financial sector could be unleashed to ensure companies could be taken over. There could even someday be leveraged buyout firms that would take over companies in hostile bids, though as Manne noted, "American commercial banks are generally forbidden to lend money for this purpose." Rules like that, however, could be changed.[15]

This new wave of thinking continued through the 1970s, and perhaps reached its apex in 1976, when the economists Michael Jensen and William Meckling published their paper "Theory of the Firm," which remains one of the most cited papers in the study of business. Jensen and Meckling describe the firm as simply a marketplace in its own right. Like any market, in the view of the law and economics movement, it is efficient and based on maximizing behavior. For Jensen and Meckling, firms weren't social creations, or active entities in the economy and their communities. They were instead an abstraction that intersected numerous individual contracts, all of them efficient in their own right. In their view, "it makes little or no sense to try to distinguish those things that are 'inside' the firm (or any other organization) from those things that are 'outside' of it." That corporations were sites of private government for workers, or had any kind of obligation or relationship to their broader communities, all dissolved in this acidic market thinking.[16]

It also presupposes that shareholders own the firm, and that they have hired managers to execute the firm for them. Using the increasingly dominant language of economics, the shareholders are principals, and the managers are their agents. The question becomes how to align the incentives of the agents with those of the principals. For Jensen and Meckling, the question was one of agency costs. Shareholders had to cover the costs of monitoring and directing their principals, and their central problem, as Jensen would later describe it, was "how to motivate managers to disgorge the cash" rather than "wasting it on organization" priorities. What if the law was deployed to minimize these costs and motivate managers to strictly serve shareholders? Instead of managers trying to run an enterprise, balancing the needs of labor, suppliers, and others, the power of law could force firms to become the mere property of their shareholders.[17]

These ideas were firmly in place in time to take advantage of the economic malaise of the 1970s. Not at all afraid of using the state to carry out a new notion of property, economists rebuilt the entire legal framework surrounding corporations and the power of shareholders. Consider several actions that were carried out in the 1980s alone. Rules surrounding investments, especially limitations on how institutional funds could act, were relaxed, allowing them to provide massive funding for the wave of leveraged buy-outs. Courts overturned state-level laws that slowed down hostile takeovers, chilling the ability of any new laws to try to address worries about abuses. The Reagan administration significantly stopped antitrust scrutiny of mergers, allowing for a greater concentration of corporations. The legal framework was rapidly overturned to set the stage for a revolution.[18]

These changes opened up a brand new economy, one built around the financial sector and shareholders. Between 1980 and 1990, a quarter of Fortune 500 manufacturers went through a takeover attempt, a wave that was largely hostile and against the wishes of management. It was also successful. Nearly a third of companies disappeared. But the bigger focus was creating intense concentration in each industry. Firms were broken down into individual business lines, and then waves of mergers took each industry and concentrated it into fewer and fewer businesses.[19]

We are living in the aftermath of this revolution, with concentration and shareholder pressure suffocating the economy. Over the past two decades, 75 percent of industries have seen a significant increase in concentration. Corporate profits are also up, and both concentration and profitability are at levels that existed in the 1970s and before. You see it in the aggregate numbers. The number of public companies has decreased, from around 5,000 in 1973 to 3,600 now. Corporate profits as a percentage of the economy were around 8 percent in 1965, while in 2018 they are at 10 percent. More sophisticated indicators of concentration and profitability, such as those measuring high-end concentration and market power, also show the highest levels in decades.[20]

The revolution was successful in changing who the economy works for. It now works better for owners, the CEOs who are now aligned with them, and the financial sector that executes it, rather than workers and everyday people. CEO pay was relatively flat from the 1930s through the 1970s. Beginning with the shareholder revolution, CEO pay has skyrocketed, largely because they are paid in large stock options that encourage them to boost share prices and serve shareholders. Finance has also been handsomely rewarded for ensuring the freedom of shareholders and owners. Finance professionals have doubled their presence in the top 1 percent since the early 1980s, earning large premiums compared with other educated workers. But the economy mostly works for shareholders. Before 1980, money from profits and loans would largely go to investments. Now there is no such relationship. Instead the cash goes to shareholders—this is just the world that theorists of shareholder freedom wanted to create.[21]

It's not just corporations that have been reimagined as a type of property, but also our knowledge and ideas themselves. The public domain, the vast depository of all our ideas that aren't subject to property claims, has come under attack in the past several decades, on the basis of the notion that our ideas should be turned into intellectual property, and that intellectual property should be protected as strongly as any other property.

From the time of the nation's founding, there was a strong rejection of the notion that property in ideas was the same as any other property. As Thomas Jefferson wrote in 1813, "If nature has made any one thing less susceptible than all others of exclusive property, it is the action of the thinking power called an idea, which an individual may exclusively possess as long as he keeps it to himself; but the moment it is divulged, it forces itself into the possession of every one, and the receiver cannot dispossess himself of it. Its peculiar character, too, is that no one possesses the less, because every other possesses the whole of it."[22]

Though these economic terms were not in use at the time, Jefferson pointed to the fact that ideas contain the two essential parts of being a truly public good. Property is a horizontal relationship among people, enforced by people being able to exclude others from using a particular thing. However, if one person enjoys or benefits from an idea, it doesn't prevent anyone else from

using from it, and once an idea spreads one cannot naturally prevent someone from enjoying it. That is, unless you deploy the state
to make ideas excludable and encase them to prevent people from
using them without permission. Jefferson understood the concept
of property in ideas as something that would give people some rewards and incentives for creating and developing them. "Society
may give an exclusive right to the profits arising from [ideas and
inventions], as an encouragement to men to pursue ideas which
may produce utility, but this may or may not be done, according to
the will and convenience of the society," he wrote. But this benefit
was for society as a whole, not just individuals, and should never
be confused with other types of property.[23]

Treating intellectual property as any other property has become a political project in the past several decades. The creation
and expansion of property rights into everything from culture to
the human genome is so widespread it's been referred to as a "second enclosure movement." You can see its beginnings in 1982, the
year Jack Valenti, the president of the Motion Picture Association
of America, testified before Congress that "reasonable men and
women" agree on one fundamental principle: "Creative property
owners must be accorded the same rights and protection resident
in all other property owners in the nation." Property is property,
and all property should be treated as sacrosanct, including property in ideas.[24]

Valenti was building on changes that were already in motion.
When it came to copyright ownership, or intellectual property in
ideas and media, the real change began with the Copyright Act
of 1976. This act extended copyright to unpublished work and
meant that authors no longer were forced to register or place a
notification on their work. The way copyright was enforced also
changed, with private lawsuits replaced by criminal prosecutions
by the government. Fines and sentences for violations not only
were created but dramatically expanded in subsequent laws.[25]

After expanding the scope of copyright, the government did

the same for the length of copyright. What was originally a four-teen-year term with an option for fourteen more years in 1790 is now far more expansive, lasting for the life of the author plus an additional seventy years, or ninety-five years for corporate work. This expansion was the result of nearly a dozen different laws over the last fifty years. One law, notable for its large lobbying campaign, was the Sonny Bono Copyright Term Extension Act of 1998, named after the performer turned representative. This law extended the term of all existing and future copyrights by an additional twenty years at the time, designed as such to protect Disney from having Mickey Mouse enter the public domain.[26]

As Senator Orrin Hatch, a Republican from Utah, argued while advocating for this major expansion, "The first principle of a contemporary copyright philosophy should be that copyright is a property right that ought to be respected as any other property right." Describing his frustration with the rest of Congress, he noted he couldn't even understand those who would think there was a difference. "Some of my colleagues, who are ardent protectors of real property, are considerably cooler toward intangible property. This has always been difficult for me to understand and has been a source of frustration." Hatch went even further, arguing that "copyright protection should be expanded unless the extent of such protection would hamper creativity or the wide dissemination of works." The notion of any public interest in ideas wasn't even a consideration. Ideas are property, and freedom comes from being able to use your property as you wish. Hatch won these arguments, and the lawmakers locked down our ideas just as the internet gave us the possibility to give them free rein.[27]

Patents, which create exclusive rights on inventions, also expanded, especially in the aftermath of the 1982 creation of a special appeal court to handle patent cases. The annual number of patent grants exploded, going from around 60,000 in 1983 to 300,000 in 2013, a 500 percent increase. More patents were issued in that thirty-year period than in the two centuries before then.

This resulted from the creation of new digital and computer technology that could now be patented, but it also expanded because the standards for what could be patented were lowered.[28]

Patents could be deployed in the business world to shut down competition and lock up business practices. Patent Assertion Entities, more generally known as patent trolls, don't actually produce anything. Instead they use their patents to sue firms and create a bottleneck in the innovation process. Patent trolls tripled their lawsuits in the early 2010s, being responsible for an estimated 62 percent of infringement lawsuits in 2013. That's over one hundred thousand companies threatened in one year. One study found that nearly $20 billion was spent on patent lawsuits from 2010 to 2012 in the smartphone industry alone. Spending by Apple and Google on patent lawsuits and patent purchases in 2011 exceeded spending on research and development for new products.[29]

The contrast between the middle of the twentieth century and the present is telling. In the aftermath of the New Deal, regulators and officials would force companies to open up their patents as part of a more aggressive implementation of antitrust policy. Look at the Bell System of the 1950s. In 1956, American Telephone and Telegraph (AT&T) owned or controlled 98 percent of all long-distance telephone services and 85 percent of all local telephone services. AT&T also owned Western Electric, which provided more than 90 percent of the telephone equipment used for phone calls. All of this was researched and created by Bell Laboratories, the research center owned by AT&T. This tightly integrated set of companies was known as the Bell System, and it controlled phone systems in the United States. AT&T was the largest private company in the world, employing nearly 598,000 people, with revenues of almost 1 percent of GDP. In 1950, it employed around 1 percent of all scientists and engineers in the country. One reason for the dominance of the Bell System was the incredible number of patents it held. Through the mid-century period it was responsible for around 1 percent of all U.S. patents each year. Going back to the 1920s, Bell Labs had pioneered everything from the transistor, to solar cells, to the laser. But the key patents it held were on all the components of the telecommunications infrastructure. It had very little interest in allowing startups to use them.

The U.S. federal government filed an antitrust lawsuit against the company in 1949 trying to break it apart, arguing that it held a monopoly on telecommunications equipment. The lawsuit failed to split apart the company, partially owing to the Department of Defense coming to its aid. But it did successfully force the company to license all of its patents to other businesses. As Judge Stanley N. Barnes said of the decision, "The patent relief in itself opens wide the door to hundreds of small businesses to attempt to supply these companies." Rather than letting the Bell System use its patents to lock down innovation and create a bottleneck for the major scientific breakthroughs of the time, the courts forced patents to be accessible. This is in line with how Jefferson saw intellectual property: something that should be used for the benefit of all and adjusted when necessary.[30]

As a result of this government action the electric transistor, the key building block of all electronic devices, was opened up to new businesses. Initially, AT&T had the patent on the electric transistor and kept it from being available to other competitors that could potentially use it to develop superior phone technology. But then, upon facing more antitrust scrutiny, AT&T started to license the right to use and develop its transistor patent to thirty-five companies. The transistor became the basis of all of our computer technology, and it was these small businesses that led the way. Some of the companies that licensed this technology were Texas Instruments, Motorola, and Fairchild, all of whom pushed the technology further and made it commercially available. This would not have been possible without government intervention and the assumption that dominant firms were required to make their patents available to competitors.

There were more examples of the government using mid-century antitrust law to keep large businesses from stockpiling knowledge and information to the detriment of the economy. In the 1960s IBM unbundled hardware, software, and services in response to antitrust pressure. This opened up the space for other companies to sell independent software. In the 1970s, Xerox used its patents to stop other companies from entering the copier market, until the Department of Justice forced it to make its patents available. The results, according to one economist, were "a great deal of innovative activity from entrants and Xerox." Because of this competition, "Xerox introduced new products in all segments." Ironically, much of the innovation and growth of the last century—a process we are told must come from markets left to their own devices—came from the active suppression of property by the state.[31]

The projects of shielding both the public corporation and intellectual property from any kind of democratic challenge or accountability have been successful in our age of market dependency.[32] But another achievement of those who see freedom in the market has been the stripping of public obligation for businesses that control essential economic markets. Nowhere is this more dire than with the companies that provide our electricity, gas, water, communications, information, transportation, financial services, and other key infrastructure that keeps the economy together. The idea of a "public utility" had guided laws, courts, and our economy for a century, but then came under rapid assault in the 1970s and 1980s in favor of markets alone. This erasure has left a void in our imagination regarding how to manage a market economy and the kinds of obligations and responsibilities we can demand, leaving only profits and property in its place.

There's a narrow definition in use today of a public utility, one that defines it in terms of size and scale. A public utility, in this view, is a business that requires regulation because it has large fixed costs associated with starting the business, and also benefits from large economics of scale—so much so that a firm will tend to be sole producer, or a natural monopoly. Since it would be inefficient to have multiple providers, this is a rare case where there's room for either a publicly run and publicly owned firm or regulations on pricing and activities.[33]

But this definition is a recent one. In the industrial era, certain key business were defined broadly as having public purposes and thus public obligations. One definition given in 1911 by the legal scholar Bruce Wyman was that a public utility operates on the principle that "all must be served, adequate facilities must be provided, reasonable rates must be charged, and no discriminations must be made."[34] An example of how this definition is deployed is the idea of a common carrier, a type of public-utility regulation. A common carrier is a requirement that a business involved in the transportation of a certain thing has to be indifferent to what is being carried and whom it is serving. A railroad that is subject to common carrier regulation can't charge a higher price to one business than another business for carrying the same load. This prevents utilities from punishing some to the benefit of others. The same rationale governs the principle of net neutrality in today's information economy. Net neutrality, drawing on the public-utility tradition, requires that your internet company be indifferent to the source of web traffic, which prevents already established websites from gaining a better foothold and access to households than smaller startups.

This kind of regulation has existed for centuries, and even our courts have understood it as an essential part of maintaining the economy. In 1871, the state of Illinois set maximum rates that companies could charge for the storage and transport of agricultural products. The concern was that farmers were being exploited and squeezed by those who would carry and transport their products. Instead, leaders argued, the grain elevators should be subject to a common carrier regulation. A series of laws, known as the "Granger Laws," regulating the railroads were a focal point of the Populist movement, which aimed to balance the power of large corporations against everyday people. The grain elevators sued, and the case went to the Supreme Court.

In its 1877 decision in *Munn v. Illinois*, the Supreme Court upheld the maximum-rate law. They reasoned that the police powers of the state gave Illinois more than ample room to decide this case. This kind of public-utility regulation was not a new invention, but one the court saw as building on centuries of law. The Supreme Court noted that it has been "customary in England from time immemorial, and in this country from its first colonization, to regulate ferries, common carriers, hackmen, bakers, millers, wharfingers, innkeepers, &c., and, in so doing, to fix a maximum of charge to be made for services rendered, accommodations furnished, and articles sold." [35]

What distinguished these businesses? The Court argued that regulations like these could be upheld when it came to businesses "affected with a public interest." When "one devotes his property to a use in which the public has an interest, he, in effect, grants to the public an interest in that use, and must submit to be controlled by the public for the common good, to the extent of the interest he has thus created." Markets in discriminatory pricing can, and often should, be suppressed for businesses that we all depend on. [36]

As the legal historian William Novak has found, this decision allowed for a flourishing of experimentation during the early 1900s to try to rein in the exploitativeness of the growing corporate world. From bridges and ferries to stock yards and grain elevators, from gas and electric to railroads and canals, key industries now saw limitations placed on their ability to marketize every element of their business. Legal advocates at the time believed that businesses with a public interest should provide their services without discrimination. These businesses could be private entities, having all the normal interests in returns and profits, but the public had a veto on how they could carry out their business. It was a way to harness the dynamism of markets while checking the potential for abuses, such as insider dealing to incumbents and the already well-off, and ensuring basic access for all.[37]

The question of which businesses should face these extra requirements is one citizens of a democracy need to decide, but there are clear guidelines. As law professor K. Sabeel Rahman notes, the industries that should be subjected to public-utility requirements usually have three key characteristics. The first is that they have some scale—bigger companies can produce more efficiently than smaller ones, and in extreme cases one firm will dominate all others. But that is only a precondition for the real worries. The second is that they host or are essential to significant downstream uses. They themselves act as inputs to further production, creation, and industry. Nobody enjoys electricity in and of itself; they use it to power and create other things. A chokehold by a private firm at these spots can do real harm to our economic and social lives. The third is that the firms are capable of causing abuses, cutting off or limiting access when people are vulnerable. If it is profitable to cause blackouts, a private energy utility will do it, causing massive harm. There needs to be protections put into place to prevent this from happening. This goes beyond the question of monopolies, as reformers understood that everyday firms could also pose these problems through secret knowledge, inequalities, fraud, preying on people's desperation, and more.[38]

This view of public utilities came under attack starting in the 1960s and 1970s. Two lines of argument stand out. The first was the prioritization of efficiency over fairness as the normative claim for these key firms. Before this period, the fundamental requirement of a public utility was that it prevent discrimination in the pricing of services. Think again of the common carrier railroad that needs to be indifferent to what it is carrying. In this view, a fair procedure that ensures everyone has access was the model for the regulation. It suppressed the ability of firms to charge for priority. But in the new view, drawing inspiration from the law and economics movement, the ability to price things and to discriminate against customers led to presumed efficiency gains in the economy. The economy became less an arena where we should ensure a level of fairness and more one where prices and market activity ensure freedom.

The second line of argument about public utilities was an attack on government itself. This criticism saw the government not just as a failure at regulating the economy, but one that was actively hostile to suitable regulations. And it was essentially just another rent-seeking entity, creating regulations that protect powerful incumbents to the detriment of everyday people. Those who made this argument completely suppressed the long history of the government, from the founders onward, trying to balance the economy among many different interests. This view depended on the assumption that markets simply take care of themselves, they aren't created by the government, and competition and new businesses would be able to check any abuses. This was not a call to update regulations or reevaluate what works and what doesn't in light of new theories and evidence. It was an agenda of removing all checks on the marketplace and reengineering the laws and code of the economy to create freedom for businesses and owners.[39]

We are living with the consequences of this revolution in market thinking. The 2008 financial crisis was one result. There was a bipartisan push by politicians and political elites since the 1980s to allow financial markets to engage in lending and borrowing that had been reserved for well-regulated ordinary banks, creating a "shadow banking sector" that existed outside of New Deal regulations. New Deal regulations that structured finance as a kind of public utility, with certain financial market activities suppressed for the benefit of the economy as a whole, were seen as too restrictive and outdated in this new era. This led to a wave of bad lending, predatory packaging of financial instruments, a banking run and panic, and then an economic collapse, similar to the wave of collapse that the New Deal was devised to stop in the first place.[40]

But the problems go beyond the financial sector. With no new system to suppress and check the market, consolidation, abuses, and stagnation have run rampant over the past several decades. Competition is down and prices are up among major industries. As the economist Thomas Philippon summarizes:

> First, US markets have become less competitive: concentration is high in many industries, leaders are entrenched, and their profit rates are excessive. Second, this lack of competition has hurt US consumers and workers: it has led to higher prices, lower investment and lower productivity growth. Third, and contrary to common wisdom, the main explanation is political, not technological: I have traced the decrease in competition to increasing barriers to entry and weak antitrust enforcement, sustained by heavy lobbying and campaign contributions.[41]

This has occurred during a period of low interest rates and high corporate profits. Conventional economic theory predicts that in this situation new businesses should start and other businesses should expand their investments in order to take advantage of those rates and try to compete for the excessive profits of incumbent businesses. This wave hasn't happened. Instead of an era of start-ups, there's actually been a decline in the number of new businesses being formed. The lack of investment forces the entire economy into a kind of quasi-permanent stagnation. But none of these broader concerns matter when the economic liberty of shareholders is the only freedom that matters.[42]

The romance of markets as self-correcting, dynamic, and resilient machines has made us forget about the crises, collapses, and depressions that have always come with capitalism. But it has also made us forget how necessary the legal and political environment is to creating innovation and prosperity, and how vulnerable it becomes when the economy is treated as the mere property of owners. Building a prosperous and innovative economy is harder if owners

are positioned to demand immediate payouts through constrict-
ing competition and sitting on safe profits. It is impossible if our
collective ideas and inventions are locked down by people who
only want to squeeze everyone else, and if the infrastructure and
essential businesses that create the lifeblood of our economy have
no public obligation whatsoever. There were safeguards in place
before, which were ripped out quickly under glib definitions of
freedom and free markets. They can be put back again.

8

FREE EDUCATION

To see how neoliberalism has overhauled the way we view markets and freedom, just reflect on the broken way we carry out social insurance today. You worry about your retirement, and you are meant to address it with a 401(k) savings program. Managing your fund requires knowing an arcane subfield of terms and concepts: net asset value, expense ratios, both gross and net, portfolio weights, and more. You wonder what life would be like if you had so much money you could actively seek to hide it in tax-free accounts, or if you had the sophistication to not be a mark for the financial companies skimming off you. The bigger worry you'll have in retirement is that you might live too long and exhaust these savings, a morbid indictment of the richest country in history. Yet this is the only way you know how to have a safe retirement.

As a new parent, you struggle with how to balance working—earning money—with providing for your child. Day care is expensive and eats up much of what you earn. You can deduct some of that, however. An additional child tax credit helps too. But it doesn't help enough, and you pay out the nose to give your kids a slight advantage. Mostly you wish there were better options than there are now. You worry about your child's college education, and you probably worry about your own student loans. You had to take out large loans to attend a good school, and paying them back plus interest is preventing you from saving up enough for your own child's future. You read about public college tuition going up year after year, and you look to your tax-advantaged 529 college savings plan, knowing you don't have the extra money needed to save your kid from the indenture of student loans.

You get sick. Your health care is provided through one of the Obamacare exchanges. You only had one option to choose from, or you chose a cheaper plan to try to save some money. You feel it later though, when you can't afford the deductibles for your insurance. You laugh when someone brings up investing in a "health savings account" to try to balance those costs, yet another of the multitude of options to save the money you don't have. "Don't get sick" sounds like a more realistic option. To really understand all these options professionals normally have to spend years studying taxes, accounting, and insurance. You are expected to learn and do all this complicated work in between dinner and putting the kids to sleep. Mostly you ignore it, hoping for the best.

There are any number of problems with this kind of safety net. It benefits those with the highest incomes, those who employ their own experts to help them manage the system, have ample disposable cash to sock away, and have the time and ability to run their own personal safety net. Over a third of the value of the employer-provided health care deduction goes to the top 20 percent; and two-thirds of the value of deductions for personal savings, like 401(k) accounts, go to that top fifth as well, with half of that concentrated in the very top 5 percent of earners.[1]

But the biggest problem is that this kind of safety net forces market dependency on us. Neoliberalism isn't just a top-down process to strip the public out of the economy. It's also a bottom-up process to reorganize ourselves so that we view ourselves as little firms, and to reorganize all of society such that it functions like a marketplace. This process was also carried out by law, with the ultimate result that the serious risks we face have devolved to each of us to handle by ourselves.

You can see this across the political landscape. In the case *Citizens United v. FEC*, the Supreme Court struck down campaign finance laws to, in the words of Justice Anthony Kennedy, preserve a "political marketplace." Workers are increasingly not legally employed by the companies they actually work for, instead working for subcontractors or as independent agents, acting as their own little firms. This forces workers to face even more market pressure through state-condoned legal fictions, as employers usually use this subterfuge to evade employment law. These are all examples of the state extending market logic to where it didn't exist before.[2]

But in recent decades, one of the main transformations that has bound ordinary people to markets has occurred through student loans. Student loans are the primary way young people access our higher education system. Higher education is now seen as an individual investment one makes in oneself, and student loans are the way to unlock this potential investment in your own human capital. But this is a recent hijacking of the idea of higher education in the United States—a complete reversal of a century and a half of this country's efforts to ensure a free, broadly accessible system of higher education. Though this was always a compromised and incomplete project, it was a genuine one, and it was successful in broadening who education could serve. The United States was building public universities for a long time before it started letting them crumble. Their collapse was the result of specific campaigns against the idea of a public system, but it also was fed by an ideology that saw the role of the state as locking citizens into markets. To understand what we've lost, we need to know where we started.

The creation of mass, free higher education dates to the beginning of the United States. The 1816 Constitution of the state of Indiana, for example, required the state "to provide, by law, for a general system of education, ascending in a regular gradation, from township schools to a state university, wherein tuition shall be gratis, and equally open to all." James Angell, president of the University of Michigan in the 1880s, described that state's system as one that would provide "an uncommon education for the common man." In Wisconsin there was a similar idea: its public university formed part of "the soul of the state," as the "state owns the university; and every citizen feels himself to be a stockholder in that ownership."[3]

But the most important investment in public higher education in the nineteenth century was through the 1862 Land-Grant College Act, often referred to as the Morrill Act. Justin Smith Morrill was the son of a blacksmith who was elected to Congress in 1854 as a Whig representative from Vermont. In the mid-1850s he became one of the founders of the Republican Party. Given his humble upbringing, Morrill worried that college would only benefit the well-off. He proposed that the federal government grant lands to states, which in turn could use the profits from them to establish public colleges. Morrill introduced this bill in 1856; it passed the House and Senate in 1859 but, like the Homestead Act, this higher education bill was vetoed by President James Buchanan. Morrill reintroduced the bill on December 9, 1861, this version stating that it was an "Act donating Public Lands to the several States and Territories which may provide Colleges for the Benefit of Agriculture and the Mechanic Arts." It offered states thirty thousand acres of public land for each senator and representative. Each acre could be sold for $1.25, the revenue from which could be used to establish funds for colleges. The bill passed Congress and was signed by President Abraham Lincoln on July 2, 1862.[4]

The matter of how to implement the Morrill Act was decided by the states, and as such there was a wide set of experiments in how to structure the new colleges. Some states built public universities quickly, such as Kansas State University, the first such college. Some states used the land grant money to prod private wealth toward investing in building colleges alongside the public funds. The founding of Cornell, for instance, relied on this kind of partnership. One requirement from the Act was that it would make education available in the mechanical and agricultural sciences in addition to the liberal arts. The advancement of well-funded public universities trained in providing both classical and scientific methods prompted older institutions like Yale and Harvard to invest more in science. Yale's Sheffield Scientific School, for instance, was the state of Connecticut's main Morrill Act school through 1892, and this funding and state resources helped move the university toward a stronger investment in sciences.[5]

A powerful vision animated this wave of higher education expansion: the government should collapse the distinction between elite education and mass education. As the president of the University of Michigan described it, "Have an aristocracy of birth if you will, or of riches if you wish, but give our plain boys from the log cabins a chance to develop their minds with the best learning and we fear nothing from your aristocracy." Or as Morrill described decades later, the goal was that "a higher and broader education should be placed in every State within the reach of those" who would see it. This education would be broad, "not limited to a superficial and dwarfed training, such as might be supplied by a foreman of a workshop or by a foreman of an experimental farm." Our citizens deserve more than "a school with equal scraps of labor and of instruction," and it was up to the state to provide it.[6]

One of the biggest public investments in higher education came with the Servicemen's Readjustment Act of 1944, often called the GI Bill of Rights. President Franklin Roosevelt was looking at plans to support veterans when they came back from the war. The GI Bill funded and supported many elements of middle-class life in the aftermath of World War II, and higher education was a central element of it.

Officials were worried about the volume of education that had been lost during the war. By one estimate, 1.5 million years of higher education instruction were lost due to mass conscription during the war. In response, the GI Bill fueled a wave of college students in the war's aftermath: between 1947 and 1948, nearly half of all college students were veterans. In 1949 there were around 2.5 million college students, a million more than any year before World War II.[7]

Much of the funding of the GI Bill was designed to be controlled locally and run through private institutions. This was intentional, as it was written by segregationists who wanted to protect Jim Crow. This strategy was evident with mortgage guarantees for veterans, which relied on private banks whose policies bolstered segregation. One report, studying thirteen Mississippi cities in 1947, found that only 2 of the 3,229 loans the Veterans Administration guaranteed went to black veterans. This mechanism was similar to Hill-Burton funding for hospitals, which found a role for the federal government, but only through boosting private institutions to maintain racial segregation and undermine public programs.

But the eligibility for education and training was federally defined, which made it harder for the South to exclude black veterans. Monthly allowances for veteran students were determined by family size, not by race. Black veterans were more likely to use the education benefits, with a 49 percent usage rate compared with 43 percent for whites. However, black veterans were excluded from many colleges and universities, especially in the South, and as such were more likely to use vocational schools. These were often predatory, fraudulent institutions that offered poor education while charging exactly the highest rate of tuition that the GI Bill would cover.

But even with these exclusions, the GI Bill helped create a demand for greater democracy and racial inclusion. Among a survey of black veterans, those who used GI Bill benefits were over four times more likely to be involved in the civil rights movement. They were also twice as likely to be involved in politics, from working on campaigns to serving in office. The GI Bill, by being universal for veterans, helped empower citizens to make more affirmative demands from the government for democracy.[8]

In the mid-twentieth century it was understood that government had a key role in providing higher education, a system designed to collapse the distance between elite education and what everyday people could access, with nearly free tuition. This system is gone now. Higher education would come under assault from two political movements. In California a neoconservative movement headed by Governor Ronald Reagan set the playbook for attacks on free higher education that are sustained to this day. In New York, free higher education would come under assault by neoliberal technocrats managing austerity. Both movements helped reframe our understanding of how Americans should be able to access higher education—and by extension, the mobility that it enables.

The higher education system of California was born from the Morrill Act. Within a few years of the Act's 1862 passage, the state of California was using the funding to locate and build colleges. Daniel Coit Gilman, the third president of the University of California, gave a sense of the promise of this endeavor in the speech he gave upon taking over in 1872: "It is not the University of Berlin, or of New Haven," nor "the University of Oakland, or San Francisco, it is the University of the State which created it." The schools they would build "must be adapted to its people, to their public and private schools, to their peculiar geographic position, to their undeveloped resources. It is not the foundation of an ecclesiastical body, or of private individuals. It is of the people and for the people—not in any low or unworthy sense, but in the highest and noblest relation to their intellectual and moral well-being."[9]

When Gilman gave this speech, the University of California school system was just two buildings hidden in the hills of Berkeley, educating 182 students, of which 39 were women. Liberal Republicans like Hiram Johnson and Earl Warren laid the foundations and expanded the college throughout the first half of the twentieth century. There was a network of influence interested in expanding this system, from citizens who wanted an education to regional Chambers of Commerce who wanted more educated workers.[10]

The century-long expansion of higher education in California culminated in the 1960 Donahoe Act, better known as the Master Plan for Higher Education. Brought to fruition by academic labor economist and University of California president Clark Kerr, the Master Plan was, under all the administrative work, a promise to the state of California to educate any and all students who wanted an education. It created a three-part system of community colleges, state colleges, and universities designed such that students could transfer among them. In theory and in practice, a student could move from the bottom to the top within it. With enough skill and effort, a Californian could get a degree from one of the best universities in the world for nearly free. The pronounced social and economic mobility of the postwar period would have been unthinkable without institutions of mass higher education, like this one, provided at public expense.

Ronald Reagan ran for governor of California in 1966, one of many conservatives who ran in opposition to the Great Society. One of his main targets was the UC system. On the campaign trail Reagan vowed to "clean up that mess in Berkeley"; warned audiences of "sexual misconduct" that was "so bad, so contrary to our standards of decent human behavior that I cannot recite them to you"; complained that "a small minority of beatniks, radicals and filthy speech advocates" were bringing left-wing subversion into the college system; and called upon the state government to investigate "Communism and blatant sexual misbehavior on the campus." He also ran on an anti-tax platform and promised to put the state's finances in order by "throw[ing] the bums off welfare." But it was the University of California at Berkeley that provided the most useful political foil, crystallizing all of his conservative ideological themes into a single figure of subversive disorder.[11]

Reagan had two allies in his battle against free college: cops and economists. Within days of being elected governor in 1967, Reagan contacted the San Francisco FBI office to ask for help with "the Berkeley situation." Though hesitant, FBI director J. Edgar

Hoover intervened to order to help Reagan; Reagan and Hoover knew each other from when the actor was an informant for the FBI's investigations into communism in Hollywood. The FBI handed off confidential information it had been compiling on student activists like Mario Savio, as well as UC president Clark Kerr. Hoover had taken a personal interest in removing Kerr and damaging his reputation, as he blamed the UC president for failing to fight left-leaning academics and student protesters. Reagan wanted to coordinate with the FBI on surveillance against those who would oppose his plan on raising tuition.[12]

The UC system had no tuition at this point, with students having to cover only small fees. Reagan's initial budget for the university system proposed big cuts and also opened the door to tuition. Reagan wanted to set annual tuition and fees at $675, which would be around $5,000 in today's dollars. Though hard to believe now, this would have made a California public university the most expensive public university in the country at that point. Reagan immediately moved to have Kerr fired as president of UC after Kerr made it clear the damage this would do to the system. After being forced out, Kerr, who had built the mid-century jewel of the state, joked, "I left the presidency as I entered it—fired with enthusiasm."[13]

While pushing for public school tuition, Reagan received some ideological backing from newly assertive conservative economists. Milton Friedman used his weekly *Newsweek* column to attack free college. For "low-income taxpayers and youngsters not in college," he wrote, " 'free' tuition is highly inequitable to them." Economist James M. Buchanan argued that free college played an important role "in creating at least part of the chaos that we witness in our major universities." Reagan was unsuccessful in his tuition campaign, but he did manage to raise fees to the point of normalizing university cost increases.[14]

These gains by conservatives depended on two arguments that would be deployed over the next half century. The first argument framed public goods such as free education as a kind of ploy to redistribute resources away from honest, everyday people and to the undeserving. The second held that free goods, by removing the discipline of the marketplace, created disorder and chaos. This latter argument would be deployed even more aggressively in 1970s New York.

New York City faced a different set of constraints, ones no less ideological and that would also come to define the political horizon. New York City's public colleges date back to 1847, when the state funded the "Free Academy." In his appeal to the state legislature for the institution's funding, the then president of New York City's Board of Education wrote, "Open the doors to all— let the children of the rich and the poor take their seats together, and know of no distinction, save that of industry, good conduct and intellect." The state system continuously expanded through the twentieth century, adding Hunter College, a women's college, a number of two- and four-year community colleges, and a postgraduate university called the Graduate Center. The state schools provided an important avenue for immigrants and working-class students to access higher education.[15]

In the 1970s, New York City faced a crisis when the city was unable to roll over its debt. As part of an emergency loan settlement to avoid bankruptcy, the city was forced into a special governing commission that pressured it into austerity. But rather than just focusing on balancing the books, this commission explored the idea that the very relationship between citizens and the city would have to change. This was no longer a question of revenues and expenses, but what kind of city New York City would be to its citizens.

One of the commission's central concerns was the "expansive university system" of public colleges and the need to impose tuition on its students. As Felix Rohatyn, a banker who helped execute the austerity plan, said, deep, structural spending cuts needed to be "overkill" and display "shock impact" in order to show to the capital markets that the city was serious about its budgetary commitments. Mayor Abe Beame noted that implementing tuition fees would raise very little money. Rohatyn responded that it wasn't the money but instead the message it would send. The city needed to change its "lifestyle" regarding generous social services. The message was received, as protests broke out, though they ultimately lost the battle against tuition fees.[16]

It wasn't just college that was under attack. Budgetary planners argued that the city could no longer afford a "large and underutilized hospital system" and spending strategies from "the federally sponsored social services revolution of the 1960s." The cuts were felt across the city. John L.S. Holloman, who helped lead the desegregation of Southern hospitals by working with government officials in charge of Medicare, later became president of the Health and Hospitals Corporation in New York. The HHC was a semi-independent agency that oversaw the city's public hospitals. As part of the austerity drive, many public hospitals were closed to save money, which Holloman denounced. He was pressured to resign and eventually forced out. Holloman, a doctor who spent his life connecting civil rights with access to health care, was replaced with a former banker turned city budget director.[17]

These episodes revealed a new kind of government official taking over liberal politics. The new technocrats who executed austerity in New York City were not rabid conservatives. They were liberals concerned about justice and policy, but they saw their role as something new and different. They wanted the city to focus narrowly on municipal services like fire protection, policing, sanitation, and schools, rather than redistribution policies and the broader de-commodification of public housing, health care, and higher education. They touted that volunteers could take up those roles as needed. The *New York Times* described a new mentality where "citizen participation" would "sustain, as well as supplement, services seriously crippled by layoffs and attrition," though it was nowhere near sufficient to the scale of the cuts. The new technocrats would come to dominate thinking in the Democratic Party over the next generation, and one of their first targets was free tuition.[18]

These leaders were far more reluctant when it came to public programs and an active government. They had an antagonistic relationship with labor unions, making a point of being willing to stand up to them. They emphasized efficiency rather than solidarity. They also used "the market" as a mechanism to suppress bold demands, outsourcing the scope of political possibilities to the financial sector. This use of financial markets to deter political debates would come to define neoliberalism.[19]

The city mourned the loss of free college. One person to correctly identify the politics of this change was Fred M. Hechinger, an editor with the *New York Times*. Hechinger was a German immigrant who came to the United States in 1936 and was a graduate of the City College of New York. He was a beneficiary of the kind of mobility that education could create across a wide variety of people. He also correctly predicted how quickly free tuition would be buried in public memory. As he wrote in 1976: "Once free tuition is buried, the politicians will want it to be forgotten. Others who take a longer view of higher education's kinship to America as the land of opportunity will want to keep its memory alive, not as one more oddity in the nostalgia attic, but as a sensible and realistic option for a more affluent, more confident and more generous day." It would take decades to recover a glimpse of this memory.[20]

As free college disappeared under political attack, a new idea of education took over. This was the idea of education as an investment in human capital, an idea that took the economics world by storm starting in the 1970s. Human capital, as theorized by Gary Becker of the University of Chicago, is an investment one makes in oneself. In the same way a business might invest in buildings, equipment, and tools, we invest in ourselves through education and learning skills. This view has continued to expand and dominates thinking about public policy.[21]

During the 1950s, economists started to argue that education and skills were major drivers of the growth of our economy. Around this time, some economists started to use the concept of human capital in the context of the country as a whole, contending that it functioned as a societal resource. Like a strategic reserve, human capital was an appropriate object of public investment and social spending—not unlike the GI Bill. At this time, it was not about individual benefit, but rather about growth for society as a whole.[22]

In the 1970s, this view was turned on its head. The American worker, rather than embodying the laborer who works for those with capital in a process of production, now emerged as an individual form of capital, their own little firm. This was a major conceptual break, pushed by economists, from the mid-century worker ideal, where workers were protected by a union and government management of the macro-economy through active Keynesian policy. As the French philosopher Michel Foucault described, under this new view, which he described as neoliberalism, a person is an "entrepreneur, an entrepreneur of himself." Our goal as individuals is to find ways to maximize our productivity and profitability as an enterprise, as well as to be ready to subject ourselves to the ever-increasing demands of the marketplace. The role of the government isn't to shield people from the worst of the marketplace, but instead to create favorable conditions for investing in ourselves. In this conception, markets don't serve the preexisting needs of people; people are instead created to serve the market.[23]

This same conceptual transformation can be seen in the case economists made for the move to student loans as a means to self-finance higher education. Milton Friedman, in his book *Capitalism and Freedom*, developed this line of thinking clearly. The question of higher education was no longer the historical one of collapsing hierarchy and aristocracy, removing the distance between mass and elite education, and making sure there was more than scraps for everyday people. For Friedman, higher education is just "a form of investment in human capital precisely analogous to investment in machinery, buildings, or other forms of non-human capital." Building on the notion of individuals as simple businesses unto themselves, the primary question of higher education is simply: How much do individuals want to invest in themselves, and how can we get them access to the financial credit they need to do so?[24]

In this theory the problem of access wasn't one for the government to solve through public programs, but one for individuals to solve through access to financial markets. "Individuals should bear the costs of investment in themselves and receive the rewards," Friedman argued. That the financial returns to colleges were so high means there is an "underinvestment in human capital" that "presumably reflects an imperfection in the capital market." If only "capital were as readily available for investment in human beings as for investment in physical assets," then financial markets would determine the correct amount of education that should exist through the price signal. This created a role for the government to use policy for "improving the operation of the market." Friedman pictured people selling equity in themselves, like shares in a corporation, and it was this same logic that created the framework for student loans.[25]

It took time for an infrastructure for student loans to achieve the size it eventually would. The goal during the 1960s and 1970s was for grants to provide access to higher ed, not student loans. Student loans were added as an extra level of support. The original goal was for government-funded Pell grants to cover most tuition costs, with student loans as mechanisms for handling living expenses and extra costs. The average grant in the 1970s actually covered more than tuition, providing extra funding that could help with room and board. Pell grants, however, didn't keep pace with rising tuition costs, and their value eroded over time.[26]

Fred Hechinger, in a prescient 1974 column, described a "class war over tuition." He anticipated that pitting middle- and working-class families against each other "could have a corroding influence on the already deteriorating relations between the poor and the lower-middle-class." Instead of supporting higher tuition to cover grants for poorer families, "hard-pressed middle-class families are likely to react in anger and political vindictiveness." He quoted the Democratic representative from Michigan, James G. O'Hara, as saying "from the point of view of the school-teacher or the cop or the accountant or the salesman," it would be a gigantic political liability "to suggest that he ought to be forced to pay more of the money he doesn't have to send his kids to college—in the name of removing financial barriers."[27]

These two dynamics reinforced each other. By weakening public investment, through the declining value of federal aid and the retrenchment of state funds, student loans became the main way in which students would access higher education. By making higher education a personal investment that individuals make, there was less support for trying to make it more accessible to poorer people.

In 1978 Harvard raised its tuition by 18 percent. It saw no drop in the number of applications, so it pursued aggressive tuition increases over the next decade, a move that other private colleges and universities duplicated. From 1980 to 2000, tuition for private institutions increased from 20 percent of median family income to 40 percent. Private schools next began providing aid to students by discounting the tuition. This high-tuition, high-aid system became the norm for the schools and allowed them to do several things at once. First was tailoring their classes to students who were desirable, either on a merit basis or their family's ability to pay. Instead of just discounting tuition on a need basis, private schools could use it to attract star students. The resulting price discrimination gave significant advantages to private institutions, as well as those students whose families understood how to navigate this system.[28]

Public colleges and universities were squeezed on numerous fronts, with students picking up the costs. Starting in the 1980s, states appropriated less for their higher education budgets. During each recession since then, states cut funding, and have never restored it to previous levels. The result is a bleeding out of public support for higher education that has happened in waves. Students have been forced to make up the resulting lack of funds themselves: Student tuition in 1980 provided around 25 percent of what states did. Since 2010, student-paid tuition has amounted to *more* than what states provide.[29]

Student loans are what allowed this transition to work, as they now cover nearly three-quarters of tuition revenues. Emerging from their small niche within conservative economics departments, student loans have now become one of the defining experiences of young adult life. In 1989 only 9 percent of all families had student loans, and the median value of that debt was $5,600. In 2016 student loan debt more than doubled to 22 percent of all families, with a median value of $19,000. For families where the head of household is under thirty-five years of age, the proportion of families with student debt went from 17 percent in 1989 to 45 percent in 2016, nearly half of those households, with the median value growing from $5,600 to $18,500.

In the aftermath of the financial crisis people are taking far longer to pay off their student loans. Since the Great Recession, the percentage of those between the ages of thirty-five and forty-four who have student debt more than doubled. The proportion was between 11 and 13 percent from 1989 until 2001; in the aughts it hovered between 13 and 15 percent. Now it is at 34 percent. The millennial generation is carrying student debt longer, and at greater amounts, than previous generations. Student loans are coming to define the balance sheet of not just young people in their twenties, but those approaching middle age as well.[30]

Student loans put pressure on the most vulnerable and create a kind of downward mobility. When we look at student loans as a percentage of people's income, we see that the burden falls on those people in lower income brackets. According to the Federal Reserve, households with student debt in the bottom 50 percent of incomes saw their student-debt-to-income ratio more than double, from 26 percent of yearly income to 58 percent between 1995 and 2013. This ratio increased for everyone outside the top 5 percent of incomes. This is a real burden that has grown over time. And the burden is accentuated by race. Black students disproportionately carry student loans, with 42 percent of households headed by a black adult ages twenty-five to fifty-five carrying student loans in 2016, compared with 34 percent of white households. In addition, black families carry an average student loan debt that is 28 percent higher than that of white families.[31]

Debt changes people's relationship to both school and the labor market. Public colleges need to make up the lost state funding by catering to affluent students who can pay, especially students from outside their states who will pay extra. In order to make this attractive, these colleges invest more in amenities, turning higher education from a leveling place of mass education into a tiered consumer experience. Luxury campus apartments for wealthy students and campus food pantries for poorer students are growing together, as high-tuition colleges become a playground for the rich and a place where everyone else struggles to survive.[32]

Meanwhile, if you need to make high debt payments every month, then it's important to find steady lucrative work, rather than start a business or do something low-paying with a broader social purpose. One study found that student loans pushed people to take higher-salary jobs and veer away from public-interest jobs that had lower pay. Another study by the Federal Reserve Bank of Philadelphia found a correlation between increases in student loan debt and lower business formation among small businesses. Student loans create an important bias against public-sector and care work, as well as starting small businesses, all of which are already struggling in our economy.[33]

The volume of student loans people are carrying into middle age is impacting every part of their adult lives. People with more student debt are less likely to own homes, and when they do, they have less equity in them. Those with high student debt are more vulnerable to economic misfortune. Women with more student debt are less likely to be married in the years after college and are more likely to delay having children. Meanwhile, the overriding stress of how to pay for college hangs over families. Parents, often dealing with their own loans, want to give their children opportunities, as all parents do. But that is now only accessible through the dependency of debt. This is the world of freedom defined by market dependency.[34]

The former poet laureate Kay Ryan once said that "right near your home, year in and year out, a community college is quietly— and with very little financial encouragement—saving lives and minds. I can't think of a more efficient, hopeful or egalitarian machine, with the possible exception of the bicycle." Ryan's observations get at the core meaning of education's relationship to American democracy. Student loans are a recent experiment, one that undercuts nearly two centuries of our egalitarian tradition. They have replaced a theory of freedom as one of opportunity and class leveling, with one of individualized investment that ultimately has served to reinforce class divisions in America. The debt-based approach to higher ed is an experiment that has failed, and we continue to see the consequences pile up.[35]

CONCLUSION

Throughout our history people have demanded limits on the market. And they have explained these demands in terms of preserving and expanding freedom. Their demands animated the question of land ownership and working hours, and extended to the creation of social insurance. Public programs, founded on an ideal of freedom, helped bring about the end of Jim Crow in the private medical system, and created a model for valuing uncompensated care work. In short, coursing beneath our history has been a powerful vision of a free society, one that has pushed forward the most important public policy achievements of the past two hundred years.

And yet, over the past forty years, the counterattack on public programs, and the wholesale removal of limits on the market, has been swift and total. Measures that put fencing around corporations have been removed. We've been drowned by markets, and force-fed the idea that market behavior itself is an expression of freedom.

Yet, in a new historical turn, the currents of political action are changing once again. Look around, and you can see people fighting to take back their lives from the market. These battles are new—many of them are only a few years old—yet they are significant and growing. They are motivating younger people to get into politics. Their fights are forcing us to answer fundamental questions about the role of the market in our lives for the first time in decades. How quickly the ground is changing should inspire us with the belief that, despite the odds, real social transformation is possible.

We see this new energy in the workplace. The pandemic has shown us how essential workers who make the modern economy function face dangerous and difficult working conditions with little in terms of economic security. Yet even before this crisis, there has been a wave of worker activism in the last several years, all of it connected to the issue of freedom. Service sector workers demanding a $15 minimum wage and a union through the Fight for $15 movement have already won huge victories. Ideas about how low-wage, precarious work is a form of unfreedom have been at the front of these movements. At the 2016 Fight for $15 national convention in Richmond, Virginia, the Rev. William Barber noted that "it took 400 years from slavery to now to get from zero to $7.25 [an hour]. We can't wait another 400 years" to get to $15.[1]

This new activism is also happening in the public sector. Teachers have led two different strike waves since 2018. The first was notable for starting in red, conservative states such as West Virginia, Kentucky, and Oklahoma, where teachers and their unions have less power. This was followed by teachers striking in blue cities, including Chicago, Los Angeles, and Oakland. In each, teachers fought against the ideology that animated anti-public sentiments in their respective political coalitions. Red-state teachers fought against austerity and the conservative push for defunding public programs. In blue cities, teachers fought against privatization and the expansion of charter schools. They've each, in their own way, articulated how schools aren't just another market but instead are a key public service that plays a social role beyond the logic of competition and profits.[2]

The demands of the new workplace movements have extended to the demand for control over labor time. This particular protest is frequently made in reaction to the emergence of "just-in-time" scheduling, where managers give workers very little advanced notice about their volatile working schedules. These practices make a mockery of freedom, as it is impossible to commit to obligations with families, friends, community, and broader civil society if you can't predict your free time with any consistency. Many cities and towns are considering "fair workweek" hours, which require employers to give advanced notice on working hours. Our politics is finally catching up to the fundamental connection between time and freedom.[3]

There's also been energy and excitement at the level of structural reform to our labor markets, especially around the ideas of codetermination and sectoral bargaining. Codetermination is a system of corporate governance in which workers sit on corporate boards and help determine economic decision-making. It is a direct challenge to the idea that the corporation should exist only as the property of its shareholders, and it makes a statement that corporations are social and political creations that require workers to have a democratic say in their governance. Sectoral bargaining is where the terms of labor are set at the industry level, instead of at each individual firm. Common across the European countries, it's a level of democratic say within the workplace that would go beyond what the New Deal envisioned. Perhaps because things are so dire for workers, it's forced us to think bigger.[4]

Just as the question of freedom and work has come crashing back, so has the question of freedom in its relationship to the broader economy. For example, starting in the 2000s advocates for a free and open internet demanded that the principle of net neutrality governed the activities of internet service providers. Net neutrality is a public-utility policy where those who deliver the internet have to be indifferent to the content of the traffic they are sending. The rationale is that corporations who control the infrastructure of the internet shouldn't get to determine and put their thumb on the scales regarding what we get to access. At the same time, there have been demands for municipal broadband owned and administered by the public. If private companies won't provide high-quality, accessible infrastructure to everyone when it comes to the internet, local governments can do it instead. Without it, there will remain a significant digital divide between well-off and struggling communities in accessing the internet. In places where the public has provided municipal broadband, over significant opposition by industry, it's been a popular and democratizing success.[5]

These same ideas are animating a new generation of lawyers, economists, and activists who want to tackle an era of concentrated corporate power by suppressing corporations' ability to marketize and discriminate. Much of Big Tech, for instance, functions as a critical intermediary to businesses but also uses the control it has over that intermediation, as well as the information it gathers in that capacity, to provide competing services against those businesses as well. To use a sports analogy, it's like these powerful companies are both a player in the game, trying to win, but also a referee as well, making calls on all the other players as well. Ideas about public-utility regulation, once abandoned, provide a means of managing these conflicts while still allowing for innovation. What form these public requirements take will depend on the platform. But most of the major ones will require restrictions on the markets they create, including limitations on their lines of businesses and what kinds of information they can use.[6]

This same demand has come through in the renewed campaign for free college and universal health care. This was apparent in the 2016 Democratic primary election, where Bernie Sanders and Hillary Clinton each had plans for health care and education, and the same dynamic was repeated in the 2020 primary. The real divide that animated the debates wasn't about price tags or generosity. Sanders, for example, argued that "healthcare is a human right and should be guaranteed to all Americans regardless of wealth or income," and that "[e]ducation should be a right, not a privilege." This was a direct response to the normal way of talking about these topics among liberal Democrats, which is to focus on *affordable* health care and education. To state that these are rights is to claim our access to health care or education is something to be secured beyond purchasing it in the market.[7]

After a difficult political fight that almost failed at the last minute, President Barack Obama signed the Affordable Care Act (ACA) into law in 2010. Since then, it has dominated the political landscape, with the conservative movement running an extended campaign to overturn or sabotage it. First, conservatives took the battle to the Supreme Court, which made a political decision to prevent the federal government from using its funding to pressure states into expanding Medicaid. From there, Donald Trump ran for and won the presidency on providing a better alternative, saying during the election, "I am going to take care of everybody [. . .] Everybody's going to be taken care of much better than they're taken care of now." However, that promise was always going to fail, as conservatives wanted to replace the ACA not with a system that was more universal or had broader risk-sharing, but one that had individuals carrying even more risks by themselves. They managed to come close to passing a replacement, but failed. Yet what is truly striking about all these political maneuvers is how starkly the ground has shifted—how health care is now solidly viewed as something that must be shielded from unchecked market forces.[8]

The political momentum in health care has since switched from defense toward offense on expanding public insurance. The ACA's private health care exchanges have struggled to meet their expected number of enrollments, are not deep enough in rural areas to serve customers, and still end up as too expensive for many. This was exactly the limitation of private insurance I.M. Rubinow diagnosed a century ago. In a similar manner, people are again turning to voluntary mutual aid to try to fill in this gap in health care access, using social media websites for crowdsourcing donations. However, the failure of this makeshift measure to provide a sufficient and widespread level of security is even more apparent this time around. Because of the limitations of the private market in providing health care and the inability of conservatives to propose, much less enact, a better market alternative, the debate has

moved to expanding the role of the government in directly providing health care. Even more conservative Democrats have signed
onto an expansion of Medicare in the form of a public option.
And single-payer Medicare-for-All, with its ability to give everyone access while reducing overall costs, is now discussed as a serious goal in a way it hasn't been since the Truman administration.[9]

A new understanding of freedom has also changed the conversation about higher education. A generation of young people suffering under student debt have seen how this burden sharply curtails
their ability to live their lives freely. In a related vein, protests
broke out during the Great Recession over the defunding of public education. This didn't just happen in the United States: similar
protests have broken out from England to Australia to Quebec to
Chile, often facing significant police violence in response. Since
then the momentum has swung in the opposite direction, from
fighting off austerity to demanding free public college, available to
all based on their ability to achieve instead of their ability to pay,
as well as demanding the forgiveness of student debt.[10]

A focus on universal programs is also reemerging in the infrastructure for care work. New York City introduced a universal
pre-K program across the city. But rather than make it only accessible to poorer families, the city made it universal, including the
very rich. This created a significant blowback among the gatekeep-
ers who set the tone on acceptable policy, as they believed it was
subsidizing the rich and not targeted solely at the poorest parents.
Yet the program has been a huge success, in large part because of
the buy-in and defense it now has from so many people, including those with more means. That it is universal is a feature of its
success. There's no way it would have succeeded as much as it has
if it didn't have a broad base of support from across the income
spectrum.[11]

There's also been a new wave of thinking about providing a universal floor to every citizen for the basic resources necessary to live,
much like the Homestead Act tried to provide a floor in terms

of access to wealth in land. As social insurance advocates understood a century ago, capitalism only distributes income to those who work or are wealthy, leaving children, students, caregivers, the disabled, the elderly, and all those who could not or should not earn market wages to face the unfreedom of poverty. Some argue for either a guaranteed income, or a universal basic income, or a large cash grant upon reaching adulthood, similar to arguments Thomas Paine made centuries ago. There are ongoing experiments with basic income that find it doesn't leave people detached or aimless but instead provides real security and better life outcomes. There are intense debates about how to prioritize what a new baseline of economic security would require, but the fact that they are happening means there's a conversation about how to secure freedom that goes far beyond simply having access to the market.[12]

These developments and debates aren't just welcome, they are necessary, as new, reactionary, far-right forces are also fighting on this same terrain. Over the past several decades conservatives have defined market freedom as the essential freedom. Their guiding principle has been to devolve, privatize, or marketize all public programs, assuming that the state could only get in the way of freedom. Whether it was the compassionate conservatism of President George W. Bush, trying to privatize Social Security, or the libertarianism of House Speaker Paul Ryan, trying to privatize everything else, this was the dominating mindset when it came to markets and freedom on the right.

Yet there's always been a historical conservative unease with market society. The neoconservative Irving Kristol gave capitalism "two cheers" in the 1970s, but not the full three cheers. The success of capitalism, in Kristol's view, weakened people's attachment to traditional virtues and ethics, especially as the richest people often had the least attachment to notions of prudence and self-reliance. Mid-century conservatives such as Robert Nisbet were concerned that both capitalism and government action to check it would destroy civil society and unravel community. A wide range of conservative thinkers have been skeptical, even hostile, to capitalism. They all share two common worries: first, that capitalism levels tradition and hierarchies, especially those of gender, race, and status; second, that the dislocations and insecurity caused by the expansion of capitalism gives the government a justification to expand to try to address these problems, at the expense of civil and private institutions. For a conservative movement that wants to preserve hierarchies and weaken the leveling tendencies of an active state that provides economic security, capitalism is a double-edged sword.[13]

This mix of repulsion at both capitalism and government responses to alleviating its effects found its ultimate advocate with President Trump. Trump has been able to combine racism, sexism, and an economic vision beyond the market into one deceptive package. There are endless debates, usually predicated on thin survey data, over whether the grievances Trump harnesses from his supporters are racial or economic. But the reality is Trump covers both facets, because it is impossible to disentangle race and class in our society. Trump says he'll use the government to bring economic security to primarily white, male breadwinners. He promises his voters security from immigrants, from foreigners, from global trade, and from elites who conspire against them. That is, he has tapped into America's deep historical distrust of unchecked markets, and poisoned it with racial and sexist appeals, to create the mirage of a better future—for some. The concrete results are tax cuts for the rich, increased precarity for workers, and aggressive policing for the rest.

Probably owing to his personal limitations, Trump has done a poor job of building a political and ideological movement for his ideas. But the next iteration won't be so incoherent. The story told here, about how freedom requires keeping us free from the market, is capable of short-circuiting this far-right threat. A genuine movement to check the market through public action needs to be broad and welcoming, rather than walled off and for the few. Universal social insurance, free public programs, economic security, and power for workers are the things that ensure broad prosperity—they succeed because they work. The Trump ideal is yet another retreat into an anachronism, and it will fail to even help the people swayed by it.

To succeed we need to harness and build on the proud legacy created by two hundred years of battles to carve out a free space beyond the confines of the market. Battles for the future of our country and society are not won on arguments about market failures, on the balance sheets of accountants, or on narrowly tailored, incremental solutions. They are won on arguments about freedom. We've lost this fight in recent decades, and for a time it seemed as if any alternative was wiped clean from public debates. But we are starting to remember. Freedom is the fundamental battlefield that we fight on, and we need to fight on it once again.

ACKNOWLEDGMENTS

As appropriate for a book on how property is a social relationship, I couldn't have done this without help and inspiration from so many people during this time. First, my thanks to the Roosevelt Institute, my home for the past decade. Both Rob Johnson and Andrew Rich took a big chance at the beginning of the Great Recession by bringing me, a pseudonymous blogger, on board to talk about financial reform and unemployment at this new place they were starting. Roosevelt grew into the powerhouse of progressive ideas and analysis that it currently is under the leadership of Felicia Wong. Felicia has always maintained a focus on ideas and a critical eye on who gets to exercise power in our society. All my colleagues have expanded and challenged my thinking in so many different ways. Special thanks to Nellie Abernathy and Katy Milani for staffing up the financialization work with me. Now, more than at any point in my lifetime, our foundational economic and political ideas are up for grabs, and engaging directly at that level is what makes Roosevelt so unique.

This book is the culmination of arguments I've been thinking through since the Great Recession, and the book owes thanks to everyone who helped me along the way. I started blogging about the financial crisis while it was happening, and encouragement and advice from people like Ezra Klein, Chris Hayes, James Kwak, and others kept me going. Over time I was able to work with editors who helped me learn how to write and tell stories, as well as let me test run these ideas in their pages. Editors such as Bryce Covert and Tim Price at the Roosevelt Institute, Kaavya Asoka, Natasha Lewis, and Nick Serpe at *Dissent*, Rob Horning at *The*

New Inquiry, Deb Chasman and Simon Waxman at *Boston Review*, Sarah Leonard and Chris Shay at *The Nation*, the Wonkblog crew at the *Washington Post*, Chris Shea at *Vox*, and many more have taught me how to be a better writer and flesh out these ideas.

I hope both the economic blogosphere of the aughts and the rebirth of left magazines in the early 2010s are remembered for creating a whole wave of intellectual energy that continues to this day. My engagement with the latter in particular forced me to think harder and more clearly about politics. This project owes special thanks to Sarah Jaffe, Astra Taylor, and others on student debt, the topic that first started me thinking more critically along these lines. I thank J.W. Mason for discussions on the role of the corporation, the public sector, and all economics more generally; Corey Robin for helping me think through freedom as the defining battle; Aaron Bady for a summer spent thinking through why free public higher education matters and what it could still do for our society; Tim Barker for important conversations on how this book should be focused; and Peter Frase for pushing me on my Polanyi-ish, and Pollyana-ish, thinking.

This manuscript benefited from feedback from a whole range of people who read chapters and drafts, including: Nellie Abernathy, Mehrsa Baradaran, Tim Barker, Kendra Bozarth, Ed Burmila, Ben Eidelson, Henry Farrell, Andrea Flynn, Katrina Forrester, Lawrence Glickman, Erik Loomis, Dylan Matthews, Lenore Palladino, Tim Price, K. Sabeel Rahman, Tim Shenk, David Barton Smith, and Felicia Wong.

Dana Goldstein offered both a model for historically informed policy writing as well as helpful advice early in the process. Special thanks for excellent research assistance from Rosemarie Ho and Kristina Karlsson. Most of the research was conducted at the Library of Congress, a remarkable resource and public institution. Kirsten Carter at the Franklin D. Roosevelt Presidential Library and Museum helped with research into the New Deal. There are also those who helped keep me sane while I was writing. This includes Team Plunge Pool: Ed Burmila, Matt Gambino, and Erik Martin; and Dice City Games, the best gaming store in the country, for having a place to say "island, go" every week.

This book started as a pretty gonzo set of ideas. I thank my agent Mel Flashman, who shaped it into an actual proposal. Marc Favreau at The New Press took a risk on this project, and provided detailed feedback, editing, and focus over the course of the writing. Thanks to Emily Albarillo who handled the production, and Brian Baughan who did a superb job with copyediting.

And, finally, thanks to my parents, Tom and Nancy, and my brother Dave, for encouraging me through the many twists and turns and sudden moves in my life. To Odetta the Dog, the best research dog a human could hope for. But, most of all, Kendra Salois, the love of my life, who makes all of this worthwhile. From coast to coast, it's been a nonstop adventure, and I can't wait to see what's next. And for our daughter Vivian, the newest addition to our family. This book came into being alongside you, and is a hope that you inherit a better world. In many ways it is a book for you, the lessons we've found and hope to convey to the future. Some say a book about the emancipatory potential of decommodification might be a little complex for a children's book, but I don't think we should talk down to children.

NOTES

Introduction

1. Konczal, "Parsing the Data and Ideology of the We Are 99% Tumblr"; Graeber, *The Democracy Project*, 84–87.
2. Kight, "Exclusive Poll: Young Americans Are Embracing Socialism"; Salmon, "Gen Z Prefers 'Socialism' to 'Capitalism.'"
3. Wood, *The Origin of Capitalism*, 2; Wood, "The Politics of Capitalism."
4. Wood, *The Origin of Capitalism*, 6–7.
5. On the proper distribution of health care that includes those who are sick, see Williams, "The Idea of Equality."
6. Robin, "Reclaiming the Politics of Freedom"; Robin, "The New Socialists"; Foner, *The Story of American Freedom*.
7. Taylor, *Democracy May Not Exist, but We'll Miss It When It's Gone*, 33.
8. Berlin, "Two Concepts of Liberty."
9. On how Berlin's contribution has clouded the debate more than helped it, see Pettit, *Republicanism*, 17–20. On Berlin and the New Deal, see Cohen, *On the Currency of Egalitarian Justice, and Other Essays in Political Philosophy*, 171–72.
10. Tobin, "On Limiting the Domain of Inequality"; Satz, *Why Some Things Should Not Be for Sale: The Moral Limits of Markets*, 63–66. On the increasing power of economists during this period, see Appelbaum, *The Economists' Hour*. On justice within the auction, see Dworkin, "What Is Equality? Part 2: Equality of Resources." On the politics of the auction alongside an ascendant right, see Forrester, *In the Shadow of Justice*, 208–14.
11. On the negative income tax, see Friedman, *Capitalism and Freedom*, 190–95; Foucault, *The Birth of Biopolitics*, 203–4.
12. Foucault, *The Birth of Biopolitics*, 206. A full discussion of the politics of a basic income are outside the scope of this introduction. For more on basic income, see Lowrey, *Give People Money*, and Hughes, *Fair Shot*. For relevant

criticism of basic income, see Gourevitch, "The Limits of a Basic Income: Means and Ends of Workplace Democracy," and Bergmann, "A Swedish-Style Welfare State or Basic Income: Which Should Have Priority?"

13. On social meaning and goods, see Walzer, *Spheres of Justice*; Rahman, "Losing and Gaining Public Goods."

14. On inelastic providers and public provisioning, see Mason, "Public Options." More generally, see Sitaraman and Alstott, *The Public Option*.

15. Anderson, *Private Government: How Employers Rule Our Lives (and Why We Don't Talk about It)*. Freedom from arbitrary domination is from the republican tradition of liberty, though in general its recent revival has not taken a hard examination of the market. See Pettit, "Freedom in the Market." For a useful corrective, see Gourevitch, "Labor and Republican Liberty." There's been an interesting revival in applying republican theory of domination to the labor market, see Gourevitch, *From Slavery to the Cooperative Commonwealth*, and Roberts, *Marx's Inferno*.

16. Satz, *Why Some Things Should Not Be for Sale: The Moral Limits of Markets*, 94–98.

17. Polanyi, *The Great Transformation*.

18. Fraser, "Contradictions of Capital and Care."

19. Fried, *The Progressive Assault on Laissez Faire: Robert Hale and the First Law and Economics Movement*, 51–53; Cohen, "Freedom and Money"; Pistor, *The Code of Capital*, 3.

1. Free Land

1. Robbins, "Horace Greeley: Land Reform and Unemployment, 1837–1862."

2. "The Public Lands—National Reform," *New-York Daily Tribune*; Mackenzie, "A Winter Journey through the Canadas."

3. Banner, *How the Indians Lost Their Land*.

4. Sellers, *The Market Revolution*, 3–33; Gates, *History of Public Land Law Development*, 77, 86.

5. Gates, *History of Public Land Law Development*, 124–25, 145; author's calculations from U.S. Bureau of the Census, *Historical Statistics of the United States, Colonial Times to 1970*, 1106.

6. Paine, "Agrarian Justice."

7. Paine, "Agrarian Justice"; Foner, *Tom Paine and Revolutionary America*, 250–52; Spence, "The Rights of Infants."

8. Quoted in Bronstein, *Land Reform and Working-Class Experience in Britain and the United States, 1800–1862,* 25–26, 270n87.

9. Wilentz, *Chants Democratic,* 183–84; Bronstein, *Land Reform and Working-Class Experience in Britain and the United States, 1800–1862,* 37.

10. Skidmore, *The Rights of Man to Property!,* 59; Wilentz, *Chants Democratic,* 184–85.

11. Skidmore, *The Rights of Man to Property!,* 125; Howe, *What Hath God Wrought,* 528–32.

12. Skidmore, *The Rights of Man to Property!,* 137–44; Bronstein, *Land Reform and Working-Class Experience in Britain and the United States, 1800–1862,* 38; Wilentz, *Chants Democratic,* 186–87.

13. Wilentz, *Chants Democratic,* 191; Bronstein, *Land Reform and Working-Class Experience in Britain and the United States, 1800–1862,* 40.

14. Wilentz, *Chants Democratic,* 195, 198–99, 201–11, 408; Pessen, "Thomas Skidmore, Agrarian Reformer in the Early American Labor Movement."

15. Pilz, *The Life, Work and Times of George Henry Evans, Newspaperman, Activist and Reformer (1829–1849),* 11–12; Lause, *Young America,* 10–11, 16; Bronstein, *Land Reform and Working-Class Experience in Britain and the United States, 1800–1862,* 16, 120.

16. Lause, *Young America,* 3, 17; Pilz, *The Life, Work and Times of George Henry Evans, Newspaperman, Activist and Reformer (1829–1849),* 151–56.

17. Bronstein, *Land Reform and Working-Class Experience in Britain and the United States, 1800–1862,* 16–18.

18. Bronstein, 168–69; Goodman, "The Emergence of Homestead Exemption in the United States: Accommodation and Resistance to the Market Revolution, 1840–1880."

19. "The National Reformers," *New-York Daily Tribune*; Stephenson, *The Political History of the Public Lands, from 1840 to 1862,* 111.

20. Bronstein, *Land Reform and Working-Class Experience in Britain and the United States, 1800–1862,* 70–71.

21. Julian, *Speeches on Political Questions,* 59.

22. Tuchinsky, *Horace Greeley's New-York Tribune,* 2–5; Williams, *Horace Greeley,* 11.

23. Howe, *The Political Culture of the American Whigs,* 184–95; Tuchinsky, *Horace Greeley's New-York Tribune,* 181–82, 184.

24. Tuchinsky, *Horace Greeley's New-York Tribune,* 135–36; Robbins, "Horace

Greeley: Land Reform and Unemployment, 1837–1862"; Williams, *Horace Greeley*, 91–93.

25. Howe, *What Hath God Wrought*, 803. On the slaveholding South as an aspiring hemispheric power dominating foreign policy, see Karp, *This Vast Southern Empire*.

26. Snay, *Horace Greeley and the Politics of Reform in Nineteenth-Century America*, 88–90.

27. Julian, *Speeches on Political Questions*, 50–66.

28. Stephenson, *The Political History of the Public Lands, from 1840 to 1862*, 146–52.

29. Snay, *Horace Greeley and the Politics of Reform in Nineteenth-Century America*, 113–15; Schlesinger, "Was Olmsted an Unbiased Critic of the South?," 179. Greeley may have never actually paid his share for the howitzer to Olmsted. See Williams, *Horace Greeley*, 188–89, 355n27.

30. Potter, *The Impending Crisis, 1848–1861*, 246–48, 338, 418–19; Roark, "George W. Julian: Radical Land Reformer."

31. Williams, *Horace Greeley*, 94; Robbins, "Horace Greeley: Land Reform and Unemployment, 1837–1862," 40.

32. Gates, "The Homestead Law in an Incongruous Land System," 655–59, 662, 666; White, *The Republic for Which It Stands*, 141–46; Deverell, "To Loosen the Safety Valve: Eastern Workers and Western Lands."

33. Williams, "The Homestead Act: A Major Asset-Building Policy in American History."

34. Du Bois, *Black Reconstruction in America, 1860–1880*, 601–3; Foner, *Reconstruction*, 70–71, 158–63.

35. Roark, "George W. Julian: Radical Land Reformer"; Merritt, "Land and the Roots of African-American Poverty"; Gates, "Federal Land Policy in the South 1866–1888."

36. Tuchinsky, *Horace Greeley's New-York Tribune*, 177–78; Snay, *Horace Greeley and the Politics of Reform in Nineteenth-Century America*, 159, 164–65.

37. Tuchinsky, *Horace Greeley's New-York Tribune*, 165–66, 211, 224–26; Snay, *Horace Greeley and the Politics of Reform in Nineteenth-Century America*, 170–71; Richardson, *The Death of Reconstruction*, 93–104.

38. Foner, *Reconstruction*, 501–11.

2. Free Time

1. The history of the law, Frank Wigeman, his court case, and the debate over the meaning of freedom it provoked is described in detail in Sawyer, "Contested Meanings of Freedom: Workingmen's Wages, the Company Store System, and the Godcharles v. Wigeman Decision." As opposed to the workshopped names given to laws today, this law in question had the refreshingly direct title "An act to secure to operatives and laborers, engaged in and about coal mines, manufactories or iron and steel, and all other manufactories, the payment of their wages at regular intervals and in lawful money of the United States."

2. Sawyer, 297–98; Witt, "Rethinking the Nineteenth-Century Employment Contract, Again"; Orren, *Belated Feudalism: Labor, the Law, and Liberal Development in the United States.*

3. Sawyer, "Contested Meanings of Freedom: Workingmen's Wages, the Company Store System, and the Godcharles v. Wigeman Decision," 304–7.

4. Fried, *The Progressive Assault on Laissez Faire: Robert Hale and the First Law and Economics Movement*, 32, 230n18; Sawyer, "Contested Meanings of Freedom: Workingmen's Wages, the Company Store System, and the Godcharles v. Wigeman Decision," 287–88, 314–15. For a contemporaneous history of Godcharles, see Pound, "Liberty of Contract."

5. As the historian William Novak describes it, "Property rights in the early nineteenth century were social, relative, and historical, not individual, absolute and natural." See Novak, *The People's Welfare: Law and Regulation in Nineteenth-Century America*, 83–105, 111.

6. Robin, "Lavatory and Liberty: The Secret History of the Bathroom Break"; Hertel-Fernandez, *Politics at Work*; Anderson, *Private Government: How Employers Rule Our Lives (and Why We Don't Talk about It)*, 37–71.

7. For reasons why workers and the general public believed in a shorter working week, see Hunnicutt, *Work without End: Abandoning Shorter Hours for the Right to Work*, 9–15. For an excellent meditation of how the time in our finite lives defines our freedom, see Hägglund, *This Life*.

8. Text of the "Ten-Hour" Circular can be found in Commons et al., *A Documentary History of American Industrial Society*, vol. 6, 94–99.

9. Roediger and Foner, *Our Own Time: A History of American Labor and the Working Day*, 30–34; Bernstein, "The Working People of Philadelphia from Colonial Times to the General Strike of 1835," 336–39.

10. Roediger and Foner, *Our Own Time: A History of American Labor and the Working Day*, vii–viii, 120–21.

11. Dubofsky and Dulles, *Labor in America*, 82–84; Roediger and Foner, *Our Own Time: A History of American Labor and the Working Day*, 83.

12. Glickman, "Workers of the World, Consume: Ira Steward and the Origins of Labor Consumerism"; Roediger and Foner, *Our Own Time: A History of American Labor and the Working Day*, 85; Glickman, *A Living Wage: American Workers and the Making of Consumer Society*, 33–34; Dubofsky and Dulles, *Labor in America*, 95–97; Cahill, *Shorter Hours: A Study of the Movement since the Civil War*, 33–34.

13. Glickman, "Workers of the World, Consume: Ira Steward and the Origins of Labor Consumerism," 72–75; Roediger and Foner, *Our Own Time: A History of American Labor and the Working Day*, 85.

14. Glickman, "Workers of the World, Consume: Ira Steward and the Origins of Labor Consumerism," 77.

15. Glickman, 75–78. On working-class culture during this time, see Rosenzweig, *Eight Hours for What We Will: Workers and Leisure in an Industrial City, 1870–1920*.

16. For the history of the politics of "more," see Currarino, *The Labor Question in America: Economic Democracy in the Gilded Age*, 86–113, and Currarino, "The Politics of 'More': The Labor Question and the Idea of Economic Liberty in Industrial America."

17. Rosenzweig, *Eight Hours for What We Will: Workers and Leisure in an Industrial City, 1870–1920*, 1.

18. Brecher, *Strike!*, 40, 46–48.

19. Brecher, 55–58. On violence deployed against labor, see Loomis, *A History of America in Ten Strikes*, 71–90.

20. U.S. Bureau of the Census, "Selected Historical Decennial Census Population and Housing Counts—Urban and Rural Populations."

21. Tippett, "Mortality and Cause of Death, 1900 v. 2010"; Kens, *Lochner v. New York*, 6–12; Millhiser, *Injustices*, 91–94.

22. Kens, *Lochner v. New York*, 12–14, 58–59.

23. Kens, 65–67; Commons et al., *History of Labour in the United States*, vol. 2, 109–10; Dubofsky and Dulles, *Labor in America*, 96–97.

24. Kens, *Lochner v. New York*, 89–91.

25. Kens, 117, 122–23.

26. Kens, 129–32.

27. Pildes, "Democracy, Anti-Democracy, and the Cannon"; Foner, *The Second Founding.*

28. On the debate over why Lochner is wrong, see Brown, "The Art of Reading Lochner," and Balkin, "Wrong the Day It Was Decided: Lochner and Constitutional Historicism."

29. Kens, *Lochner v. New York*, 147–49.

30. Ginsburg, "Muller v. Oregon: One Hundred Years Later." On multiple eras of Lochner and giant swings, see Bernstein, "Lochner Era Revisionism, Revised: Lochner and the Origins of Fundamental Rights Constitutionalism."

31. Friedman, *A History of American Law*, 270–72; Purdy, "Neoliberal Constitutionalism: Lochnerism for a New Economy," 208–11.

32. For an excellent history and overview of the legal realism approach to law during this period, see Fried, *The Progressive Assault on Laissez Faire: Robert Hale and the First Law and Economics Movement*, 47–59.

33. On ways in which the state created an economy favorable to capital see Moss, *When All Else Fails: Government as the Ultimate Risk Manager*, 53–151. On the question of why labor was singled out by the courts, see Fried, *The Progressive Assault on Laissez Faire: Robert Hale and the First Law and Economics Movement*, 230n19.

34. Menand, *The Metaphysical Club*, 409–33.

3. Free Life

1. *Proceedings of the Casualty Actuarial and Statistical Society of America*, vol. 2, 1–10, 172; Rubinow, "Problems and Possibilities," 289; Rubinow, *The Quest for Security*, 20–21.

2. Moss, *Socializing Security: Progressive-Era Economists and the Origins of American Social Policy*, 2.

3. Bremner, *The Discovery of Poverty in the United States*, 16–30.

4. On the "New View" of poverty, see Bremner, 123–28.

5. Hunter, *Poverty*, vi, 4–5.

6. Patterson, *America's Struggle against Poverty, 1900–1980*, 6–14.

7. Witt, *The Accidental Republic: Crippled Workingmen, Destitute Widows, and the Remaking of American Law*, 2–3, 22–33, 225n30; Janocha and Hopler, "The Facts of the Faller."

8. Kreader, "Isaac Max Rubinow: Pioneering Specialist in Social Insurance";

Rose, *No Right to Be Idle: The Invention of Disability, 1840s–1930s*, 154–61; Rubinow, *Social Insurance: With Special Reference to American Conditions*, iii–iv; Lubove, *The Struggle for Social Security*, 34–35; Rodgers, *Atlantic Crossings: Social Politics in a Progressive Age*, 242–43.

9. Rodgers, *Atlantic Crossings*, 242; Kreader, "Isaac Max Rubinow: Pioneering Specialist in Social Insurance."

10. Rubinow, *Social Insurance: With Special Reference to American Conditions*. For a reference to its influence, see Epstein, *Insecurity, a Challenge to America*, vii.

11. Rubinow, *Social Insurance: With Special Reference to American Conditions*, 11, 16.

12. Rubinow, vii–viii, 17; Kreader, "Isaac Max Rubinow: Pioneering Specialist in Social Insurance," 408–10.

13. Skocpol, *Protecting Soldiers and Mothers: The Political Origins of Social Policy in the United States*, 9; Hacker, *The Divided Welfare State*, 87; Hicks, Misra, and Ng, "The Programmatic Emergence of the Social Security State," 337.

14. For a summary of the debate over why the United States developed a welfare state later than other countries, see Moss, *Socializing Security: Progressive-Era Economists and the Origins of American Social Policy*, 180n17, and Skocpol, *Protecting Soldiers and Mothers*, 254–61.

15. Lubove, *The Struggle for Social Security, 1900–1935*, 1–24.

16. Tocqueville, *Democracy in America*, 595.

17. Beito, *From Mutual Aid to the Welfare State*, 14, 31–39.

18. Balogh, *A Government Out of Sight*, 1–8; Moss, *When All Else Fails: Government as the Ultimate Risk Manager*, 56–57.

19. Katz, *In the Shadow of the Poorhouse*.

20. Skocpol, *Protecting Soldiers and Mothers*; Konczal, "The Voluntarism Fantasy."

21. Lubove, *The Struggle for Social Security, 1900–1935*, 2.

22. Lubove, 1–24; *Proceedings of the First Annual Meeting of the National Fraternal Congress of America*.

23. Rubinow, *Social Insurance: With Special Reference to American Conditions*, 247.

24. Salamon, "Of Market Failure, Voluntary Failure, and Third-Party Government: Toward a Theory of Government-Nonprofit Relations in the Modern Welfare State"; Konczal, "The Voluntarism Fantasy." Though fictional, for an important contemporary example of how private charity can predictably fail to deliver essential goods in our lives, see *The Office*, "Scott's Tots."

25. Rubinow, "Old-Age Pensions and Moral Values: A Reply to Miss Coman."

26. Seager, "Outline of a Program of Social Legislation with Special Reference to Wage-Earners," 93, 98; Seager, *Social Insurance, a Program of Social Reform*, 1–23.

27. Rubinow, *Social Insurance: With Special Reference to American Conditions*, 302–4.

28. Pigou, *The Economics of Welfare*, 162–63, 788–89.

29. Moss, *Socializing Security: Progressive-Era Economists and the Origins of American Social Policy*, 59–76.

30. Lubove, *The Struggle for Social Security, 1900–1935*, 38–44.

31. Lubove, 169–78; Moss, *When All Else Fails: Government as the Ultimate Risk Manager*, 182–88.

32. Rodgers, *Atlantic Crossings*, 257–62.

4. Free Security

1. Perkins, *The Roosevelt I Knew*, 236–39.

2. Martin, *Madam Secretary, Frances Perkins*, 41–53, 74–79; Downey, *The Woman behind the New Deal*, 11–16, 25–32.

3. Martin, *Madam Secretary, Frances Perkins*, 84–90; Downey, *The Woman behind the New Deal*, 33–36.

4. Downey, *The Woman behind the New Deal*, 88–95.

5. Rauchway, *Winter War*, 138–40; Brands, *Traitor to His Class*, 222, 236–38.

6. Roosevelt, *Public Papers of the Presidents of the United States*, vol. 6, 103, 222–25.

7. Roosevelt, 657, 746.

8. Galbraith, *The Great Crash, 1929*, 1; Kennedy, *Freedom from Fear*, 58–59; Rauchway, *The Great Depression and the New Deal*, 55.

9. Kennedy, *Freedom from Fear*, 47–48; Stein, *The Fiscal Revolution in America*, 12–13; Hawley, "Herbert Hoover, the Commerce Secretariat, and the Vision of an 'Associative State,' 1921–1928," 127, 135.

10. For the story on Herbert Hoover, voluntarism, and the early Great Depression, see Hawley, "Herbert Hoover, Associationalism, and the Great Depression Relief Crisis of 1930–1933."

11. Beito, *From Mutual Aid to the Welfare State*, 204–5, 217–20.

12. Cohen, *Making a New Deal*, 218–24, 249, 267–89.

13. Lubove, *The Struggle for Social Security, 1900–1935*, 40; Rubinow, *The Quest for Security*, 339.

14. Patterson, *America's Struggle against Poverty, 1900–1980*, 73–74; Rubinow, *The Quest for Security*, 512; Hacker, *The Divided Welfare State*, 88–90.

15. Social Security History, "Message to Congress Reviewing the Broad Objectives and Accomplishments of the Administration."

16. Kennedy, *Freedom from Fear*, 267; Perkins, *The Roosevelt I Knew*, 266–88.

17. Perkins, "Basic Idea Behind Social Security Program; Miss Perkins Outlines the Theory of Collective Aid to the Individual."

18. Brinkley, *Voices of Protest*, 222–24; Gaydowski, "Eight Letters to the Editor: The Genesis of the Townsend National Recovery Plan"; Mason, "The Townsend Movement." For contemporaneous estimates, see Twentieth Century Fund, *The Townsend Crusade*, 9–10.

19. Aikman, "Townsendism: Old-Time Religion."

20. Leuchtenburg, *Franklin D. Roosevelt and the New Deal, 1932–1940*, 103–5; Old Age Revolving Pensions, Ltd., *Old Age Revolving Pensions, a Proposed National Plan*.

21. Witte, *The Development of the Social Security Act*, 103n65; Cohen, "Random Reflections on the Great Society's Politics and Health Care Programs after Twenty-Years," 118.

22. Old Age Revolving Pensions, Ltd., *Old Age Revolving Pensions, a Proposed National Plan*; Aikman, "Townsendism: Old-Time Religion."

23. Kennedy, *Freedom from Fear*, 296; Leuchtenburg, *Franklin D. Roosevelt and the New Deal, 1932–1940*, 111–14; Zietlow, *Enforcing Equality*, 74.

24. Kennedy, *Freedom from Fear*, 297–98; Leuchtenburg, *Franklin D. Roosevelt and the New Deal*, 150–51, 262. For debates over why the Wagner Act passed, see Plotke, "The Wagner Act, Again: Politics and Labor, 1935–37," and Skocpol, Finegold, and Goldfield, "Explaining New Deal Labor Policy."

25. Zietlow, *Enforcing Equality*, 75–77.

26. Loomis, *A History of America in Ten Strikes*, 121; Kennedy, *Freedom from Fear*, 308–10.

27. Kennedy, *Freedom from Fear*, 310–15; Loomis, *A History of America in Ten Strikes*, 123–28.

28. Shesol, *Supreme Power*, 2–3; Kennedy, *Freedom from Fear*, 331–34.

29. Shesol, *Supreme Power*, 3, 221–29, 429–33; Kennedy, *Freedom from Fear*, 329–32; Brands, *Traitor to His Class*, 470–73. The Republicans were ironically the ones who ran in 1936 against the Supreme Court. Their platform included a plank to "[s]upport the adoption of state laws and interstate compacts to

abolish sweatshops and child labor, and to protect women and children with respect to maximum hours, minimum wages and working conditions. We believe that this can be done within the Constitution as it now stands." The last part was in reference to the Supreme Court attacking popular state-level minimum wage laws, which the Republicans saw as an alternative to federal ones. Herbert Hoover even agreed, stating that "something should be done to give back to the states the power they thought they already had." "Republican Party Platform"; Associated Press, "Hoover Advocates Women's Wage Law."

30. For a recent argument that the Supreme Court was largely sorting out lawyerly disagreements about the role of administration and that the switch was "less a revolution than a reconciliation between the judicial and executive branches," see Ernst, *Tocqueville's Nightmare.*

31. Witte, *The Development of the Social Security Act,* 143–44, 153; Katznelson, *When Affirmative Action Was White,* 59–60; Katznelson, *Fear Itself,* 259–60. There is significant historical debate on what drove these exclusions. For the arguments that weak administrative capacity was the driver for the Social Security old-age pension exclusions, see DeWitt, "The Decision to Exclude Agricultural and Domestic Workers from the 1935 Social Security Act," and Rodems and Shaefer, "Left Out: Policy Diffusion and the Exclusion of Black Workers from Unemployment Insurance."

32. Schickler, *Racial Realignment,* 58–60.

33. Schickler, 63–65; Wade, *The Fiery Cross,* 262–63.

34. "26 Negro Rallies Back Roosevelt," *New York Times*; Schickler, *Racial Realignment,* 50–51; High, *Roosevelt—and Then?,* 198–201; Spencer, "The Good Neighbor League Colored Committee and the 1936 Democratic Presidential Campaign."

35. Ward, "Wooing the Negro Vote."

36. Schickler, *Racial Realignment,* 129–34, 285–86.

37. Farber et al., "Unions and Inequality over the Twentieth Century: New Evidence from Survey Data."

38. Center on Budget and Policy Priorities, "Policy Basics: Top Ten Facts about Social Security"; Schmitt, "Social Security's Enduring Legacy."

39. Foner, *The Story of American Freedom,* 197; Morris, *The Limits of Voluntarism,* xv, 1–3; Putnam, *Bowling Alone,* 54–57, 69–72. There is a conservative critique that public social insurance "crowds outs" and replaces civil society. For one attempted analysis, see Gruber and Hungerman, "Faith-Based Charity

and Crowd-Out during the Great Depression." These arguments don't discuss whether private charity should play this role as insurer, or the numerous ways in which voluntary charity fails as a mechanism for security. (See Salamon, "Of Market Failure, Voluntary Failure, and Third-Party Government: Toward a Theory of Government-Nonprofit Relations in the Modern Welfare State.") More important, this argument is based on importing an intuition about the economy, that private and public investment necessarily substitute against each other, into civil society. This is not how economies themselves work. See Keynes, *The General Theory of Employment, Interest, and Money.* There is zero reason to assume this logic extends over to voluntary sector. What is more likely, as seen in the decades after the New Deal, is that public spending can crowd-in civic life, encouraging more once security is established. This was one of the original arguments for restrictions on working hours in the first place.

40. Kreader, "America's Prophet for Social Security: A Biography of Isaac Max Rubinow," 678–86, 690–98.

5. Free Care

1. Brinkley, *The End of Reform*, 259–64; Stoltzfus, *Citizen, Mother, Worker,* 24–28.
2. Stoltzfus, *Citizen, Mother, Worker,* 24–25.
3. Stoltzfus, 5–6.
4. Furman, "Child Care Plan Taken to Truman"; Fousekis, *Demanding Child Care,* 50.
5. On care work and social reproduction, see Fraser, "Contradictions of Capital and Care," and Jaffe, "The Factory in the Family."
6. Cooper, *Family Values,* 9–15.
7. Fraser, "Between Marketization and Social Protection: Resolving the Feminist Ambivalence," 232–35.
8. On wartime mobilization and the market, see Mason, "The Economy During Wartime"; Bossie and Mason, "The Public Role in Economic Transformation: Lessons from World War II."
9. Hartmann, *The Home Front and Beyond,* 15–18.
10. Hartmann, 21, 77–78; Anderson, *Wartime Women,* 6.
11. Hartmann, *The Home Front and Beyond,* 79–80.
12. Cohen, "A Brief History of Federal Financing for Child Care in the United States," 26–29.

13. Anderson, *Wartime Women*, 5; Cohen, "A Brief History of Federal Financing for Child Care in the United States," 29.

14. Anderson, *Wartime Women*, 122–24; Cohen, "A Brief History of Federal Financing for Child Care in the United States," 29.

15. Michel, *Children's Interests/Mothers' Rights: The Shaping of America's Child Care Policy*, 136–37, 142, 144; Dratch, "The Politics of Child Care in the 1940s," 179–80; Anderson, *Wartime Women*, 130–36; Carr and Stermer, *Willow Run*, 252–56.

16. Anderson, *Wartime Women*, 6, 146; Stoltzfus, *Citizen, Mother, Worker*, 40; Covert, "Here's What Happened the One Time When the U.S. Had Universal Childcare"; Herbst, "Universal Child Care, Maternal Employment, and Children's Long-Run Outcomes: Evidence from the US Lanham Act of 1940."

17. Kesselman, *Fleeting Opportunities*, 71–78; Crawford, "Daily Life on the Home Front: Women, Blacks, and the Struggle for Public Housing," 124–25.

18. Kesselman, *Fleeting Opportunities*, 80–81; Crawford, "Daily Life on the Home Front," 124–27.

19. Stoltzfus, *Citizen, Mother, Worker*, 51.

20. Stoltzfus, 38–44, 47–48, 59.

21. Stoltzfus, 55–56, 68–69, 73–74, 82.

22. Fousekis, *Demanding Child Care*, 44–45, 80–81.

23. Stoltzfus, *Citizen, Mother, Worker*, 38–41.

24. Stoltzfus, 61.

25. Stoltzfus, 61–63.

26. Fousekis, *Demanding Child Care*, 37–42, 88–89.

27. Fousekis, 51–52, 88–89, 107–8.

28. McCaffery, *Taxing Women*, 111–13; Blumberg, "Sexism in the Code: A Comparative Study of Income Taxation of Working Wives and Mothers," 63–65; Klein, "Tax Deductions for Family Care Expenses," 917–19.

29. Stoltzfus, *Citizen, Mother, Worker*, 203, 205.

30. Stoltzfus, 201–6.

31. Samansky, "Child Care Expenses and the Income Tax," 260–61; Blumberg, "Sexism in the Code: A Comparative Study of Income Taxation of Working Wives and Mothers," 72; Wolfman, "Child Care, Work, and the Federal Income Tax," 156.

32. Stoltzfus, *Citizen, Mother, Worker,* 212–13; Wolfman, "Child Care, Work, and the Federal Income Tax," 181–89.

33. For recent numbers on tax expenditures, see Center on Budget and Policy Priorities, "Policy Basics: Federal Tax Expenditures." The political science literature has several different metaphors—submerged, divided, hidden, delegated—for the obfuscating nature of this social insurance system. For multiple approaches, each with a specific focus, see Mettler, *The Submerged State;* Hacker, *The Divided Welfare State;* Howard, *The Hidden Welfare State;* and Morgan and Campbell, *The Delegated Welfare State.*

34. Esping-Andersen, *The Three Worlds of Welfare Capitalism.*

35. Hacker, *The Divided Welfare State,* 36–40; Crandall-Hollick and Falk, "The Child and Dependent Care Credit: Impact of Selected Policy Options," 6.

36. Mettler, *The Submerged State,* 26–28, 38.

37. Michel, *Children's Interests/Mothers' Rights: The Shaping of America's Child Care Policy,* 3.

6. Free Health

1. Herbers, "Medicare Drive on Rights Urged; Negroes Would Deny Funds to Segregated Hospitals."

2. Smith, *The Power to Heal,* 96–97; Dittmer, *The Good Doctors,* 135–36.

3. For more on a capabilities approach to health care, see Venkatapuram, *Health Justice.*

4. Hacker, "Bigger and Better"; Ingraham, "This Chart Is a Powerful Indictment of Our Current Health-Care System"; Rosenthal, "That Beloved Hospital? It's Driving Up Health Care Costs."

5. As the philosopher Bernard Williams describes it, "the proper ground of distribution of medical care is ill health: this is a necessary truth." See Williams, "The Idea of Equality."

6. Hacker, *The Divided Welfare State,* 223–24; Blumenthal and Morone, *The Heart of Power,* 67–69.

7. This and the following quotes are from Truman, "Special Message to the Congress Recommending a Comprehensive Health Program."

8. Starr, *The Social Transformation of American Medicine,* 283–85.

9. Starr, 285–88.

10. Starr, 287–89; Hacker, *The Divided Welfare State,* 222–25, 230–31.

11. Hacker, *The Divided Welfare State,* 237–41.

12. Hacker, 225; Starr, *The Social Transformation of American Medicine*, 348–51.

13. Quadagno and McDonald, "Racial Segregation in Southern Hospitals: How Medicare 'Broke the Back of Segregated Health Services,' " 120–21.

14. Rosenberg, *The Hollow Hope*, 42–43.

15. Rosenberg, 49–52.

16. Rosenberg, 10–21, 50.

17. Quadagno and McDonald, "Racial Segregation in Southern Hospitals: How Medicare 'Broke the Back of Segregated Health Services,' " 121–24.

18. Quadagno and McDonald, 125–26.

19. Hicks, "New Chief of Hospitals: John Lawrence Sullivan Holloman Jr."; "Defender of Health Care for Poor," *New York Times*; Martin, "Dr. John L. S. Holloman Jr. Is Dead at 82; Fought to Improve Health Care for the Poor."

20. Dittmer, *The Good Doctors*, 12–14.

21. Talese, "Selma 1990."

22. Gluck and Reno, "Reflections on Implementing Medicare," 7.

23. Gluck and Reno, 4–5, 49; Zorn, "Ronald Reagan on Medicare, circa 1961. Prescient Rhetoric or Familiar Alarmist Claptrap?"

24. US Commission on Civil Rights, "Title VI, One Year After," 5–6, 14.

25. Quadagno and McDonald, "Racial Segregation in Southern Hospitals: How Medicare 'Broke the Back of Segregated Health Services,' " 127; Gluck and Reno, "Reflections on Implementing Medicare," 8.

26. Smith, *The Power to Heal*, 105–8; Reynolds, "The Federal Government's Use of Title VI and Medicare to Racially Integrate Hospitals in the United States, 1963 through 1967," 1853.

27. Smith, *The Power to Heal*, 109–12, 115; Gluck and Reno, "Reflections on Implementing Medicare," 8.

28. Smith, *The Power to Heal*, 110–12, 116–17.

29. Smith, 121–22.

30. Smith, 128–29.

31. Dittmer, *The Good Doctors*, 133–40; Smith, *The Power to Heal*, 129–30.

32. Tidwell, "The Quiet Revolution"; Smith, *The Power to Heal*, 131.

33. Smith, *The Power to Heal*, 132–33; Reynolds, "The Federal Government's Use of Title VI and Medicare," 1853–55; Gluck and Reno, "Reflections on Implementing Medicare," 8–9.

34. Smith, *The Power to Heal*, 134–35; Reynolds, "The Federal Government's Use of Title VI and Medicare," 1855.

35. Quadagno and McDonald, "Racial Segregation in Southern Hospitals: How Medicare 'Broke the Back of Segregated Health Services,' " 129; Reynolds, "The Federal Government's Use of Title VI and Medicare," 1856; Cohen, "Random Reflections on the Great Society's Politics and Health Care Programs after Twenty-Years."

36. Almond, Chay, and Greenstone, "Civil Rights, the War on Poverty, and Black-White Convergence in Infant Mortality in the Rural South and Mississippi"; U.S. Central Intelligence Agency, "The World Factbook: Country Comparison: Infant Mortality Rate."

37. From an early 2019 estimate, fourteen states did not expand Medicaid, leaving 2.5 million uninsured adults caught in the "coverage gap" between making too much to qualify for Medicaid and not enough to be eligible for ACA exchange subsidies. See Garfield, Orgera, and Damico, "The Coverage Gap: Uninsured Poor Adults in States That Do Not Expand Medicaid." On the purely political maneuvering John Roberts executed on the ACA, see Biskupic, *The Chief,* 221–48.

7. Free Economy

1. Although histories of neoliberalism in the United States often start in the 1980s, examining the 1970s is just as important to understanding how quickly things changed. See Cowie, *Stayin' Alive*; Krippner, *Capitalizing on Crisis*; Stein, *Pivotal Decade*; Barker, "Other People's Blood." On New York City, see Phillips-Fein, *Fear City*.

2. Phillips-Fein, *Invisible Hands*; Hacker and Pierson, *American Amnesia*, 201–37. For more on conservative think tanks as ideological actors, see Rich, *Think Tanks, Public Policy, and the Politics of Expertise*, and Stahl, *Right Moves*.

3. Peck and Tickell, "Neoliberalizing Space."

4. Slobodian, *Globalists*, 2–3. For an important dive into understanding conservatism not as a temperament but as a nostalgic ideological drive for restoring lost power, see Robin, *The Reactionary Mind*.

5. Moss, *When All Else Fails: Government as the Ultimate Risk Manager*, 56–57.

6. Berle and Means, *The Modern Corporation and Private Property*, 1, 3.

7. Berle and Means, 121.

8. Berle and Means, 340–44, emphasis in original.

9. Berle and Means, 140–41, 158–59.

10. Berle and Means, 356. There is a wide range of ideas on how to read Berle

and Means on the weakening of shareholder control. This needs to be contextualized by their book responding to multiple debates at the time, those arguments unfolding under the massive crisis of the Great Depression, and subsequent evolution of their arguments. For one overview of the debates, see Bratton and Wachter, "Shareholder Primacy's Corporatist Origins: Adolf Berle and the Modern Corporation."

11. Hansmann and Kraakman, "The End of History for Corporate Law."

12. Friedman, "A Friedman Doctrine: The Social Responsibility of Business Is to Increase Its Profits," 33.

13. Friedman, 123–126.

14. Stout, *The Shareholder Value Myth*, 37–44; Stout, "Bad and Not-so-Bad Arguments for Shareholder Primacy"; Róna, "Letter in Response to Jensen"; Henwood, *Wall Street: How It Works and for Whom*, 72–76; Mason, "Understanding Short-Termism," which finds that "[t]otal shareholder payouts in 2014 were over $1.2 trillion, while general estimates show that money going from investors to businesses in the form of IPOs and venture capital (VC) is less than $200 billion. This implies that for every $1 invested by finance more than $6 is taken out by finance."

15. Manne, "Mergers and the Market for Corporate Control"; Carney, "The Legacy of the Market for Corporate Control and the Origins of the Theory of the Firm"; Davis, *Managed by the Markets*, 43–44.

16. Meckling and Jensen, "Theory of the Firm: Managerial Behavior, Agency Costs and Ownership Structure," 311.

17. Meckling and Jensen, "Theory of the Firm: Managerial Behavior, Agency Costs and Ownership Structure"; Palladino, "The Economic Argument for Stakeholder Corporations"; Henwood, *Wall Street: How It Works and for Whom*, 269.

18. Mason, "Disgorge the Cash"; Mason, "Disgorge the Cash: The Disconnect between Corporate Borrowing and Investment."

19. Davis, *Managed by the Markets*, 84–85.

20. Grullon, Larkin, and Michaely, "Are US Industries Becoming More Concentrated?"; Konczal, "There Are Too Few Companies and Their Profits Are Too High."

21. Frydman and Saks, "Executive Compensation: A New View from a Long-Term Perspective, 1936–2005"; Bakija, Cole, and Heim, "Jobs and Income Growth of Top Earners and the Causes of Changing Income Inequality:

Evidence from US Tax Return Data"; Philippon and Reshef, "Wages and Human Capital in the US Finance Industry: 1909–2006"; Mason, "Disgorge the Cash," which finds that "[i]n the 1960s and 1970s, an additional dollar of earnings or borrowing was associated with about a 40-cent increase in investment. Since the 1980s, less than 10 cents of each borrowed dollar is invested [. . .] Today, there is a strong correlation between shareholder payouts and borrowing that did not exist before the mid-1980s."

22. Sinnreich, *The Essential Guide to Intellectual Property*, 38–39.

23. Sinnreich, 39.

24. Lessig, *Free Culture*, 116–19; Boyle, "The Second Enclosure Movement and the Construction of the Public Domain."

25. Lindsey and Teles, *The Captured Economy*, 65–66.

26. Sinnreich, *The Essential Guide to Intellectual Property*, 42–43; Gifford, "The Sonny Bono Copyright Term Extension Act."

27. Hatch, "Toward a Principled Approach to Copyright Legislation at the Turn of the Millennium."

28. Sinnreich, *The Essential Guide to Intellectual Property*, 48–49; Lindsey and Teles, *The Captured Economy*, 67.

29. Duhigg and Lohr, "In Technology Wars, Using the Patent as a Sword"; U.S. Executive Office of the President, "Patent Assertion and US Innovation."

30. Watzinger et al., "How Antitrust Enforcement Can Spur Innovation"; U.S. Congress House Committee on the Judiciary, *Report of the Antitrust Subcommittee (Subcommittee No. 5) of the Committee on the Judiciary, House of Representatives, Eighty-Sixth Congress on Consent Decree Program of the Department of Justice*, 317.

31. Lynn, "Estates of Mind."

32. It's tempting to think that simply making ideas and information free and accessible is sufficient to check abuses. But data can only be used by those with the tools and resources to actively deploy it. The larger conversation about how the political movement for restoring the information commons has to reckon with the "romance of the public domain" is outside the scope of this book, though in an age of big data and social media, it should be much more front and center. To start, see Chander and Sunder, "The Romance of the Public Domain"; Taylor, *The People's Platform: Taking Back Power and Culture in the Digital Age*, 172–76; and Mueller, "Digital Proudhonism."

33. Brown and Sibley, *The Theory of Public Utility Pricing*, 1–2; Pepall, Richards,

and Norman, *Industrial Organization*, 70–71; Crew and Kleindorfer, *Public Utility Economics*, 3.

34. Novak, "The Public Utility Idea and the Origins of Modern Business Regulation," 159.

35. Munn v. Illinois, 94 U.S. 113 (1877).

36. Novak, "The Public Utility Idea and the Origins of Modern Business Regulation," 160–63.

37. Novak, "The Public Utility Idea and the Origins of Modern Business Regulation."

38. Rahman, "Infrastructural Regulation and the New Utilities"; Rahman, *Democracy Against Domination*. For this in the context of medicine, see Bagley, "Medicine as a Public Calling." As Bagley notes, "An extraordinary range of market features—the costs of shopping around, bargaining inequalities, informational disadvantage, rampant fraud, collusive pricing, emergency conditions, and more—could all frustrate competition and [. . .] warrant state intervention." This is similar to many of the arguments deployed today around monopsony, the minimum wage, and more.

39. Crew and Kleindorfer, *Public Utility Economics*, 4–5; Brown and Sibley, *The Theory of Public Utility Pricing*, 2–5; Rossi and Ricks, "Foreword to Revisiting the Public Utility"; Appelbaum, *The Economists' Hour*, 136–46, 161–65.

40. For an example of the celebration of lending through the capital markets and the idea that New Deal regulations had become outdated, see Litan and Rauch, *American Finance for the 21st Century*. On the financial crisis as a bank run, see Gorton, *Slapped by the Invisible Hand*.

41. Philippon, *The Great Reversal*, 205.

42. Gutierrez and Philippon, "Investmentless Growth: An Empirical Investigation"; Eggertsson, Robbins, and Wold, "Kaldor and Piketty's Facts: The Rise of Monopoly Power in the United States"; Konczal and Steinbaum, "Declining Entrepreneurship, Labor Mobility, and Business Dynamism: A Demand-Side Approach."

8. Free Education

1. U.S. Congressional Budget Office, "The Distribution of Major Tax Expenditures in the Individual Income Tax System."

2. Brown, *Undoing the Demos*, 155–73; Weil, *The Fissured Workplace: Why Work Became So Bad for So Many and What Can Be Done to Improve It*.

3. Douglass, *The Conditions for Admission*, 5.

4. Richardson, *The Greatest Nation of the Earth*, 155–60.

5. Nemec, *Ivory Towers and Nationalist Minds*, 47–76; Mettler, *Degrees of Inequality*, 6.

6. Association of Public and Land-Grant Universities, "The Land-Grant Tradition."

7. Loss, *Between Citizens and the State*, 112–14.

8. For numbers and the debate over how to interpret race, education, and the GI Bill, see Katznelson and Mettler, "On Race and Policy History: A Dialogue about the GI Bill."

9. Douglass, *The Conditions for Admission*, 5.

10. Douglass, 5–6.

11. Bady and Konczal, "From Master Plan to No Plan: The Slow Death of Public Higher Education"; Reagan, *The Creative Society: Some Comments on Problems Facing America*, 125–27.

12. Rosenfeld, *Subversives*, 1–8, 229–31, 370–72.

13. Rosenfeld, 369, 372–76.

14. Cooper, *Family Values*, 236–38.

15. Phillips-Fein, *Fear City*, 242–43.

16. Phillips-Fein, 138–39, 170.

17. Phillips-Fein, 170, 212–15.

18. Phillips-Fein, 220.

19. Phillips-Fein, 8–9, 211, 218–20. On outsourcing political decisions to financial markets, see Krippner, *Capitalizing on Crisis*.

20. Gelder, "Fred Hechinger, Education Editor and Advocate, Dies at 75"; Hechinger, "Who Killed Free Tuition?"; Phillips-Fein, *Fear City*, 255.

21. Becker, *Human Capital*.

22. Cooper, *Family Values*, 219–23.

23. Foucault, *The Birth of Biopolitics*, 226; Konczal, "How to Waste a Crisis." On the Keynesian ideal of a worker who is also a saver, see Payne, *The Consumer, Credit and Neoliberalism*.

24. Friedman, *Capitalism and Freedom*, 100. The original quotes are about vocational and professional schools, though the logic quickly expanded to all higher education.

25. Friedman, 98–107.

26. Mettler, *Degrees of Inequality*, 52–53; Geiger, *American Higher Education since World War II*, 281–82.

27. Hechinger, "Class War Over Tuition."

28. Geiger, *American Higher Education since World War II*, 285–87.

29. Geiger, 292–93.

30. Geiger, 319; U.S. Federal Reserve Board, "2016 SCF Chartbook."

31. Yellen, "Perspectives on Inequality and Opportunity from the Survey of Consumer Finances"; McKernan et al., "Nine Charts about Wealth Inequality in America."

32. Goldberg, "This Is What Happens When You Slash Funding for Public Universities."

33. Rothstein and Rouse, "Constrained after College: Student Loans and Early-Career Occupational Choices"; Ambrose, Cordell, and Ma, "The Impact of Student Loan Debt on Small Business Formation."

34. Nau, Dwyer, and Hodson, "Can't Afford a Baby?" For a summary of student loan studies, see Fullwiler et al., "The Macroeconomic Effects of Student Debt Cancellation." For a more recent study of the impact of loans on families today, see Zaloom, *Indebted*.

35. Krajeski, "It Takes a Community College."

Conclusion

1. Pyke, "Taking the Fight for $15 to the Old Confederacy."

2. Goldstein, "It's More Than Pay: Striking Teachers Demand Counselors and Nurses"; Goldstein, "West Virginia Teachers Walk Out (Again) and Score a Win in Hours"; Cohen, "Los Angeles Teachers Poised to Strike."

3. Wykstra, "The Movement to Make Workers' Schedules More Humane."

4. Holmberg, "Workers on Corporate Boards? Germany's Had Them for Decades"; Block and Sachs, "Clean Slate for Worker Power: Building a Just Economy and Democracy"; Campbell, "Warren Just Released the Most Ambitious Labor Reform Platform of the 2020 Campaign."

5. Wu, "Network Neutrality, Broadband Discrimination"; Malmgren, "The New Sewer Socialists."

6. Tarnoff, "A Socialist Plan to Fix the Internet." For an important paper that rebooted much of this conversation, see Khan, "Amazon's Antitrust Paradox." Senator Elizabeth Warren phrases the sports analogy this way: "You can run

the platform—that is, you can be the umpire in the baseball game and you can run an honest platform. Or you can be a player, that is, you can have a business or you can have a team in the game. But you don't get to be the umpire and have a team in the game." See Beauchamp, "Elizabeth Warren's Really Simple Case for Breaking up Big Tech."

7. Iber and Konczal, "Karl Polanyi for President."

8. Jackson, "6 Promises Trump Has Made about Health Care."

9. Heller, "The Hidden Cost of GoFundMe Health Care"; Petersen, "The Real Peril of Crowdfunding Health Care."

10. The international scope of the protests against the marketization of higher education gets lost in US discussions. For excellent coverage, see Jaffe, "Red Squares Everywhere"; Loofbourow, "No to Profit."

11. Goldstein, "Bill de Blasio's Pre-K Crusade."

12. Bruenig, "Who Was Poor in 2016 and Why Our System Keeps Failing Them." On the effects of basic income experiments, see Marinescu, "No Strings Attached: The Behavioral Effects of U.S. Unconditional Cash Transfer Programs."

13. Kolozi, *Conservatives Against Capitalism*, 12–21, 145–47.

BIBLIOGRAPHY

Aikman, Duncan. "Townsendism: Old-Time Religion." *New York Times Maga-zine*, March 8, 1936.

Almond, Douglas, Kenneth Y. Chay, and Michael Greenstone. "Civil Rights, the War on Poverty, and Black-White Convergence in Infant Mortality in the Rural South and Mississippi," MIT Department of Economics Working Paper No. 07-04, December 31, 2006.

Ambrose, Brent W., Larry Cordell, and Shuwei Ma. "The Impact of Student Loan Debt on Small Business Formation." FRB of Philadelphia Working Paper No. 15-26, July 22, 2015.

Anderson, Elizabeth. *Private Government: How Employers Rule Our Lives (and Why We Don't Talk About It)*. Princeton, NJ: Princeton University Press, 2017.

Anderson, Karen. *Wartime Women: Sex Roles, Family Relations, and the Status of Women During World War II*. Westport, CT: Greenwood Press, 1981.

Appelbaum, Binyamin. *The Economists' Hour: False Prophets, Free Markets, and the Fracture of Society*. New York: Little, Brown and Company, 2019.

Associated Press. "Hoover Advocates Women's Wage Law." *New York Times*, June 7, 1936.

Association of Public and Land-Grant Universities. "The Land-Grant Tradition." Washington, DC: Association of Public and Land-Grant Universities, 2012.

Bady, Aaron, and Mike Konczal. "From Master Plan to No Plan: The Slow Death of Public Higher Education." *Dissent* 59, no. 4 (Fall 2012): 10–16.

Bagley, Nicholas. "Medicine as a Public Calling." *Michigan Law Review* 114 (2015): 57–106.

Bakija, Jon, Adam Cole, and Bradley T. Heim. "Jobs and Income Growth of Top Earners and the Causes of Changing Income Inequality: Evidence from US Tax Return Data," April 2012.

Balkin, Jack M. "Wrong the Day It Was Decided: Lochner and Constitutional Historicism." *Boston University Law Review* 85 (2005): 677–725.

Balogh, Brian. *A Government Out of Sight: The Mystery of National Authority in Nineteenth-Century America*. Cambridge: Cambridge University Press, 2009.

Banner, Stuart. *How the Indians Lost Their Land: Law and Power on the Frontier*. Cambridge, MA: Harvard University Press, 2005.

Barker, Tim. "Other People's Blood." *N+1*, Spring 2019. https://nplusonemag .com/issue-34/reviews/other-peoples-blood-2.

Beauchamp, Zack. "Elizabeth Warren's Really Simple Case for Breaking Up Big Tech." *Vox*, April 22, 2019.

Becker, Gary S. *Human Capital: A Theoretical and Empirical Analysis, with Special Reference to Education*. Chicago: University of Chicago Press, 2009.

Beito, David T. *From Mutual Aid to the Welfare State: Fraternal Societies and Social Services, 1890–1967*. Chapel Hill: University of North Carolina Press, 2000.

Bergmann, Barbara R. "A Swedish-Style Welfare State or Basic Income: Which Should Have Priority?" *Politics & Society* 32, no. 1 (March 2004): 107–18.

Berle, Adolf A., and Gardiner C. Means. *The Modern Corporation and Private Property*. New York: Macmillan, 1933.

Berlin, Isaiah. "Two Concepts of Liberty." In *Liberty Reader*, edited by David Miller, 33–57. Boulder, CO: Paradigm Publishers, 2006.

Bernstein, David E. "Lochner Era Revisionism, Revised: Lochner and the Origins of Fundamental Rights Constitutionalism." *Georgetown Law Journal* 92, no. 1 (April 2003).

Bernstein, Leonard. "The Working People of Philadelphia from Colonial Times to the General Strike of 1835." *The Pennsylvania Magazine of History and Biography* 74, no. 3 (July 1950): 322–39.

Biskupic, Joan. *The Chief: The Life and Turbulent Times of Chief Justice John Roberts*. New York: Basic Books, 2019.

Blumberg, Grace. "Sexism in the Code: A Comparative Study of Income Taxation of Working Wives and Mothers." *Buffalo Law Review* 21 (1971): 49–98.

Blumenthal, David, and James Morone. *The Heart of Power: Health and Politics in the Oval Office*. Berkeley: University of California Press, 2009.

Bossie, Andrew, and J.W. Mason. "The Public Role in Economic Transformation: Lessons from World War II." Roosevelt Institute, March 2020.

Boyle, James. "The Second Enclosure Movement and the Construction of the Public Domain." *Law and Contemporary Problems* 66, no. 1 (Winter–Spring 2003): 33–74.

Brands, H. W. *Traitor to His Class: The Privileged Life and Radical Presidency of Franklin Delano Roosevelt.* New York: Anchor Books, 2009.

Bratton, William W., and Michael L. Wachter. "Shareholder Primacy's Corporatist Origins: Adolf Berle and the Modern Corporation." *Journal of Corporate Law* 34 (2008): 99–152.

Brecher, Jeremy. *Strike!* Oakland, CA: PM Press, 2014.

Bremner, Robert H. *The Discovery of Poverty in the United States.* New Brunswick, NJ: Transaction Publishers, 1992.

Brinkley, Alan. *The End of Reform: New Deal Liberalism in Recession and War.* New York: Vintage Books, 1996.

———. *Voices of Protest: Huey Long, Father Coughlin, and the Great Depression.* New York: Vintage Books, 1983.

Bronstein, Jamie L. *Land Reform and Working-Class Experience in Britain and the United States, 1800–1862.* Stanford, CA: Stanford University Press, 1999.

Brown, Rebecca L. "The Art of Reading Lochner." *NYU Journal of Law & Liberty* 1, no. 1 (Summer 2005): 570–89.

Brown, Stephen J., and David S. Sibley. *The Theory of Public Utility Pricing.* Cambridge: Cambridge University Press, 1986.

Brown, Wendy. *Undoing the Demos: Neoliberalism's Stealth Revolution.* New York: Zone Books, 2015.

Bruenig, Matt. "Who Was Poor in 2016 and Why Our System Keeps Failing Them." *People's Policy Project*, September 12, 2017. https://www.peoplespolicy project.org/2017/09/12/who-was-in-poverty-in-2016.

Cahill, Marion Cotter. *Shorter Hours: A Study of the Movement Since the Civil War.* New York: Columbia University Press, 1932.

Campbell, Alexia Fernández. "Warren Just Released the Most Ambitious Labor Reform Platform of the 2020 Campaign." *Vox*, October 3, 2019.

Carney, William J. "The Legacy of the Market for Corporate Control and the Origins of the Theory of the Firm." *Case Western Reserve Law Review* 50, no. 2 (1999): 215–44.

Carr, Lowell Juilliard, and James Edson Stermer. *Willow Run: A Study of Industrialization and Cultural Inadequacy.* New York: Harper, 1952.

Center on Budget and Policy Priorities. "Policy Basics: Federal Tax Expenditures." Center on Budget and Policy Priorities, November 18, 2019. https://www .cbpp.org/research/federal-tax/policy-basics-federal-tax-expenditures.

———. "Policy Basics: Top Ten Facts about Social Security." Center on

Budget and Policy Priorities, August 14, 2019. https://www.cbpp.org/research /social-security/policy-basics-top-ten-facts-about-social-security.

Chander, Anupam, and Madhavi Sunder. "The Romance of the Public Domain." *California Law Review* 92 (2004): 1331–74.

Cohen, Abby J. "A Brief History of Federal Financing for Child Care in the United States." *The Future of Children* 6, no. 2 (Summer/Fall 1996): 26–40.

Cohen, G. A. "Freedom and Money." In *On the Currency of Egalitarian Justice, and Other Essays in Political Philosophy*, 166–92. Princeton, NJ: Princeton University Press, 2011.

Cohen, Lizabeth. *Making a New Deal: Industrial Workers in Chicago, 1919–1939*. Cambridge: Cambridge University Press, 1990.

Cohen, Rachel M. "Los Angeles Teachers Poised to Strike." *The American Prospect*, January 7, 2019.

Cohen, W. "Random Reflections on the Great Society's Politics and Health Care Programs After Twenty-Years." In *The Great Society and Its Legacy: Twenty Years of United States Social Policy*, edited by Marshall Kaplan and Peggy Cuciti, 113–20. Durham, NC: Duke University Press, 1986.

Commons, John R., Ulrich B. Phillips, Eugene A. Gilmore, Helen L. Sumner, and John B. Andrews, eds. *A Documentary History of American Industrial Society*. Vol. 6. Cleveland, OH: Arthur H. Clark, 1910.

Commons, John R., David J. Saposs, Helen L. Sumner, E.B. Mittelman, H.E. Hoagland, John B. Andrews, and Selig Perlman. *History of Labour in the United States*. Vol. 2. New York: Macmillan, 1918.

Cooper, Melinda. *Family Values: Between Neoliberalism and the New Social Conservatism*. New York: Zone Books, 2017.

Covert, Bryce. "Here's What Happened the One Time When the U.S. Had Universal Childcare." *Think Progress* (blog), September 30, 2014. https:// thinkprogress.org/heres-what-happened-the-one-time-when-the-u-s-had-uni versal-childcare-c965a3178112.

Cowie, Jefferson. *Stayin' Alive: The 1970s and the Last Days of the Working Class*. New York: New Press, 2010.

Crandall-Hollick, Margot L., and Gene Falk. "The Child and Dependent Care Credit: Impact of Selected Policy Options." Congressional Research Service, December 5, 2017.

Crawford, Margaret. "Daily Life on the Home Front: Women, Blacks, and the Struggle for Public Housing." In *World War II and the American Dream*, edited by Donald Albrecht, 90–143, Cambridge, MA: National Building Museum, 1995.

Crew, Michael A., and Paul R. Kleindorfer. *Public Utility Economics*. New York: St. Martin's Press, 1979.

Currarino, Rosanne. *The Labor Question in America: Economic Democracy in the Gilded Age*. Urbana: University of Illinois Press, 2011.

———. "The Politics of 'More': The Labor Question and the Idea of Economic Liberty in Industrial America." *The Journal of American History* 93, no. 1 (June 2006): 17–36.

Davis, Gerald F. *Managed by the Markets: How Finance Reshaped America*. Oxford: Oxford University Press, 2009.

Deverell, William F. "To Loosen the Safety Valve: Eastern Workers and Western Lands." *The Western Historical Quarterly* 19, no. 3 (August 1988): 269–85.

DeWitt, Larry. "The Decision to Exclude Agricultural and Domestic Workers from the 1935 Social Security Act." *Social Security Bulletin* 70, no. 4 (2010): 49–68.

Dittmer, John. *The Good Doctors: The Medical Committee for Human Rights and the Struggle for Social Justice in Health Care*. New York: Bloomsbury Press, 2009.

Douglass, John Aubrey. *The Conditions for Admission: Access, Equity, and the Social Contract of Public Universities*. Stanford, CA: Stanford University Press, 2007.

Downey, Kirstin. *The Woman Behind the New Deal: The Life and Legacy of Frances Perkins—Social Security, Unemployment Insurance, and the Minimum Wage*. New York: Anchor Books, 2010.

Dratch, Howard. "The Politics of Child Care in the 1940s." *Science & Society* 38, no. 2 (Summer 1974): 167–204.

Du Bois, W.E.B. *Black Reconstruction in America, 1860-1880*. New York: The Free Press, 1998.

Dubofsky, Melvyn, and Foster Rhea Dulles. *Labor in America: A History*. 8th ed. Wheeling, IL: Harlan Davidson, 2010.

Duhigg, Charles, and Steve Lohr. "In Technology Wars, Using the Patent as a Sword." *New York Times*, October 7, 2012.

Dworkin, Ronald. "What Is Equality? Part 2: Equality of Resources." *Philosophy & Public Affairs* 10, no. 4 (Autumn 1981): 283–345.

Eggertsson, Gauti B., Jacob A. Robbins, and Ella Getz Wold. "Kaldor and Piketty's Facts: The Rise of Monopoly Power in the United States." Washington Center for Equitable Growth, February 2018.

Epstein, Abraham. *Insecurity, a Challenge to America: A Study of Social Insurance in the United States and Abroad.* New York: H. Smith and R. Haas, 1933.

Ernst, Daniel R. *Tocqueville's Nightmare: The Administrative State Emerges in America, 1900–1940.* Oxford: Oxford University Press, 2014.

Esping-Andersen, Gøsta. *The Three Worlds of Welfare Capitalism.* Princeton, NJ: Princeton University Press, 1990.

Farber, Henry S., Daniel Herbst, Ilyana Kuziemko, and Suresh Naidu. "Unions and Inequality over the Twentieth Century: New Evidence from Survey Data." National Bureau of Economic Research, May 2018.

Foner, Eric. *Reconstruction: America's Unfinished Revolution, 1863–1877.* New York: Harper & Row, 1988.

———. *The Second Founding: How the Civil War and Reconstruction Remade the Constitution.* New York: W.W. Norton, 2019.

———. *The Story of American Freedom.* New York: W.W. Norton, 1998.

———. *Tom Paine and Revolutionary America.* New York: Oxford University Press, 1976.

Forrester, Katrina. *In the Shadow of Justice: Postwar Liberalism and the Remaking of Political Philosophy.* Princeton, NJ: Princeton University Press, 2019.

Foucault, Michel. *The Birth of Biopolitics: Lectures at the Collège de France, 1978–1979.* Edited by Michel Senellart. Translated by Graham Burchell. Basingstoke, UK: Palgrave Macmillan, 2008.

Fousekis, Natalie M. *Demanding Child Care: Women's Activism and the Politics of Welfare, 1940–1971.* Urbana: University of Illinois Press, 2011.

Fraser, Nancy. "Between Marketization and Social Protection: Resolving the Feminist Ambivalence." In *Fortunes of Feminism: From State-Managed Capitalism to Neoliberal Crisis.* Brooklyn, NY: Verso Books, 2013.

———. "Contradictions of Capital and Care." *New Left Review* 100 (August 2016): 99–117.

Fried, Barbara. *The Progressive Assault on Laissez Faire: Robert Hale and the First Law and Economics Movement.* Cambridge, MA: Harvard University Press, 1998.

Friedman, Lawrence M. *A History of American Law.* 3rd ed. New York: Simon and Schuster, 2005.

Friedman, Milton. "A Friedman Doctrine: The Social Responsibility of Business Is to Increase Its Profits." *New York Times Magazine*, September 13, 1970, 32–33, 123–26.

———. *Capitalism and Freedom*. Chicago: University of Chicago Press, 1962.

Frydman, Carola, and Raven E. Saks. "Executive Compensation: A New View from a Long-Term Perspective, 1936–2005." *The Review of Financial Studies* 23, no. 5 (2010): 2099–2138.

Fullwiler, Scott, Stephanie A. Kelton, Catherine Ruetschlin, and Marshall Steinbaum. "The Macroeconomic Effects of Student Debt Cancellation." Levy Economics Institute, February 2018.

Furman, Bess. "Child Care Plan Taken to Truman." *New York Times*, September 26, 1945.

Galbraith, John Kenneth. *The Great Crash, 1929*. Boston: Houghton Mifflin, 1997.

Garfield, Richard, Kendal Orgera, and Anthony Damico. "The Coverage Gap: Uninsured Poor Adults in States That Do Not Expand Medicaid." Henry J. Kaiser Family Foundation, March 2019. https://www.kff.org/medicaid/issue -brief/the-coverage-gap-uninsured-poor-adults-in-states-that-do-not-expand -medicaid.

Gates, Paul Wallace. "Federal Land Policy in the South 1866–1888." *The Journal of Southern History* 6, no. 3 (August 1940): 303–30.

———. *History of Public Land Law Development*. Washington, DC: U.S. Government Printing Office, 1968.

———. "The Homestead Law in an Incongruous Land System." *The American Historical Review* 41, no. 4 (July 1936): 652–81.

Gaydowski, John Duffy. "Eight Letters to the Editor: The Genesis of the Townsend National Recovery Plan." *Southern California Quarterly* 52, no. 4 (December 1970): 365–82.

Geiger, Roger L. *American Higher Education Since World War II: A History*. Princeton, NJ: Princeton University Press, 2019.

Gelder, Lawrence Van. "Fred Hechinger, Education Editor and Advocate, Dies at 75." *New York Times*, November 7, 1995.

Gifford, Christina N. "The Sonny Bono Copyright Term Extension Act." *University of Memphis Law Review* 30 (1999): 363.

Ginsburg, Ruth Bader. "Muller v. Oregon: One Hundred Years Later." *Willamette Law Review* 45, no. 3 (Spring 2009): 359–80.

Glickman, Lawrence. "Workers of the World, Consume: Ira Steward and the Origins of Labor Consumerism." *International Labor and Working-Class History* 52 (Fall 1997): 72–86.

Glickman, Lawrence B. *A Living Wage: American Workers and the Making of Consumer Society*. Ithaca, NY: Cornell University Press, 1997.

Gluck, Michael E., and Virginia P. Reno, eds. "Reflections on Implementing Medicare." National Academy of Social Insurance, January 2001.

Goldberg, Michelle. "This Is What Happens When You Slash Funding for Public Universities." *The Nation*, May 19, 2015.

Goldstein, Dana. "Bill de Blasio's Pre-K Crusade." *The Atlantic*, September 7, 2016.

———. "It's More Than Pay: Striking Teachers Demand Counselors and Nurses." *New York Times*, October 24, 2019.

———. "West Virginia Teachers Walk Out (Again) and Score a Win in Hours." *New York Times*, February 19, 2019.

Goodman, Paul. "The Emergence of Homestead Exemption in the United States: Accommodation and Resistance to the Market Revolution, 1840–1880." *The Journal of American History* 80, no. 2 (September 1993): 470–98.

Gorton, Gary B. *Slapped by the Invisible Hand: The Panic of 2007*. Oxford: Oxford University Press, 2010.

Gourevitch, Alex. *From Slavery to the Cooperative Commonwealth: Labor and Republican Liberty in the Nineteenth Century*. New York: Cambridge University Press, 2015.

———. "Labor and Republican Liberty." *Constellations* 18, no. 3 (September 2011): 431–54.

———. "The Limits of a Basic Income: Means and Ends of Workplace Democracy." *Basic Income Studies* 11, no. 1 (June 2016): 17–28.

Graeber, David. *The Democracy Project: A History, a Crisis, a Movement*. New York: Spiegel & Grau, 2013.

Gruber, Jonathan, and Daniel M. Hungerman. "Faith-Based Charity and Crowdout During the Great Depression." *Journal of Public Economics* 91, no. 5 (June 2007): 1043–69.

Grullon, Gustavo, Yelena Larkin, and Roni Michaely. "Are US Industries Becoming More Concentrated?" *Review of Finance* 23, no. 4 (2019): 697–743.

Gutierrez, German, and Thomas Philippon. "Investmentless Growth: An Empirical Investigation." *Brookings Papers on Economic Activity*, Fall 2017: 89–169.

Hacker, Jacob S. "Bigger and Better." *The American Prospect*, April 19, 2005.

———. *The Divided Welfare State: The Battle over Public and Private Social Benefits in the United States*. New York: Cambridge University Press, 2002.

Hacker, Jacob S., and Paul Pierson. *American Amnesia: How the War on Government Led Us to Forget What Made America Prosper*. New York: Simon and Schuster, 2016.

Hägglund, Martin. *This Life: Secular Faith and Spiritual Freedom*. New York: Pantheon Books, 2019.

Hansmann, Henry, and Reinier Kraakman. "The End of History for Corporate Law." *Georgetown Law Journal* 89 (2001): 439–68.

Hartmann, Susan M. *The Home Front and Beyond: American Women in the 1940s*. Boston: Twayne Publishers, 1982.

Hatch, Orrin G. "Toward a Principled Approach to Copyright Legislation at the Turn of the Millennium." *University of Pittsburgh Law Review* 59 (1997): 719–34.

Hawley, Ellis W. "Herbert Hoover, Associationalism, and the Great Depression Relief Crisis of 1930–1933." In *With Us Always: A History of Private Charity and Public Welfare*, edited by Donald T. Critchlow and Charles H. Parker, 161–90. Lanham, MD: Rowman and Littlefield Publishers, 1998.

———. "Herbert Hoover, the Commerce Secretariat, and the Vision of an 'Associative State,' 1921–1928." *The Journal of American History* 61, no. 1 (June 1974): 116–40.

Hechinger, Fred M. "Class War over Tuition." *New York Times*, February 5, 1974.

———. "Who Killed Free Tuition?" *New York Times*, May 18, 1976.

Heller, Nathan. "The Hidden Cost of GoFundMe Health Care." *New Yorker*, July 1, 2019.

Henwood, Doug. *Wall Street: How It Works and for Whom*. London: Verso, 1997.

Herbers, John. "Medicare Drive on Rights Urged; Negroes Would Deny Funds to Segregated Hospitals." *New York Times*, December 17, 1965.

Herbst, Chris M. "Universal Child Care, Maternal Employment, and Children's Long-Run Outcomes: Evidence from the US Lanham Act of 1940." *Journal of Labor Economics* 35, no. 2 (April 2017): 519–64.

Hertel-Fernandez, Alex. *Politics at Work: How Companies Turn Their Workers into Lobbyists*. New York: Oxford University Press, 2018.

Hicks, Alexander, Joya Misra, and Tang Nah Ng. "The Programmatic Emergence of the Social Security State." *American Sociological Review* 60, no. 3 (June 1995): 329–49.

Hicks, Nancy. "New Chief of Hospitals: John Lawrence Sullivan Holloman Jr." *New York Times*, March 15, 1974.

High, Stanley. *Roosevelt—and Then?* Freeport, NY: Books for Libraries Press, 1971.

Holmberg, Susan R. "Workers on Corporate Boards? Germany's Had Them for Decades." *New York Times,* January 6, 2019.

Howard, Christopher. *The Hidden Welfare State.* Princeton, NJ: Princeton University Press, 1997.

Howe, Daniel Walker. *The Political Culture of the American Whigs.* Chicago: University of Chicago Press, 1979.

———. *What Hath God Wrought: The Transformation of America, 1815–1848.* New York: Oxford University Press, 2007.

Hughes, Chris. *Fair Shot: Rethinking Inequality and How We Earn.* New York: St. Martin's Press, 2018.

Hunnicutt, Benjamin Kline. *Work without End: Abandoning Shorter Hours for the Right to Work.* Philadelphia: Temple University Press, 1988.

Hunter, Robert. *Poverty.* New York: Macmillan, 1904.

Iber, Patrick, and Michael Konczal. "Karl Polanyi for President." *Dissent,* May 23, 2016.

Ingraham, Christopher. "This Chart Is a Powerful Indictment of Our Current Health-Care System." *Washington Post,* March 8, 2017.

Jackson, Henry C. "6 Promises Trump Has Made About Health Care." *Politico,* March 13, 2017. https://politi.co/2Ok3ASP.

Jaffe, Sarah. "Red Squares Everywhere." *In These Times,* July 9, 2012. http://inthese times.com/article/13470/red_squares_everywhere.

———. "The Factory in the Family." *The Nation,* March 14, 2018.

Janocha, Jill, and Caleb Hopler. "The Facts of the Faller: Occupational Injuries, Illnesses, and Fatalities to Loggers 2006–2015." *Beyond the Numbers: Workplace Injuries* 7, no. 5 (April 2018). https://www.bls.gov/opub/btn/volume-7 /the-facts-of-the-faller-occupational-injuries-illnesses-and-fatalities-to-log gers-2006-2015.htm.

Julian, George Washington. *Speeches on Political Questions.* New York: Hurd and Houghton, 1872.

Karp, Matthew. *This Vast Southern Empire.* Cambridge, MA: Harvard University Press, 2016.

Katz, Michael B. *In the Shadow of the Poorhouse: A Social History of Welfare in America.* New York: Basic Books, 1996.

Katznelson, Ira. *Fear Itself: The New Deal and the Origins of Our Time.* New York: Liveright Publishing, 2013.

———. *When Affirmative Action Was White: An Untold History of Racial Inequality in Twentieth-Century America.* New York: W.W. Norton, 2005.

Katznelson, Ira, and Suzanne Mettler. "On Race and Policy History: A Dialogue About the GI Bill." *Perspectives on Politics* 6, no. 3 (September 2008): 519–37.

Kennedy, David M. *Freedom from Fear: The American People in Depression and War, 1929–1945.* New York: Oxford University Press, 1999.

Kens, Paul. *Lochner v. New York: Economic Regulation on Trial.* Lawrence: University Press of Kansas, 1998.

Kesselman, Amy Vita. *Fleeting Opportunities: Women Shipyard Workers in Portland and Vancouver During World War II and Reconversion.* Albany: State University of New York Press, 1990.

Keynes, John Maynard. *The General Theory of Employment, Interest, and Money.* New York: Springer, 2018.

Khan, Lina M. "Amazon's Antitrust Paradox." *Yale Law Journal* 126, no. 3 (January 2017): 710–805.

Kight, Stef W. "Exclusive Poll: Young Americans Are Embracing Socialism." *Axios,* March 10, 2019. https://www.axios.com/exclusive-poll-young-americans-em bracing-socialism-b051907a-87a8-4f61-9e6e-0db75f7edc4a.html.

Klein, William A. "Tax Deductions for Family Care Expenses." *Boston College Industrial and Commercial Law Review* 14 (1972): 917–41.

Kolozi, Peter. *Conservatives Against Capitalism: From the Industrial Revolution to Globalization.* New York: Columbia University Press, 2017.

Konczal, Mike. "How to Waste a Crisis." *The New Inquiry,* November 26, 2013. https://thenewinquiry.com/how-to-waste-a-crisis.

———. "Parsing the Data and Ideology of the We Are 99% Tumblr." *Rortybomb* (blog), October 9, 2011. https://rortybomb.wordpress.com/2011/10/09/pars ing-the-data-and-ideology-of-the-we-are-99-tumblr.

———. "The Voluntarism Fantasy." *Democracy,* no. 32 (Spring 2014).

———. "There Are Too Few Companies and Their Profits Are Too High." *The Nation,* July 12, 2019.

Konczal, Mike, and Marshall Steinbaum. "Declining Entrepreneurship, Labor Mobility, and Business Dynamism: A Demand-Side Approach." Roosevelt Institute, July 2016.

Krajeski, Jenna. "It Takes a Community College." *New Yorker*, October 27, 2009.

Kreader, J. Lee. "America's Prophet for Social Security: A Biography of Isaac Max Rubinow." PhD diss., University of Chicago, 1988.

———. "Isaac Max Rubinow: Pioneering Specialist in Social Insurance." *Social Service Review* 50, no. 3 (1976): 402–25.

Krippner, Greta R. *Capitalizing on Crisis: The Political Origins of the Rise of Finance.* Cambridge, MA: Harvard University Press, 2011.

Lause, Mark A. *Young America: Land, Labor, and the Republican Community.* Urbana: University of Illinois Press, 2005.

Lessig, Lawrence. *Free Culture: How Big Media Uses Technology and the Law to Lock Down Culture and Control Creativity.* New York: Penguin, 2004.

Leuchtenburg, William Edward. *Franklin D. Roosevelt and the New Deal, 1932–1940.* New York: Harper & Row, 1963.

Lindsey, Brink, and Steven M. Teles. *The Captured Economy: How the Powerful Enrich Themselves, Slow Down Growth, and Increase Inequality.* New York: Oxford University Press, 2017.

Litan, Robert E., and Jonathan Rauch. *American Finance for the 21st Century.* Washington, DC: Brookings Institution Press, 1998.

Loofbourow, Lili. "No to Profit." *Boston Review*, May 16, 2013. http://boston review.net/world/%E2%80%9Cno-profit%E2%80%9D.

Loomis, Erik. *A History of America in Ten Strikes.* New York: New Press, 2018.

Loss, Christopher P. *Between Citizens and the State: The Politics of American Higher Education in the 20th Century.* Princeton, NJ: Princeton University Press, 2012.

Lowrey, Annie. *Give People Money: How a Universal Basic Income Would End Poverty, Revolutionize Work, and Remake the World.* New York: Crown, 2018.

Lubove, Roy. *The Struggle for Social Security, 1900–1935.* 2nd ed. Pittsburgh, PA: University of Pittsburgh Press, 1986.

Lynn, Barry C. "Estates of Mind." *Washington Monthly*, July/August 2013.

Mackenzie, W. "A Winter Journey Through the Canadas." *New-York Tribune*, April 24, 1849.

Malmgren, Evan. "The New Sewer Socialists." *Logic*, December 1, 2017.

Manne, Henry G. "Mergers and the Market for Corporate Control." *Journal of Political Economy* 73, no. 2 (April 1965): 110–20.

Marinescu, Ioana. "No Strings Attached: The Behavioral Effects of U.S. Unconditional Cash Transfer Programs." Roosevelt Institute, May 2017.

Martin, Douglas. "Dr. John L. S. Holloman Jr. Is Dead at 82; Fought to Improve Health Care for the Poor." *New York Times*, March 2, 2002.

Martin, George Whitney. *Madam Secretary, Frances Perkins.* Boston: Houghton Mifflin, 1976.

Mason, Bruce. "The Townsend Movement." *The Southwestern Social Science Quarterly* 35, no. 1 (June 1954): 36–47.

Mason, J.W. "Disgorge the Cash." *The New Inquiry*, April 21, 2014. https://the newinquiry.com/disgorge-the-cash.

———. "Disgorge the Cash: The Disconnect Between Corporate Borrowing and Investment." Roosevelt Institute, February 2015.

———. "Public Options: The General Case." *The Slack Wire* (blog), September 5, 2010. https://jwmason.org/slackwire/public-options-general-case.

———. "The Economy During Wartime." *Dissent* 64, no. 4 (Fall 2017): 140–44.

———. "Understanding Short-Termism." Roosevelt Institute, November 2015.

McCaffery, Edward J. *Taxing Women.* Chicago: University of Chicago Press, 2007.

McKernan, Signe-Mary, Caroline Ratcliffe, C. Eugene Steuerle, Caleb Quakenbush, and Emma Kalish. "Nine Charts About Wealth Inequality in America." Urban Institute, October 5, 2017. http://urbn.is/wealthcharts.

Meckling, William H., and Michael C. Jensen. "Theory of the Firm: Managerial Behavior, Agency Costs and Ownership Structure." *Journal of Financial Economics* 3, no. 4 (October 1976): 305–60.

Menand, Louis. *The Metaphysical Club.* New York: Farrar, Straus, and Giroux, 2001.

Merritt, Keri Leigh. "Land and the Roots of African-American Poverty." *Aeon*, March 11, 2016. https://aeon.co/ideas/land-and-the-roots-of-african-american -poverty.

Mettler, Suzanne. *Degrees of Inequality: How the Politics of Higher Education Sabotaged the American Dream.* New York: Basic Books, 2014.

———. *The Submerged State: How Invisible Government Policies Undermine American Democracy.* Chicago: University of Chicago Press, 2011.

Michel, Sonya. *Children's Interests/Mothers' Rights: The Shaping of America's Child Care Policy.* New Haven, CT: Yale University Press, 1999.

Millhiser, Ian. *Injustices: The Supreme Court's History of Comforting the Comfortable and Afflicting the Afflicted.* New York: Nation Books, 2015.

Morgan, Kimberly J., and Andrea Louise Campbell. *The Delegated Welfare State:*

Medicare, Markets, and the Governance Of Social Policy. New York: Oxford University Press, 2011.

Morris, Andrew J. F. *The Limits of Voluntarism: Charity and Welfare from the New Deal Through the Great Society.* Cambridge: Cambridge University Press, 2009.

Moss, David A. *Socializing Security: Progressive-Era Economists and the Origins of American Social Policy.* Cambridge, MA: Harvard University Press, 1996.

———. *When All Else Fails: Government as the Ultimate Risk Manager.* Cambridge, MA: Harvard University Press, 2002.

Mueller, Gavin. "Digital Proudhonism." *boundary 2,* July 31, 2018. https://www.boundary2.org/2018/07/mueller.

Munn v. Illinois, 94 U.S. 113 (1877).

Nau, Michael, Rachel E. Dwyer, and Randy Hodson. "Can't Afford a Baby? Debt and Young Americans." *Research in Social Stratification and Mobility* 42 (December 1, 2015): 114–22.

Nemec, Mark R. *Ivory Towers and Nationalist Minds: Universities, Leadership, and the Development of the American State.* Ann Arbor: University of Michigan Press, 2006.

New York Times. "26 Negro Rallies Back Roosevelt," September 22, 1936.

———. "Defender of Health Care for Poor," October 21, 1976.

New-York Daily Tribune. "The National Reformers," October 11, 1845.

———. "The Public Lands—National Reform," January 23, 1846.

Novak, William J. *The People's Welfare: Law and Regulation in Nineteenth-Century America.* Chapel Hill: University of North Carolina Press, 1996.

———. "The Public Utility Idea and the Origins of Modern Business Regulation." In *The Corporation and American Democracy,* edited by Naomi R. Lamoreaux and William J. Novak, 139–76. Cambridge, MA: Harvard University Press, 2017.

Old Age Revolving Pensions, Ltd. *Old Age Revolving Pensions, a Proposed National Plan.* Long Beach, CA: Old Age Revolving Pensions, 1934.

Orren, Karen. *Belated Feudalism: Labor, the Law, and Liberal Development in the United States.* Cambridge: Cambridge University Press, 1991.

Paine, Thomas. "Agrarian Justice." https://www.ssa.gov/history/paine4.html.

Palladino, Lenore. "The Economic Argument for Stakeholder Corporations." Roosevelt Institute, July 2019.

Patterson, James T. *America's Struggle Against Poverty, 1900–1980.* Cambridge, MA: Harvard University Press, 1981.

Payne, Christopher. *The Consumer, Credit and Neoliberalism: Governing the Modern Economy.* London: Routledge, 2012.

Peck, Jamie, and Adam Tickell. "Neoliberalizing Space." *Antipode* 34, no. 3 (July 2002): 380–404.

Pepall, Lynne, Dan Richards, and George Norman. *Industrial Organization: Contemporary Theory and Empirical Applications.* 5th ed. Hoboken, NJ: Wiley, 2014.

Perkins, Frances. "Basic Idea Behind Social Security Program; Miss Perkins Outlines the Theory of Collective Aid to the Individual." *New York Times,* January 27, 1935.

———. *The Roosevelt I Knew.* New York: Penguin Books, 2011.

Pessen, Edward. "Thomas Skidmore, Agrarian Reformer in the Early American Labor Movement." *New York History* 35, no. 3 (July 1954): 280–96.

Petersen, Anne Helen. "The Real Peril of Crowdfunding Health Care." *BuzzFeed News,* March 11, 2017.

Pettit, Philip. "Freedom in the Market." *Politics, Philosophy & Economics* 5, no. 2 (2006): 131–49.

———. *Republicanism: A Theory of Freedom and Government.* Oxford: Clarendon Press, 1997.

Philippon, Thomas. *The Great Reversal: How America Gave Up on Free Markets.* Cambridge, MA: Harvard University Press, 2019.

Philippon, Thomas, and Ariell Reshef. "Wages and Human Capital in the US Finance Industry: 1909–2006." *The Quarterly Journal of Economics* 127, no. 4 (November 2012): 1551–1609.

Phillips-Fein, Kim. *Fear City: New York's Fiscal Crisis and the Rise of Austerity Politics.* New York: Metropolitan Books, 2017.

———. *Invisible Hands: The Making of the Conservative Movement from the New Deal to Reagan.* New York: W.W. Norton, 2009.

Pigou, A. C. *The Economics of Welfare.* London: Macmillan and Co., Ltd, 1920.

Pildes, Richard H. "Democracy, Anti-Democracy, and the Cannon." *Constitutional Commentary* 17 (2000): 295–319.

Pilz, Jeffrey J. *The Life, Work and Times of George Henry Evans, Newspaperman, Activist and Reformer (1829–1849).* Lewiston, NY: Edwin Mellen Press, 2001.

Pistor, Katharina. *The Code of Capital: How the Law Creates Wealth and Inequality.* Princeton, NJ: Princeton University Press, 2019.

Plotke, David. "The Wagner Act, Again: Politics and Labor, 1935–37." *Studies in American Political Development* 3 (Spring 1989): 104–56.

Polanyi, Karl. *The Great Transformation: The Political and Economic Origins of Our Time*. Boston: Beacon Press, 2001.

Potter, David Morris. *The Impending Crisis, 1848–1861*. Edited by Don Edward Fehrenbacher. New York: Harper & Row, 1976.

Pound, Roscoe. "Liberty of Contract." *Yale Law Journal* 18, no. 7 (May 1909): 454–87.

Proceedings of The Casualty Actuarial and Statistical Society of America. Vol. 2. Lancaster, PA: Press of The New Era Printing Company, 1916.

Proceedings of the First Annual Meeting of the National Fraternal Congress of America, 1914.

Purdy, Jedediah. "Neoliberal Constitutionalism: Lochnerism for a New Economy." *Law and Contemporary Problems* 77, no. 4 (2014): 195–213.

Putnam, Robert D. *Bowling Alone: The Collapse and Revival of American Community*. New York: Simon and Schuster, 2000.

Pyke, Alan. "Taking the Fight for $15 to the Old Confederacy." *Think Progress* (blog), August 16, 2016. https://thinkprogress.org/fight-for-15-richmond -convention-1dbc73e24183.

Quadagno, Jill, and Steve McDonald. "Racial Segregation in Southern Hospitals: How Medicare 'Broke the Back of Segregated Health Services.'" In *The New Deal and Beyond: Social Welfare in the South Since 1930*, edited by Elna C. Green, 119–37. Athens: University of Georgia Press, 2003.

Rahman, K. Sabeel. *Democracy Against Domination*. New York: Oxford University Press, 2017.

———. "Infrastructural Regulation and the New Utilities." *Yale Journal on Regulation* 35, no. 3 (2018): 911–39.

———. "Losing and Gaining Public Goods." *Boston Review*, September 5, 2017.

Rauchway, Eric. *The Great Depression and the New Deal: A Very Short Introduction*. Oxford: Oxford University Press, 2008.

———. *Winter War: Hoover, Roosevelt, and the First Clash over the New Deal*. New York: Basic Books, 2018.

Reagan, Ronald. *The Creative Society: Some Comments on Problems Facing America*. New York: Devin-Adair, 1968.

Pepperdine School of Public Policy. "Republican Party Platform," June 11, 1936.

https://publicpolicy.pepperdine.edu/academics/research/faculty-research/new-deal/1930s-party-platforms/repub36.htm.

Reynolds, P. Preston. "The Federal Government's Use of Title VI and Medicare to Racially Integrate Hospitals in the United States, 1963 through 1967." *American Journal of Public Health* 87, no. 11 (November 1997): 1850–58.

Rich, Andrew. *Think Tanks, Public Policy, and the Politics of Expertise.* Cambridge: Cambridge University Press, 2004.

Richardson, Heather Cox. *The Death of Reconstruction.* Cambridge, MA: Harvard University Press, 2001.

———. *The Greatest Nation of the Earth: Republican Economic Policies During the Civil War.* Cambridge, MA: Harvard University Press, 1997.

Roark, James L. "George W. Julian: Radical Land Reformer." *Indiana Magazine of History* 64, no. 1 (March 1968): 25–38.

Robbins, Roy M. "Horace Greeley: Land Reform and Unemployment, 1837–1862." *Agricultural History* 7, no. 1 (January 1933): 18–41.

Roberts, William Clare. *Marx's Inferno: The Political Theory of Capital.* Princeton, NJ: Princeton University Press, 2017.

Robin, Corey. "Lavatory and Liberty: The Secret History of the Bathroom Break." *Boston Globe,* September 29, 2002.

———. "The New Socialists." *New York Times,* August 24, 2018.

———. *The Reactionary Mind: Conservatism from Edmund Burke to Donald Trump.* 2nd ed. New York: Oxford University Press, 2018.

———. "Reclaiming the Politics of Freedom." *The Nation,* April 6, 2011.

Rodems, Richard, and H. Luke Shaefer. "Left Out: Policy Diffusion and the Exclusion of Black Workers from Unemployment Insurance." *Social Science History* 40, no. 3 (Fall 2016): 385–404.

Rodgers, Daniel T. *Atlantic Crossings?: Social Politics in a Progressive Age.* Cambridge, MA: Harvard University Press, 1998.

Roediger, David R., and Philip S. Foner. *Our Own Time: A History of American Labor and the Working Day.* London: Verso, 1989.

Róna, Peter. "Letter in Response to Jensen." *Harvard Business Review* 89 (1989): 6–7.

Roosevelt, Franklin D. *Public Papers of the Presidents of the United States: F.D. Roosevelt, 1937.* Vol. 6. Washington, DC: United States Government Printing Office, 1941.

Rose, Sarah F. *No Right to Be Idle: The Invention of Disability, 1840s–1930s.* Chapel Hill: University of North Carolina Press, 2017.

Rosenberg, Gerald N. *The Hollow Hope: Can Courts Bring About Social Change?* 2nd ed. Chicago: University of Chicago Press, 2008.

Rosenfeld, Seth. *Subversives: The FBI's War on Student Radicals, and Reagan's Rise to Power.* New York: Farrar, Straus, and Giroux, 2013.

Rosenthal, Elisabeth. "That Beloved Hospital? It's Driving Up Health Care Costs." *New York Times*, September 1, 2019.

Rosenzweig, Roy. *Eight Hours for What We Will: Workers and Leisure in an Industrial City, 1870–1920.* Cambridge: Cambridge University Press, 1983.

Rossi, Jim, and Morgan Ricks. "Foreword to Revisiting the Public Utility." *Yale Journal on Regulation* 35, no. 3 (2018): 711–19.

Rothstein, Jesse, and Cecilia Elena Rouse. "Constrained After College: Student Loans and Early-Career Occupational Choices." *Journal of Public Economics* 95 (2011): 149–63.

Rubinow, Isaac Max. "Old-Age Pensions and Moral Values: A Reply to Miss Coman." *Survey*, February 28, 1914.

———. "Problems and Possibilities." *The Market World and Chronicle* 9, no. 9 (February 27, 1915): 286–89.

———. *The Quest for Security.* New York: H. Holt, 1934.

———. *Social Insurance: With Special Reference to American Conditions.* New York: H. Holt, 1913.

Salamon, Lester M. "Of Market Failure, Voluntary Failure, and Third-Party Government: Toward a Theory of Government-Nonprofit Relations in the Modern Welfare State." *Nonprofit and Voluntary Sector Quarterly* 16 (January 1987): 29–49.

Salmon, Felix. "Gen Z Prefers 'Socialism' to 'Capitalism.' " *Axios*, January 27, 2019. https://www.axios.com/socialism-capitalism-poll-generation-z-preference -1ffb8800-0ce5-4368-8a6f-de3b82662347.html.

Samansky, Allan J. "Child Care Expenses and the Income Tax." *Florida Law Review* 50 (April 1998): 245–94.

Satz, Debra. *Why Some Things Should Not Be for Sale: The Moral Limits of Markets.* New York: Oxford University Press, 2010.

Sawyer, Laura Phillips. "Contested Meanings of Freedom: Workingmen's Wages, the Company Store System, and the Godcharles v. Wigeman Decision." *The Journal of the Gilded Age and Progressive Era* 12, no. 3 (July 2013): 285–319.

Schickler, Eric. *Racial Realignment: The Transformation of American Liberalism, 1932–1965.* Princeton, NJ: Princeton University Press, 2016.

Schlesinger, Arthur M. "Was Olmsted an Unbiased Critic of the South?" *The Journal of Negro History* 37, no. 2 (April 1952): 173–87.

Schmitt, Mark. "Social Security's Enduring Legacy: Adaptability." *Roosevelt Institute* (blog), August 14, 2012. https://rooseveltinstitute.org/social-securitys -enduring-legacy-adaptability.

Seager, Henry Rogers. "Outline of a Program of Social Legislation with Special Reference to Wage-Earners." In *American Association for Labor Legislation: Proceedings of the First Annual Meeting.* Madison, 1908.

———. *Social Insurance, a Program of Social Reform.* New York: Macmillan, 1910.

Sellers, Charles. *The Market Revolution: Jacksonian America, 1815–1846.* New York: Oxford University Press, 1991.

Shesol, Jeff. *Supreme Power: Franklin Roosevelt vs. the Supreme Court.* New York: W.W. Norton, 2010.

Sinnreich, Aram. *The Essential Guide to Intellectual Property.* New Haven, CT: Yale University Press, 2019.

Sitaraman, Ganesh, and Anne L. Alstott. *The Public Option: How to Expand Freedom, Increase Opportunity, and Promote Equality.* Cambridge, MA: Harvard University Press, 2019.

Skidmore, Thomas E. *The Rights of Man to Property!: Being a Proposition to Make It Equal Among the Adults of the Present Generation, and to Provide for Its Equal Transmission to Every Individual of Each Succeeding Generation on Arriving at the Age of Maturity.* New York: printed for the author by Alexander Ming, 1829.

Skocpol, Theda. *Protecting Soldiers and Mothers?: The Political Origins of Social Policy in the United States.* Cambridge, MA: Harvard University Press, 1992.

Skocpol, Theda, Kenneth Finegold, and Michael Goldfield. "Explaining New Deal Labor Policy." *American Political Science Review* 84, no. 4 (1990): 1297–1315.

Slobodian, Quinn. *Globalists: The End of Empire and the Birth of Neoliberalism.* Cambridge, MA: Harvard University Press, 2018.

Smith, David Barton. *The Power to Heal: Civil Rights, Medicare, and the Struggle to Transform America's Health Care System.* Nashville, TN: Vanderbilt University Press, 2016.

Snay, Mitchell. *Horace Greeley and the Politics of Reform in Nineteenth-Century America.* Lanham, MD: Rowman & Littlefield, 2011.

Social Security History. "Message to Congress Reviewing the Broad Objectives and Accomplishments of the Administration," June 8, 1934. https://www.ssa .gov/history/fdrcon34.html.

Spence, Thomas. "The Rights of Infants." Marxists Internet Archive, 1797.

Spencer, Thomas T. "The Good Neighbor League Colored Committee and the 1936 Democratic Presidential Campaign." *The Journal of Negro History* 63, no. 4 (October 1978): 307–16.

Stahl, Jason. *Right Moves: The Conservative Think Tank in American Political Culture Since 1945.* Chapel Hill: University of North Carolina Press, 2016.

Starr, Paul. *The Social Transformation of American Medicine.* New York: Basic Books, 1982.

Stein, Herbert. *The Fiscal Revolution in America.* Chicago: University of Chicago Press, 1969.

Stein, Judith. *Pivotal Decade: How the United States Traded Factories for Finance in the Seventies.* New Haven, CT: Yale University Press, 2010.

Stephenson, George Malcolm. *The Political History of the Public Lands, from 1840 to 1862: From Pre-Emption to Homestead.* Boston: R.G. Badger, 1917.

Stoltzfus, Emilie. *Citizen, Mother, Worker: Debating Public Responsibility for Child Care After the Second World War.* Chapel Hill: University of North Carolina Press, 2003.

Stout, Lynn. "Bad and Not-So-Bad Arguments for Shareholder Primacy." *Southern California Law Review* 75 (2002): 1189–1209.

———. *The Shareholder Value Myth: How Putting Shareholders First Harms Investors, Corporations, and the Public.* San Francisco: Berrett-Koehler, 2012.

Talese, Gay. "Selma 1990: Old Faces and a New Spirit." *New York Times*, March 7, 1990.

Tarnoff, Ben. "A Socialist Plan to Fix the Internet." *Jacobin*, November 30, 2019.

Taylor, Astra. *Democracy May Not Exist, but We'll Miss It When It's Gone.* New York: Metropolitan Books, 2019.

———. *The People's Platform: Taking Back Power and Culture in the Digital Age.* New York: Metropolitan Books, 2014.

The Office. "Scott's Tots." Directed by B. J. Novak. Written by Gene Stupnitsky and Lee Eisenberg. NBC, December 3, 2009.

Tidwell, Mike. "The Quiet Revolution." *American Legacy*, Fall 2000.

Tippett, Rebecca. "Mortality and Cause of Death, 1900 v. 2010." *Carolina*

Demography (blog), June 16, 2014. https://www.ncdemography.org/2014/06/16
/mortality-and-cause-of-death-1900-v-2010.

Tobin, James. "On Limiting the Domain of Inequality." *The Journal of Law and Economics* 13, no. 2 (October 1970): 263–77.

Tocqueville, Alexis de. *Democracy in America*. Translated by Arthur Goldhammer. New York: Library of America, 2004.

Truman, Harry. "Special Message to the Congress Recommending a Comprehensive Health Program." Harry S. Truman Library and Museum, November 19, 1945. https://www.trumanlibrary.gov/library/public-papers/192 /special-message-congress-recommending-comprehensive-health-program.

Tuchinsky, Adam-Max. *Horace Greeley's New-York Tribune: Civil War-Era Socialism and the Crisis of Free Labor*. Ithaca, NY: Cornell University Press, 2009.

Twentieth Century Fund, ed. *The Townsend Crusade: An Impartial Review of the Townsend Movement and the Probable Effects of the Townsend Plan*. New York: Committee on Old Age Security of the Twentieth Century Fund, 1936.

U.S. Bureau of the Census. *Historical Statistics of the United States, Colonial Times to 1970*. Bicentennial edition. Washington, DC: U.S. Government Printing Office, 1975.

———. "Selected Historical Decennial Census Population and Housing Counts— Urban and Rural Populations," n.d. https://www.census.gov/population/www /censusdata/hiscendata.html.

U.S. Central Intelligence Agency. "The World Factbook: Country Comparison: Infant Mortality Rate." Accessed December 14, 2019. https://www.cia.gov/li brary/publications/the-world-factbook/rankorder/2091rank.html.

US Commission on Civil Rights. "Title VI, One Year After: A Survey of Desegregation of Health and Welfare Services in the South." Washington, DC: U.S. Government Printing Office, 1966.

U.S. Congress House Committee on the Judiciary. *Report of the Antitrust Subcommittee (Subcommittee No. 5) of the Committee on the Judiciary, House of Representatives, Eighty-Sixth Congress on Consent Decree Program of the Department of Justice*. Washington, DC: U.S. Government Printing Office, 1959.

U.S. Congressional Budget Office. "The Distribution of Major Tax Expenditures in the Individual Income Tax System," May 29, 2013. https://www.cbo.gov /publication/43768.

U.S. Executive Office of the President. "Patent Assertion and US Innovation." Washington, DC: U.S. Government Printing Office, 2013.

U.S. Federal Reserve Board. "2016 SCF Chartbook." Federal Reserve, October 16, 2017. https://www.federalreserve.gov/econres/files/BulletinCharts.pdf.

Venkatapuram, Sridhar. *Health Justice: An Argument from the Capabilities Approach*. Cambridge: Polity Press, 2011.

Wade, Wyn Craig. *The Fiery Cross: The Ku Klux Klan in America*. New York: Oxford University Press, 1998.

Walzer, Michael. *Spheres Of Justice: A Defense of Pluralism and Equality*. New York: Basic Books, 1983.

Ward, Paul W. "Wooing the Negro Vote." *The Nation*, August 1, 1936.

Watzinger, Martin, Thomas A. Fackler, Markus Nagler, and Monika Schnitzer. "How Antitrust Enforcement Can Spur Innovation: Bell Labs and the 1956 Consent Decree." SSRN Scholarly Paper. Rochester, NY: Social Science Research Network, February 27, 2017.

Weil, David. *The Fissured Workplace: Why Work Became So Bad for So Many and What Can Be Done to Improve It*. Cambridge, MA: Harvard University Press, 2014.

White, Richard. *The Republic for Which It Stands: The United States During Reconstruction and the Gilded Age, 1865–1896*. New York: Oxford University Press, 2017.

Wilentz, Sean. *Chants Democratic: New York City and the Rise of the American Working Class, 1788–1850*. 20th anniversary ed. London: Oxford University Press, 2004.

Williams, Bernard. "The Idea of Equality." In *Problems of the Self*, 230–49. Cambridge: Cambridge University Press, 1973.

Williams, Robert Chadwell. *Horace Greeley: Champion of American Freedom*. New York: New York University Press, 2006.

Williams, Trina. "The Homestead Act: A Major Asset-Building Policy in American History." Center for Social Development, 2000.

Witt, John Fabian. *The Accidental Republic?: Crippled Workingmen, Destitute Widows, and the Remaking of American Law*. Cambridge, MA: Harvard University Press, 2004.

———. "Rethinking the Nineteenth-Century Employment Contract, Again." *Law and History Review* 18, no. 3 (Fall 2000): 627–57.

Witte, Edwin Emil. *The Development of the Social Security Act: A Memorandum on the History of the Committee on Economic Security and Drafting and Legislative History of the Social Security Act*. Madison: University of Wisconsin Press, 1962.

Wolfman, Brian. "Child Care, Work, and the Federal Income Tax." *American Journal of Tax Policy* 3 (1984): 153–93.

Wood, Ellen Meiksins. *The Origin of Capitalism: A Longer View*. London: Verso, 2017.

———. "The Politics of Capitalism." *Monthly Review* 51, no. 4 (September 1999).

Wu, Tim. "Network Neutrality, Broadband Discrimination." *Journal of Telecommunications and High Technology Law* 2 (2003): 141–76.

Wykstra, Stephanie. "The Movement to Make Workers' Schedules More Humane." *Vox*, November 5, 2019.

Yellen, Janet. "Perspectives on Inequality and Opportunity from the Survey of Consumer Finances." Presented at the Conference on Economic Opportunity and Inequality, Federal Reserve Bank of Boston, Boston, MA, October 17, 2014. https://www.federalreserve.gov/newsevents/speech/yellen20141017a.htm.

Zaloom, Caitlin. *Indebted: How Families Make College Work at Any Cost*. Princeton, NJ: Princeton University Press, 2019.

Zietlow, Rebecca E. *Enforcing Equality: Congress, the Constitution, and the Protection of Individual Rights*. New York: New York University Press, 2006.

Zorn, Eric. "Ronald Reagan on Medicare, Circa 1961. Prescient Rhetoric or Familiar Alarmist Claptrap?" *Chicago Tribune—Change of Subject* (blog), September 2, 2009. https://blogs.chicagotribune.com/news_columnists_ezorn/2009/09/ronald-reagan-on-medicare-circa-1961-prescient-rhetoric-or-familiar-alarmist-claptrap-.html.

INDEX

ABOUT THE AUTHOR

Mike Konczal is a director at the Roosevelt Institute, where he focuses on economics, inequality, and the role of public power in a democracy. He is a co-author, with Joseph Stiglitz, of *Rewriting the Rules of the American Economy*. Described as having "a cult following among progressives" by the *New York Times Magazine*, his writing has been featured in the *Washington Post*, *Vox*, *Dissent*, and *The Nation*. He is a sought-after commentator on the U.S. economy and has appeared on CNN, MSNBC, *All Things Considered*, *Planet Money*, and *Lovett or Leave It*. Born and raised in Chicago, he now lives in Takoma Park, Maryland with his wife, daughter, and pit bull.

Rachel Cusk

Near Misses

KATHERINE LUCKY

W e've heard this story before: *A stranger arrives, bringing trouble. The stranger leaves. Things have changed.* But in Rachel Cusk's hands, a simple plot becomes deep and mysterious, like the "distant blue shape of the receded tide." The stranger in her eleventh novel, *Second Place*, is a renowned painter named L, whose arrival at the titular "second place"—a cottage for visiting artists built by the narrator, M, and her second husband, Tony—disturbs the peace on the marsh where they live. Middle-aged M is struggling with the sense that her life has "been a near miss." She's written a few "little books" that "hardly made any money." Her daughter, Justine, is all grown up. Where M is restless, Tony, a day laborer, is frustratingly stubborn and good, happy to spend his time working with his hands. Her invitation to L to come and paint at the marsh is an act of resistance to his contentment. L's paintings changed M's life years earlier, when she saw them exhibited in a sunlit Paris gallery. At the time, she was "a young mother on the brink of rebellion," about to divorce her first husband. The paintings gave her courage. They felt like a discovery of her "true origins"—as if she "was not alone in what, until then, I had held secret to myself." Now, perhaps, L will recognize and adore her as a kindred spirit. Perhaps he will change her life once again.

But the visit doesn't go as planned. L rudely brings a guest without asking, a beautiful young woman who makes M jealous. He takes down the cottage's curtains and paints on its walls. He treats M with scorn; at times, it's as if he despises her. She worries that he finds

SECOND PLACE
A Novel

RACHEL CUSK
Farrar, Straus and Giroux
$25 | 192 pp.

political commentary, which too often treats eruptions of populist sentiment as arising *ex nihilo* and as reversible through appeals to "normalcy," even if underlying economic problems remain unaddressed.

Freedom from the Market offers a refreshing corrective to this kind of "anti-Polanyian" thinking. In this sense, its perspectives on political economy, and even its idea of freedom as requiring far more than just the absence of external coercion, lines up quite well with that of Catholic social thought (though Konczal never refers to Catholic sources). But perhaps this isn't surprising, because others have noted a resemblance between Church teaching on the economy and the work of Polanyi—a Christian convert from Judaism. The late Canadian theologian Fr. Gregory Baum wrote of the "affinity" that exists between the thought of Polanyi and that of Pope Francis, even if there exists no evidence of a direct influence of the former on the latter. Likewise, an article published in the *Atlantic* a few months after Francis's election commented on the efforts

unions. Against anti-union proponents of so-called "right-to-work" laws, pro-union activists tried to sell their effort as one designed to expand liberty.

Unfortunately, this type of branding is still fairly uncommon. Attacks on liberals and the Left often involve scare-mongering about twentieth-century state Communism or political authoritarianism more generally, but the reflexive response, whether from mainstream liberals like Barack Obama or leftists like Bernie Sanders, has usually been to wave away these guilt-by-association tactics and calmly insist that a progressive program has nothing to do with central planning. In a 2016 speech at Georgetown University defining his understanding of democratic socialism, Sanders laughed off the idea that he would ever propose having the government "own the grocery store down the street."

But this is a defensive reaction, one that reinforces the idea that conservatives are the ones who "support freedom" and that their critics believe in less freedom, even if that still turns out

the future of our country and society are not won on arguments about market failures, on the balance sheets of accountants, or on narrowly tailored, incremental solutions. They are won on arguments about freedom. We've lost this fight in recent decades.... But we are starting to remember. Freedom is the fundamental battlefield that we fight on, and we need to fight on it once again.

Freedom from the Market is an impressive book, easily one of the best I've read in the past several years. I cannot recommend it highly enough. My hope is that Mike Konczal's careful study of American history can help recover a forgotten tradition in our politics, and that his "Polanyi-ish and Pollyanna-ish" lens can reveal to a wider audience the many ways in which contemporary ideologies obscure important truths about the economy and society. ◎

MATT MAZEWSKI *is a PhD student in economics at Columbia University, the rapporteur of the University Seminar on Catholicism, Culture, and Modernity, and a columnist for* Commonweal.

tured by it. Even in those areas where government appears to take a hands-off approach, it still plays a critical role in sustaining economic activity by virtue of the fact that it sets the "rules of the game"—for example, by establishing laws governing incorporation, bankruptcy, or labor relations. Without such acts of *creatio continua*, the market would devolve into Hobbesian chaos.

The second key argument of *The Great Transformation* is that, in the words of Konczal and Iber, "the move to markets is inherently destabilizing":

Rather than a font of liberty and freedom, markets are also a source of coercion, instability, precarity, and worse. Subjecting all of life to the market wouldn't result in the freest society but instead one defined by the collapse of social life.... [P]eople resist being turned into commodities. When they are exposed to too much of the market—when markets try to "disembed" from society—people resist, demanding protection from excessive commodification. Lives are more than commodities for those who are living them.

area of Texas and California combined. And although Konczal acknowledges problems with the law—including that much of this "free government land" was "only 'free' when it was taken, with force, from the people already living there," namely, Native Americans—he nevertheless credits it with providing "a floor of opportunity for all those who were able to use it." Republican politicians always like to remind everyone that the GOP is the "Party of Lincoln," but can anyone imagine a modern Republican president overseeing such a gargantuan redistribution of wealth to ordinary Americans?

In a chapter titled "Free Time," Konczal examines how labor organizers in the nineteenth and early twentieth centuries fought for, and ultimately won, shorter working hours and a shorter workweek. One of the greatest obstacles to progress in this regard was a conservative judiciary that routinely struck down limits on working time, most infamously in the 1905 Supreme Court decision *Lochner v. New York*, on

but also how it has been used historically as an instrument to combat other forms of inequality and discrimination. Most of the chapter is devoted to recounting how the implementation of Medicare gave progressives an opportunity to force the racial integration of hospitals in the Jim Crow South, by threatening to bar from the program any medical institution that remained segregated and thereby deprive it of a lucrative income stream. According to Wilbur Cohen, who worked in the Kennedy and Johnson administrations, "on the day that Medicare went into effect in the South, all those signs [reading "White" and "Colored"]...began to come down. This I think was a singular achievement of Medicare. In one day Medicare and Medicaid broke the back of segregated health services."

In the book's acknowledgements, Konczal credits an acquaintance with helping him to refine his "Polanyi-ish, and Pollyanna-ish, thinking," a

ty necessarily involves a constriction of freedom, and to show that such beliefs

Illinois homesteaders, 1916

without state action, like that required to enforce contracts, protect property rights, or maintain a stable currency.

Polanyi-ish

MATT MAZEWSKI

E
veryone has an opinion about "the free market." To some, it's a shining ideal; to others, an anarchic nightmare. But even for many of those who associate *laissez-faire* with the law of the jungle, it's only the idea of a *completely* free market that causes alarm. By this way of thinking, as long as the market is tamed with the right regulations, it can be channeled in ways that promote the common good. What both of these views seem to take for granted, however, is that there is always a tradeoff between economic liberty and state intervention. Both advocates and critics of the free market often tend to operate from the same assumptions about what "freedom" really entails.

FREEDOM FROM THE MARKET
America's Fight to Liberate Itself from the Grip of the Invisible Hand

MIKE KONCZAL
The New Press
$25.99 | 256 pp.

are in fact an historical anomaly. In *Freedom from the Market: America's Fight to Liberate Itself from the Grip of the Invisible Hand*, the Roosevelt Institute's Mike Konczal sets out to demonstrate how, "for all the language about how markets open up opportunities, they also create dependencies as well."

"People have used markets for trading and exchange for centuries," he writes, but "what is unique today is how the economy has been restructured to extend our reliance on markets into all aspects of society." He quotes an observation by the historian Ellen Meiksins Wood: "What defines our current way of dealing with markets is not opportunity or choice, but, on the contrary, compulsion. The things we need to live our lives"—healthcare, childcare, pensions— "are forced into markets where we are compelled to obtain them, at the mercy of private, profit-seeking actors and our own ability to pay."

In his introduction, Konczal lays out five key reasons why "freedom requires the suppression of the market": (1) markets allocate even essential and life-sustaining goods on the basis of ability to pay, rather than need; (2) they are less effective and efficient than the state at providing certain goods and services, such as health insurance, because of the logic of what economists would refer to as "market failures"; (3) market interactions, and in particular the employment relationship, can often be occasions of "domination by the will of others"; (4) the creeping commodification of everything "leaves no reward for things that don't function as commodities," such as the unpaid ach chapter of *Freedom from the Market* takes up a different domain of public policy and shows how social reformers have historically fought for progress in that area by "articulating a different idea of freedom," one rooted in "resisting dependency on markets." In "Free Land," Konczal traces the history of movements for the redistribution of land and the wealth of landowners, from Thomas Paine's 1796 pamphlet, "Agrarian Justice," which argued that landowners owed the public treasury a "ground-rent" and that taxes on land inheritance should be used to finance what amounted to a universal basic income, to the passage of the Homestead Act of 1862, which provided 160 acres of free government-owned land to anyone willing to build a dwelling on the tract and live there for at least five years.

The Homestead Act constituted one of the largest wealth transfers in U.S. history: in the decades after its passage, a total of 246 million acres was granted to 1.5 million people. This represented the grounds that they interfered with "freedom of contract" —that is, the freedom of capitalists to dictate the terms of contracts to workers. But those agitating for reform were not content to cede the mantle of liberty to their opponents, often framing their demands as efforts to *increase* the freedom of the working class by countering the tyranny of bosses. The "Ten-Hour Circular," a manifesto released in 1835 by a group of laborers in Boston calling for a ten-hour workday, solemnly declared that "we claim, by the blood of our fathers, shed on our battle-fields, in the War of the Revolution, the rights of American Freemen, and no earthly power shall resist our righteous claims with impunity." Even the most florid progressive rhetoric today generally stops short of depicting the labor movement as an extension of the American Revolution.

In "Free Health," Konczal highlights not only how public provision of health insurance can make everyone more free reference to the twentieth-century Austro-Hungarian political economist Karl Polanyi, whose ideas permeate the book. Although Konczal only explicitly references Polanyi a handful of times, he has written elsewhere about the enduring relevance of his thought. "Karl Polanyi for President," a 2016 article in *Dissent* that Konczal coauthored with Patrick Iber, is a useful companion piece to *Freedom from the Market*, and helps illuminate the intellectual genealogy of its arguments.

As Konczal and Iber explain, Polanyi's most famous work, *The Great Transformation* (1944), is devoted in large part to a critique of the idea that the so-called "free market" is a precondition for, and guarantor of, freedom more generally. "Polanyi's work dismantles this argument in two important ways," they write, first by showing that "markets are planned everywhere they exist." As Polanyi puts it, even *laissez-faire* "was the product of deliberate state action"; the economy is not

Polanyi referred to this process as "the double movement": the destabilization wrought by marketization produces backlash, sometimes in the form of socialist or progressive movements that work to provide refuge from the market, but at other times in the form of fascist or reactionary movements.

I'm always surprised at how much of our current discourse treats "the economy" as something wholly separate from society, rather than as the system by which society seeks to meet the material needs of its members. One of the major problems with neoliberalism, according to Konczal, is that its vision is one in which "markets don't serve the preexisting needs of people; people are instead created to serve the market." Talk of how efforts to suppress the pandemic "hurt the economy," when of course society and its members are hurt far more by allowing a deadly virus to spread unchecked, is one example of the absurdities that result from a failure to appreciate the "embeddedness"

to label the pope a Marxist, and instead offered "a case for the pontiff's debt not to Karl Marx but to Karl Polanyi."

K onczal's book excels not just as a work of history and a meditation on political economy, but also as a call to action. Among its many strengths is the strategic advice it offers to progressives, socialists, and leftists of all stripes: specifically, that advocates of a more humane economic system should deliberately steer clear of the framing I alluded to earlier, in which an economy based on solidarity is seen to be necessarily "less free" than the alternative. In fact, as Konczal convincingly shows, exactly the opposite is true.

There are already good examples of egalitarian economic policy being presented in a way that emphasizes how it bolsters rather than limits freedom. One such example was the "Employee Free Choice Act," introduced in Congress during the Obama adminis-

to be somewhat more freedom than the Soviet Politburo or the Chinese Communist Party. Why not turn the tables, and make the Right answer for Chile under Augusto Pinochet, or Singapore under Lee Kuan Yew? If socialists are forced to explain why their ideology does not logically lead to political oppression and the loss of civil liberties, capitalists should be challenged to do the same.

Plus, any social movement that aspires to make real change in the United States needs to reckon with the preeminent place that freedom occupies in the American political imagination. Following the authors of the "Ten-Hour Circular," the modern Left should not shy away from claiming, "by the blood of our fathers, shed on our battle-fields, in the War of the Revolution, the rights of American Freemen." Here's Konczal, in the closing paragraph of the book:

To succeed we need to harness and build on the proud legacy created by two hundred